**DO NOT REMOVE
CARDS FROM POCKET**

BOOMERANG

Other Books by Theda Skocpol

STATES AND SOCIAL REVOLUTIONS
A Comparative Study of France, Russia, and China

PROTECTING SOLDIERS AND MOTHERS
The Political Origins of Social Policy in the United States

SOCIAL REVOLUTIONS IN THE MODERN WORLD

SOCIAL POLICY IN THE UNITED STATES
Future Possibilities in Historical Perspective

STATE AND PARTY IN AMERICA'S NEW DEAL
(with Kenneth Finegold)

VISION AND METHOD IN HISTORICAL SOCIOLOGY
(editor)

BRINGING THE STATE BACK IN
(co-editor with Peter Evans and Dietrich Rueschemeyer)

THE POLITICS OF SOCIAL POLICY IN THE UNITED STATES
(co-editor with Margaret Weir and Ann Shola Orloff)

AMERICAN SOCIETY AND POLITICS
Institutional, Historical, and Theoretical Perspectives
(co-editor with John L. Campbell)

STATES, SOCIAL KNOWLEDGE, AND THE ORIGINS
OF MODERN SOCIAL POLICIES
(co-editor with Dietrich Rueschemeyer)

BOOMERANG

Clinton's Health Security Effort and the

Turn against Government

in U.S. Politics

THEDA SKOCPOL

W. W. Norton & Company

New York   London

Copyright © 1996 by Theda Skocpol
All rights reserved
Printed in the United States of America
First Edition

For information about permission to reproduce selections from this book, write to
Permissions, W. W. Norton & Company, Inc., 500 Fifth Avenue, New York, NY 10110.

The text of this book is composed in Electra, with the display set in Bureau Empire
and Helevetica Black. Composition and manufacturing by
The Maple-Vail Book Manufacturing Group.
Book design by Charlotte Staub

Library of Congress Cataloging-in-Publication Data

Skocpol, Theda.
    Boomerang: Clinton's health security effort and the turn
against government in U.S. politics / Theda Skocpol.
        p.   cm.
    Includes bibliographical references and index.
    ISBN 0-393-03970-6
    1. Health care reform—United States.   2. Social security—United
States—History.   3. United States—Social policy—1993–   4. United
States—Politics and government—1993–   I. Title.
RA395.A3S56   1996
362.1′0973—dc20   95-39074   CIP

W. W. Norton & Company, Inc., 500 Fifth Avenue, New York, N.Y. 10110
http://web.wwnorton.com
W. W. Norton & Company Ltd., 10 Coptic Street, London WC1A 1PU
1 2 3 4 5 6 7 8 9 0

For Bill and Michael

CONTENTS

NATIONAL HEALTH CARE?

✔ **The compassion of the IRS!**
✔ **The efficiency of the post office!**
✔ **All at Pentagon prices!**

Bumper sticker on an aging Chevrolet pickup in Maine, summer 1994.

PREFACE

In 1992 Americans elected to the presidency a moderate Democrat, Bill Clinton of Arkansas, who promised to deliver a plan for comprehensive health care reform along with measures to spur national economic growth. President Clinton proceeded to do pretty much what he had said he would do; and the launching of his Health Security proposal in September 1993 occurred to much acclaim. But by September 1994, the Health Security plan lay in congressional ruin. Soon thereafter, American voters delivered stinging blows to President Clinton and his fellow Democrats, while giving apparent electoral approval to a conservative Republican revolt against federal interventions in the domestic economy and social order.

The effort of Health Security, it suddenly seemed, had not only failed to extend the New Deal's security guarantees for Americans, as President Clinton had intended, but might instead trigger the outright unraveling of such prior programs as Medicare, Medicaid, and Social Security itself. How did this sudden turnaround in U.S. politics happen? What did the 1993–94 conflicts over health care reform contribute to the larger political turnaround?

This book tells the story of the failed Health Security effort of 1993–94 and uses the story as a window into the past and future of U.S. domestic politics. *Boomerang* shares insights and arguments that I—quite unexpectedly—found myself working out in the aftermath of the reform debacle and the November 1994 elections. As struggles over the Clinton Health Security proposal reached their culmination during 1994, I was at my summer home on Mount Desert island in Maine happily doing research about the past. Little did I suspect that, within a few months, I would be drawn into an investigation of the rise and resounding demise of the Clinton Health Security effort. I certainly did not expect to spend several months in 1995 writing this book on a very contemporary set of concerns.

My first step into an unplanned project came in September 1994, when the well-known economist Henry Aaron called from the Brookings Institution in Washington, D.C. He was organizing a conference on "Health Reform: Past and Future" to be held in January 1995, and wondered if I would agree to write a paper offering a historical perspective on the failure of the Health Security effort. I am not a specialist on health policy; but Henry said that did not matter. He wanted a broader perspective, and the paper did not have to be very long. Well, I had been gathering newspaper clippings during all 1993 and 1994, imagining that someday I might write about the Health Security debate. During 1994–95 I was on research leave from my professorship at Harvard University. So I decided to rearrange my schedule to accept Henry's invitation; I would spend about a month on a brief paper for his conference.

During December 1994 and January 1995, I found myself drawn more and more into the story of Health Security. As I delved into what had happened, I was struck by the ironies. Bill Clinton and his health policy planners had obviously struggled to be fiscally responsible, combining federal deficit reduction and cost saving for the private sector with the extension of health insurance to millions of uninsured Americans and the enhancement of protections for those already insured. What is more, Clinton was no flaming liberal. He had responded to strong popular interest in the reform of health care financing by coming up with a plan that looked like a middle way between market tendencies and governmental involvements in health care. Despite his efforts, the entire effort had boomeranged politically—both on him and on the Democratic Party he was trying to renovate for the future.

It helped me to think about the Health Security effort of the early 1990s in contrast to the planning and enactment of Social Security in the middle 1930s, as well as in the context of changes in U.S. politics and public policies since the 1960s. My prior scholarly research and writing let me put recent political events in perspective.

In the shorter term, there had been portentious shifts in the U.S. electoral and fiscal landscape. Democrats approached health care reform while struggling to overcome racial splits and the erosion of the party's base over several decades. A determined antigovernment insurgency was on the march within the Republican party. And any health care financing reform had to cope with a growing federal budget deficit and deepening popular distrust of the federal government—legacies handed down with a vengeance from the 1960s and the Reagan era of the 1980s.

In longer historical perspective, I was struck by the contrast between Social Security and Health Security. The two omnibus programs had been devised in similar ways by intragovernment planning groups. But the New Deal's Social Security legislation had promised to deliver new, federally financed benefits to states, localities, and many individual citizens; and the new benefits were to be accompanied by loose federal regulations. In contrast, the Clinton Health Security proposal surrounded its promised benefits for average Americans with tight, new regulations intended to push employers, doctors, hospitals, and insurance companies toward cost cutting. Established interests in the health care economy became very worried about their profits and freedom of maneuver. And more privileged middle-class Americans who already had some kind of health coverage began to think that Clinton's Health Security plan might make their health care more costly and cumbersome.

Ironically, much of this happened because President Clinton was trying so hard to be a fiscally responsible reformed Democrat. Determined to cut the federal deficit inherited from the 1980s, Clinton assiduously avoided the "tax and spend" modalities of traditional New Deal liberalism—only to fall victim instead to the political pitfalls of substituting regulations for spending, of trying to use government quietly and indirectly.

Because it embodied an intricate set of cost-cutting regulations, the Health Security bill as it was submitted to Congress and the public in the fall of 1993 inadvertently amounted to an ideal foil for concerted antigovernmental countermobilization. By the early 1990s, ideologically committed conservatives had amassed many material and intellectual resources in U.S. politics. They had plans to win elections and begin to cut or eliminate federal domestic programs. What these conservatives needed was a cause to help them woo middle-class public opinion, and a target to help them rally and unite locally widespread groups in opposition to the federal government as well as the Democratic Party. Inadvertently, the Clinton Health Security plan gave antigovernment conservatives exactly what they needed. The basis was laid for an electoral upheaval in November 1994, bringing to power hard-line conservatives determined to dismantle rather than extend the U.S. federal government's contributions to security for the American people.

As I developed these ideas, the paper I was preparing for the Brookings conference got out of hand. I found myself collecting more materials than I could possibly use—including dozens of cartoons and illustrations not really appropriate for the buttoned-up atmosphere of a gathering of "experts." Right after the Brookings conference, I had to cut my colorful 70-page paper to a 25-page article for immediate publication in the journal *Health Affairs*. While doing this, I passed the longer paper around. People liked it and encouraged me to write more, especially about the broader political issues (nobody wanted to hear much more about the technical details of alternative health reform proposals). So I decided to go ahead and write a short book.

Just as I was arriving at this decision, another fateful development intervened. I was included in a group of scholars and social thinkers invited to come to Camp David to meet with President Clinton, Vice President Gore, Mrs. Clinton, Mrs Gore, and some of their advisors. There were informal discussions and a three-hour seminar about the changing role of government in U.S. society, all as background for the President's thinking about his State of the Union Address and additional speeches he planned to give during 1995. Of course it was a great honor to be at Camp David. In addition, during supper I had the opportunity to talk informally with the First Lady, Hillary Rodham Clinton. I asked if I could send her my paper on "The Rise and Resounding Demise of the Clinton Health Security Plan." She agreed and said she would also show it to Ira Magaziner, who had helped her to direct planning for Health Security.

After that, my decision to proceed with a book was soon reinforced. Mrs. Clinton and Ira Magaziner (whom I had never met before) assented to talk with me about their perspectives on what had happened in 1993 and 1994. They didn't fully agree with the arguments of my paper, some of which were very critical of the Clinton administration. But they were willing to try to set me straight and answer the questions I posed, sometimes bluntly. In due course, they also let me look at confidential internal White House memos. I could not have copies of these materials, but I could take notes from them during visits to Washington.

The overall arguments of this book were already sketched out before I ever talked with people who had been involved with the administration's Health Security effort. Even so, it was very helpful to me to get contemporaneous information about how key policy planners viewed the politics of health care reform while it was happening. I asked for and received access to 1993–94 memos and strategy documents that dealt with how White House people and their political advisors understood, and tried to deal with, public opinion, Congress, and the concerns of the hundreds of groups that had a stake in the U.S. health care system. I did not explore all the technical byways of policy planning, for my concern was with the politics of what had happened during 1993–94.

As I wrote *Boomerang*, I wanted to make certain citations to, and quotations from, the White House documents I had seen. Because I am a scholar, I did not want to use these materials surreptitiously, "on background" only. Fortunately, when I asked permission to make specific quotations and citations, it was granted in every case but one (which was a minor matter from my point of view).

Unlike some other books that are being written on the Health Security episode, *Boomerang* is *not* based on extensive retrospective interviews with dozens of people in Congress, interest groups, and the executive branch. I have paid very little attention to interpersonal maneuvers, to who did what to whom, to who disagreed with whom, to who was "right" and who was "wrong." Such matters are, of course, fascinating. But they are best left to memoirs and interview-based accounts; and issues of who was right and wrong cannot be settled now, anyway. My effort has been to achieve a more-distanced perspective, looking through the prism of changing U.S. political and governmental arrangements, while still presenting the actions and outlooks of key protagonists correctly. As I see it, people mostly acted as one would expect, given their institutional locations, the political resources they had at their disposal (or not), and their ideas as one can see them in contemporaneous writings. I have not relied on retrospective accounts of motives or conflicts unless I could validate them against contemporaneous information.

Aside from scholarly works on U.S. politics and the White House documents I was able to review, my main sources of evidence have been articles or reports on public-opinion data, along with group manifestos, governmental documents, position papers, and other writings that were produced as Health Security was being planned and debated. A number of memoirs already published (or distributed) by key actors have also been useful, especially when they put me on to things I could dig up more on myself. I have drawn very extensively on the marvellous political reporting of journalists from 1991 to 1994, often borrowing quotations they got from key actors at the time. The steady stream of detailed articles written by Julie Kosterlitz for the *National Journal* were especially helpful to me. In addition, I relied heavily on articles from the *New York Times, Wall Street Journal, Boston Globe, Washington Post*, and scattered other magazines and newspapers.

Finally, I learned a lot from the hundreds of political cartoons that I collected during the health reform debate, some of which I have gotten permission to include at appropriate points in this book. To make people laugh, cartoonists have to capture social truths—and pinpoint political ironies. So cartoons are an excellent source for a scholar trying to understand and write vividly about the deeper meanings of current events.

Acknowledgments

I am grateful to many groups and people for helping me to produce as good and as vividly written a book as possible in a short time. I thank Henry Aaron, the Brookings Institution, and the editors of *Health Affairs* for getting me started. I am also grateful to those in and around the Clinton administration who, without demanding that I agree with them, talked with me and gave me access to documents. Months before I decided to write anything about Health Security, I received a three-year grant from the "Investigator Awards in Health Policy Research" program of the Robert Wood Johnson Foundation, resources to support historical research on the politics of U.S. health insurance reforms from the 1930s to the present. As it turned out, the award helped make it possible for me to write this book during 1995.

Several groups of colleagues gave me stimulating feedback on presentations leading to this book, including the January 1995 Brookings conference mentioned above, a discussion among Robert Wood Johnson investigators, a meeting of the Boston-area Workshop on American Political Development, a seminar at Harvard's Center for Business and Government, a discussion at the 1995 Newman Lecture sponsored by the Department of Government at Cornell University, a seminar at the Russell Sage Foundation, a session of the New Majority Project, and a session at the 1995 meeting of the Netherlands American Studies Association.

Lots of individuals helped, too. As the relevant people know, I was not always willing to take advice or correction. Yet I greatly appreciate the comments on drafts generously given by Henry Aaron, Michael Aronson, Derek Bok, Heather Booth, Alan Brinkley, Judy Feder, Morris Fiorina, Stan Greenberg, Jacob Hacker, Lawrence Jacobs, Ira Magaziner, Mark Peterson, Paul Peterson, Jason Solomon, Rick Valelly, Margaret Weir, and Joseph White. Denise Ricketson helped with many arrangements and factual details. Timely research assistance was provided by Sherwin Chen, James Diehl, Marshall Ganz, Julia Rubin, Kira Sanbonmatsu, and Juliet Sanger. At W. W. Norton and Company, both Donald Lamm and Mary Cunnane made suggestions useful for the final revision of the book manuscript, and many others helped in the production process.

Finally, I lovingly thank Bill Skocpol and our seven-year-old son, Michael, for putting up with me as I simultaneously wrote this book, did research for another book, and watched the O. J. Simpson trial. Through their generous good humor, I was able to alternate writing and watching over several months, combining production with distracting relaxation as I completely immersed myself in the poignancies of politics and society in America today. For some reason, the combination helped me to finish *Boomerang* very quickly.

BOOMERANG

A PIVOTAL EPISODE

On September 22, 1993, President Bill Clinton gave a stirring speech about "Health Security."[1] As he stood before Congress and reached out via television to all the American people, Mr. Clinton was launching the most important initiative of his presidency. He called for legislators and citizens to work with him "to fix a health care system that is badly broken ... giving every American health security—health care that's always there, health care that can never be taken away." "Despite the dedication of millions of talented health professionals," the President explained, health care "is too uncertain and too expensive. . . . Our health care system takes 35 percent more of our income than any other country, insures fewer people, requires more Americans to pay more and more for less and less, and gives them fewer choices. There is no excuse for that kind of system, and it's time to fix it."

Historic associations resonated as President Clinton spoke that September evening, particularly with the broad-based federal initiatives launched by another Democratic president, Franklin Delano Roosevelt, half a century earlier during the New Deal. The very title of Clinton's "Health Security" proposal harkened back to the Social Security Act of 1935. And the "Health Security card" that the president said every American would receive if his reforms were enacted was obviously meant to encourage a sense of safe and honorable entitlement such as Americans feel they have in Social Security. In soaring rhetoric near the end of his speech, President Clinton projected a vision of a new founding moment for U.S. social provision reminiscent of the enactment of Social Security. "It is hard to believe," the President told his fellow citizens,

> that there was once a time—even in this century—when retirement was nearly synonymous with poverty, and older Americans died in our streets. That is unthinkable today because over half a century ago Americans had the courage to change—to create a Social Security system that ensures that no Americans will be forgotten in their later years.
>
> I believe that forty years from now our grandchildren will also find it unthinkable that there was a time in our country when hardworking families lost their homes and savings simply because their child fell ill, or lost their health coverage when they changed jobs. Yet our grandchildren will only find such things unthinkable if we have the courage to change today.

President Clinton's invocation of the precedent of Social Security symbolized a faith that problems shared by a majority of Americans could be effectively addressed through a comprehensive initiative of the federal government. As the President and his advisors knew, Social Security is the most successful of the federal government's domestic policies, a program that enjoys broad support across lines of class, race, and partisan orientation. Middle-class Americans feel that they have a stake in Social Security, and the protections it offers are seen as "deserved benefits," not pilloried as "welfare handouts." Like the Social Security retirement insurance program of 1935, the Health Security proposal of 1993 was designed to address the needs—and capture the political support—of middle-class as well as less economically privileged Americans.

Indeed, throughout his carefully crafted speech, President Clinton spoke directly to—and about—hardworking middle-class citizens. He never once explicitly mentioned the poor, who had been the targets of many recent federal social programs supported by Democrats. Instead, he spoke of the insecurities that more-privileged Americans were increasingly facing in the "broken" U.S. arrangements for financing health care.

"Every one of us," Clinton reminded his audience, "knows someone who has worked hard and played by the rules but has been hurt by this system that just doesn't work. Let me tell you about just one."

Cover of *Health Security: The President's Report to the American People,*
October 1993

Kerry Kennedy owns a small furniture franchise that employs
seven people in Titusville, Florida. Like most small business owners,
Kerry has poured his sweat and blood into that company. But over
the last few years, the cost of insuring his seven workers has skyrock-
eted, as did the coverage for himself, his wife, and his daughter. Last

year, however, Kerry could no longer afford to provide coverage for all his workers because the insurance companies had labeled two of them high risk simply because of their age. But you know what? Those two people are Kerry's mother and father, who built the family business and now work in the store.

"That story speaks for millions of others," the President stressed, as he reminded his listeners of other sympathetic situations:

Millions of Americans are just a pink slip away from losing their health coverage, and one serious illness away from losing their life savings. Millions more are locked in the wrong kinds of jobs because they'd lose their coverage if they left their companies. And on any given day over 37 million of our fellow citizens, the vast majority of them children or hardworking adults, have no health insurance at all. And despite all of this, our medical bills are growing at more than twice the rate of inflation.

President Clinton promised to solve the problems he had dramatized. "Before this Congress adjourns next year," he declared, "I will sign a new law to create health security for every American." "Under our plan," the President promised, "every American will receive a health security card that will guarantee you a comprehensive package of benefits over the course of your lifetime that will equal the benefits provided by most Fortune 500 corporations. . . . With this card,

If you lose your job or switch jobs, you're covered.
If you leave your job to start a small business, you're covered.
If you are an early retiree, you're covered.
If you or someone in your family has a preexisting medical condition, you're covered.
If you get sick or a member of your family gets sick, even if it's a life-threatening illness, you're covered.
And if an insurance company tries to drop you for any reason, you'll still be covered—because that will be illegal.

Tens of millions of Americans watched the September 1993 Health Security address, and polls taken right afterward and over the next few weeks registered strong support for the President's general vision of reform.[2] So well did things go that opinion analyst and CNN political correspondent Bill Schneider soon published a positively gushy analysis of "Health Reform: What Went Right?"[3] "The reviews are in and the box office is terrific," declared Schneider, as he praised the President for his "intellect" and "sense of complete conviction" and Hillary Rodham Clinton for her "compassion and concern." "The plan also plays to the Democratic party's strength," noted Schneider. "Democrats believe in great government enterprises to solve great problems. A lot of people have lost faith in government's ability to do that. But Clinton deliberately evoked the imagery of the big Democratic success stories of the past. . . ." The President was also praised for showing bipartisan flexibility and building "a broad coalition" behind his reform.

Also well received were the first presentations of the Health Security plan made by First Lady Hillary Rodham Clinton to five congressional committees. "The Clinton Plan Is Alive on Arrival" trumpeted the *New York Times* on October 3.[4] Both Democratic and Republican congressional leaders were quoted offering euphoric praise of the Clintons. Mrs. Clinton was presented by the *Times* not only as intellectually "dazzling" but also as charming and conciliatory, as "breaking down the mentality that says there's a contradiction between being a warm, fuzzy mom and an expert on health care." " 'The need for health care is not a partisan issue,' she told the Senate Finance Committee. 'We want to work with you,' she told one Republican after another." Republican Senator John Danforth typified the response of moderate Republicans, who seemed open to compromise in the national interest: "We will pass a law next year," he told the *Times*. "The answers she [Hillary Clinton] gives and the answers that Ira Magaziner gives indicate that they want to work things out."

President Clinton, proclaimed House Ways and Means Chairman Dan Rostenkowski, "has succeeded in changing the debate from whether we should have reform to what type of reform we should have." Moderates as well as liberals agreed that "this time it could just happen," as the *Wall Street Journal* put it on September 23. "Already—even as members of both parties question the financing measures in the Clinton plan, even as powerful interest groups denounce details in the proposal—the broad outlines of a compromise can be seen that would lead to legislation that would provide universal health coverage."[5]

In short, although no one (including those who fashioned it) expected the Clinton plan to be enacted by Congress without modifications, it was initially widely accepted as an excellent starting point for the enactment of comprehensive national health care reform. "Health Security," it appeared, might indeed renovate the New Deal tradition of the federal government as guarantor of basic security needs for the majority of Americans. A Democratic president and a Democratic-led Congress might succeed in capturing popular allegiance and bipartisan support for a comprehensive new reform to address national and personal concerns.

How ironic, then, that just a bit over one year after President Clinton launched his Health Security initiative, that plan had lost public support and failed to pass Congress, even in sharply curtailed form. On September 26, 1994, death was pronounced for health reform by George Mitchell, then the Senate Majority Leader. Within weeks after the demise of health care reform the Democratic Party—legatee of the very New Deal whose achievements Clinton had hoped to imitate and extend—lay in a shambles. Voters went to the polls on November 8, 1994, and registered widespread victories for Republicans running for state legislatures, for Republican gubernatorial candidates, for Republican Senate candidates, and—most remarkably—for Republican House candidates, who took control of that chamber after four full decades of continuous Democratic ascendancy. Scores of Democratic congressional incumbents were tossed out on November 8, while not even one incumbent Republican was defeated. The breadth and depth of the Republican victories seemed to render President Clinton an irrelevant lame duck for the remaining two years of his first term and raised the very real prospect of a long-lasting pro-Republican "realignment" in U.S. electoral politics.

Many of the Republicans who won in 1994 were ideologically hostile to governmental social provision of any sort, and news commentators quickly concluded that New Deal traditions in American politics are sure to be reversed. Much attention focused on the Republicans' "Contract with America," a ten-point manifesto devised before the election to commit House Republicans to vote within the first hundred days of the 104th Congress on transformations in government procedures, regulatory cutbacks, abolition of welfare as an entitlement for the poor, and huge tax cuts, mostly benefiting business and relatively well-off families.[6] The "Contract" said not a word about health care reform, which had been such an important public priority during the 1992 election and, according to polls, remained a widespread concern.[7] Instead, the Republican Contract unabashedly aimed to hobble permanently the domestic capacities of government.

Right after the November 1994 election the chief architect of the Republican congressional victories, incoming Speaker of the House Newt Gingrich of Georgia, loudly promised to carry through his long-nurtured determination to dismantle America's "failed" welfare state.[8] "Gingrich Declares War on Social Programs" announced a November 12 headline in the Boston Globe, where the Speaker-to-be denounced "Great Society social programs" as a "disaster" for "ruining the poor" and creating "a culture of poverty and a culture of violence which is destructive of this civilization."[9] Within a few more weeks, Speaker Gingrich also went on record promising to fundamentally revamp Medicare from a universal public health insurance program for older citizens into more-limited subsidies for participation in private health plans.[10] Only Social Security seemed to be off limits for the dismantling that Gingrich and his fellow conservative Republicans had in mind—but apparently only for a while.[11]

The collapse of President Clinton's attempted Health Security reform lurked like a brooding ghost throughout the electoral upheavals of the fall of 1994 and the conservative Republican attacks on federal social programs that followed. To be sure, there were other issues and moods at work in the election. "Sour" and "skeptical" Americans blamed everyone in Washington, D.C., for many things—including the health reform debacle.[12] Polls following the November election showed that many voters were punishing Democrats for having been in charge during a time when the federal government was in unappealing disarray and not delivering desired results.[13] A crucial minority of voters—particularly "swing" Independents and former Ross Perot voters—were disappointed in President Clinton in part because they believed he had proposed a "big-government solution" to health care reform.[14]

Reservations about Clinton and the Democrats were fueled by the perceptions of health care reform that had jelled by late summer. "Comprehensive health-care reform" was probably "beyond saving," concluded analyst William Schneider on August 14, because, as Congress had grappled with the Clinton plan and various alternatives to it over the past several months, the middle class had come to see possible legislative action as more threatening than the failure of comprehensive reform. "People's biggest fear about the Administration's health-care plan is that it will take what they already have [i.e., employer-provided insurance] and make it worse."[15] Subsequently, an election-night survey of voters sponsored by the Kaiser Family Foundation found that a substantial majority (and especially those who voted Republican) believed that the Democrats' reform plans entailed too much "government bureaucracy" and could have reduced the quality of their own health care.[16]

Media assessments of an unstoppable "Republican revolution" after the November 1994 elections were hasty and overwrought. During 1995 and early 1996, many House Republican efforts to slash government spending and trim taxes on the better-off ran into trouble in the Senate and among Americans who shared with pollsters their worries about undoing successful federal efforts such as nutrition programs, Medicare, and educational loans. Part of the time, at least, President Clinton held his own in legislative sparring with the Republicans, and the eventual outcome of the 1996 presidential contest remained open.

Nevertheless, the year 1994 was an important turning point in U.S. politics. In the wake of the demise of the Clinton Health Security plan and the midterm elections, congressional and public debates about government moved sharply to the right. Debates henceforth focused on *how* to reduce federal spending and balance the budget, whether to eliminate or merely sharply cut domestic federal programs. The focus of attention is no longer on how to create or even sustain national guarantees of security for the American citizenry. The Democratic Party, long confident in its hold on Congress and many subnational public offices, is clearly on the defensive, both electorally and intellectually. Democrats are uncertain about the contributions, if any, that public social programs can make to security and opportunity for American families. The national and Democratic Party moods are a far cry from what they were when President Clinton spoke so eloquently on September 22, 1993.

The demise of President Bill Clinton's Health Security plan was, in short, not just an attempted policy change that fizzled out. The presentation and decisive defeat of the Clinton plan in 1993–94 was a pivotal moment in the history of the U.S. governmental and political system. It is too soon to tell how sharp or unwavering the changes of 1994 will prove to be. But we are unlikely ever to return to the *status quo ante*, to the partisan, institutional, or public policy situations that existed before the rise and resounding demise of the Health Security effort. The agenda of politics has changed.

To understand why the 1993–94 attempt at comprehensive health insurance reform backfired so badly on its sponsors, we must ask why President Clinton devised a plan that was not only defeated in Congress but also inadvertently helped to fuel a massive electoral and governmental upheaval. The reasons for this, as we shall see, turn out to be revealing about the limits and intractable tensions of U.S. politics and governing processes since the 1970s. Moreover, only against the backdrop of the political and governmental upheavals spurred by the defeat of Clinton's ambitious Health Security plan, can we make sense of challenges and possibilities in U.S. politics and social policymaking in the foreseeable future.

What Went Wrong?

Some have argued that there is little to investigate about the failure of the Clinton Health Security plan. Soon after George Mitchell, then the Democratic Majority Leader of the Senate, called it quits in the quest for any health legislation in September 1994, "obvious" explanations spewed forth to account for an attempted reform that backfired. Instant judgments came above all from Washington insiders and members of the "punditocracy" of media commentators and policy experts who appear daily on television and in the editorial and op-ed pages of newspapers and magazines. A year before, such commentators had been certain that President Clinton had irreversibly aroused a national commitment to some sort of universal health insurance. After the President's effort failed, the pundits became equally sure that his venture had never had any chance of popular acceptance or legislative enactment. We knew it all along, they said.

For many commentators, flaws in the personalities of key actors in the Clinton administration make sense of what happened. According to this story line, foolish and arrogant policy planners launched a liberal, government-takeover scheme that was doomed to fail. The debacle was "what happens," the editors of New Republic assure us, "when you cross the worst management consultancy blather with paleoliberal ambition."[17] Commentators say that President Clinton, himself a man of unsteady character, unwisely entrusted policy planning by the President's Task Force on Health Care Reform to the joint leadership of his controversial wife, First Lady Hillary Rodham Clinton, and his business-consultant friend, Ira C. Magaziner, onetime Brown University student leader and Rhodes Scholar.[18] In the aftermath of the health reform debacle, the unfortunate Magaziner has become almost everyone's preferred scapegoat, ridiculed as grandiose and dogmatic, while Mrs. Clinton is regularly portrayed as an overly ambitious, meddling woman. In the characteristic words of Bill Schneider (who is always ready to articulate the conventional opinions of the day, even if they are 180 degrees opposite to what they earlier were),

> the Clinton administration displayed awesome political stupidity. It turned health-care reform over to a 500-person task force of self-annointed experts, meeting for months in secret, chaired by a sinister liberal activist and a driven First Lady. Who elected them? They came up with a 1,300-page document that could not have been better designed to scare the wits out of Americans. It was the living embodiment of Big Government—or Big Brother.[19]

Both Magaziner and Mrs. Clinton are retrospectively upbraided for "know it all" arrogance and an unwillingness to undertake politically necessary compromises. Many in Washington and the punditocracy believe that this "sinister" pair committed the President to a reckless drive for universal insurance coverage; they are sure that Clinton would have been successful if only he had pursued modest changes in a bipartisan fashion. Depending on who one believes, Bill Clinton pursued his health reform initiative in such an "awesomely stupid" way because he really is a 1960s radical at heart or because he is a hen-pecked husband hoodwinked by his wife and her left-wing friends or because he has no backbone and gave in to pressure from old-fashioned Democrats in Congress and liberal interest groups.

Stories about flawed personalities are fun to read, and they mesh perfectly with the overall judgements that have been registered on the Clinton presidency by such elite journalists as Bob Woodward and Elizabeth Drew.[20] From the start, elite journalists have taken a haughty and hypercritical stance toward the Clinton administration, writing a steady stream of news features and editorials revealing its alleged incompetence (or even corruption), while implying with surprisingly little subtlety that the nation would be in better hands if only the journalists were in charge instead. Retrospectives blaming the

Courtesy *Richmond Times-Dispatch*

failure of health care reform on scapegoats have easily slid into this well-worn line of condemnation.

Probing only slightly more deeply than those who attribute the failure of reform to the "awesome stupidity" of certain members of the Clinton administration, other commentators, especially academics and think-tank policy analysts, have thrown up their hands in despair about the hopeless inconsistencies of the American people. "The Gridlock Is Us," declared a *New York Times* op-ed by a leading advocate of this point of view, Professor Robert Blendon of the Harvard University School of Public Health.[21] According to Blendon, the legislative impasse that loomed by the spring of 1994 was attributable to confusions and divisions of opinion among Americans about how to achieve health care reform—and even more tellingly, to the citizenry's insistence on universal coverage without painful trade-offs such as "some limitations on our choice of medical providers, paying more in taxes or premiums, accepting some Federal intervention to control hospital, doctor and insurance costs—or all of the above." After the burial of the reform effort, a similar conclusion was put forward by policy expert Joshua M. Wiener of the Brookings Institution. Searching for the "fundamental factors" that explain "What Killed Health Care Reform?" Wiener gives pride of place to his conclusion that

Americans are schizophrenic about health care. They believe that the U.S. health care *system* needs major reform, but they are quite content with their own health care. . . . Americans want the problems fixed without making any major changes in the way their own health care is financed and delivered. But the problem cannot be fixed without significantly changing the way health care is financed and delivered.[22]

Explanations for the 1993–94 health reform debacle that stress leaders' character flaws or public fecklessness are glib and unsatisfying, however. The "gridlock is us" view implies that President Clinton was rash to take on health care reform at a time when Americans were "not yet ready" to make the necessary sacrifices and trade-offs to enable coverage to be extended and costs to be contained. Americans are presumed to have been, all along, unwilling to accept changes in their health care arrangements. But this makes little sense in an era when medical care provision is being rapidly transformed by market forces

Courtesy Universal Press Syndicate

above the heads and beyond the control of most ordinary patients.

Americans are *already* experiencing major changes in the financing and delivery of their health care—changes instituted by employers, health insurance companies, hospitals, and fiscally hard-pressed governments. While acquiescing in such sweeping changes, Americans at the start of the health care reform debate were quite clear in their strong expectations for government action. As opinion analysts put it, the

> public believes that guaranteeing the availability of adequate health care for all americans is an exceedingly important goal for the nation. Recent surveys show that the goal of universal coverage is the most popular aspect of current health system reform plans, with support ranging from 73% to 86%. . . . [and] nearly two thirds (65%) of the public believes that the federal government should guarantee health coverage for all Americans.[23]

By respectable majorities as well, Americans endorsed modest tax increases and employer mandates as tools for moving toward universal coverage.[24] Such support did wane during the 1993–94 debate, but only after Americans had been exposed to fierce partisan arguments against the sorts of "sacrifices" they were clearly prepared to make during 1991–92 and as President Clinton's plan was launched in 1993.[25]

More than "setting the agenda" for policymakers can hardly be expected from the citizenry as a whole. Public opinion in general never chooses among exact policy options; nor does it work out the details of policy innovations. These tasks are the responsibility of societal leaders and elected officials, ideally working within a general mandate given by voters and the public. The "gridlock is us" interpretation overestimates the direct role of shifting opinions on unfolding policy debates. In fact, popular views are just as readily shaped and reshaped by arguments among leaders as vice versa.[26] During the protracted 1993–94 national debate over the Clinton Health Security plan and various alternatives to it, the American people heard many elite attacks on every major reform approach, so it is hardly surprising that public opinion became more confused over time.

All too conveniently, the "gridlock is us" argument excuses America's politicians, policy intellectuals, and private-sector elites from responsibility for the failure of comprehensive and democratically inclusive reform of the nation's system for financing health care. If the citizenry as a whole is to blame for the confusions and divisions into which the 1993–94 debate degenerated, then our leaders and institutional arrangments for making civic decisions are off the hook.

We should not, however, allow our attention to be directed away from the nation's major institutions—its government, mass media, political parties, and health care and economic enterprises. These were the arenas within which our leaders—not just those in the Clinton administration, but also corporate leaders, journalists, health care providers, and Democrats and Republicans in Congress and beyond—defined their goals and maneuvered in relation to each other. Within and at the intersections of these institutions, America's leaders failed to come up with reasonable ways to address pressing national concerns about the financing of health care for everyone.

As for explanations that highlight the personality flaws and supposed "awesome stupidity" of certain people in the Clinton administration, surely these miss the forest for a few trees. Various people in and around the Clinton administration did indeed take missteps, as I shall argue. But most of their errors were not stupid ones. Most of the mistakes made by the President and his allies need to be understood in terms of the difficult choices these people inexorably faced—given sensitive economic circumstances, artificially draconian federal budgetary constraints, and the flawed modalities of politics in the United States today.

Scapegoating of the President's Task Force on Health Care Reform led by Mrs. Clinton and Ira Magaziner has been especially overdone in instant retrospectives on the events of 1993–94. President Clinton decided on his basic approach to health reform well before this task force was convened, and the general outlines of Health Security got a warm public reception during the first nine months of 1993. From a historical perpective, the planning process that fleshed out the Clinton Health Security plan was not all that different from the process run by the Committee on Economic Security in 1934–35 to draft Franklin Delano Roosevelt's Social Security legislation.[27] In both cases, governmental officials and carefully selected policy experts were at the core of the effort. Basic decisions about major policy options were made quite apart from public hearings and conferences, and a lot of attention was paid to trying to anticipate what might arouse support or opposition and make headway or not through Congress.[28]

In both the 1930s and the early 1990s, many individuals and groups whose ideas were not accepted by policy planners became angry with the fact. But what is so surprising or decisive about that? The different outcomes for Social Security in 1935 versus Health Security in 1994 surely had much more to do with the contrasting overall political dynamics of the two eras. The divergent outcomes can also be attributed, in part, to the very different sorts of governmental interventions substantively called for by Social Security versus Health Security. I will highlight such comparisons in the chapters to come.

Journalistic accounts that accuse the Clinton administration of devising a liberal, big-government approach to health care reform are simply misrepresenting the most basic aspects of what happened from 1992 through 1994. As we will see, the Clinton Health Security plan was *a compromise* between market-oriented and government-centered reform ideas. In any event, talking about the "market" versus the "government" when analyzing plans for financing health care makes little sense; what matters is the *kind* of government involvement any plan proposes, and its political implications. Markets pure and simple cannot be expected to control costs and include everyone in health care.[29] All plans for health care reform, including those that have been put forward by the very conservative Heritage Foundation, involve heavy doses of one kind or another of governmental involvement.[30] What is more, proposed changes of any variety must be inserted into a U.S. health care system that already includes huge amounts of governmentally funneled money and public regulation. Medicaid and Medicare account for about a third of all U.S. health care financing, and state and federal governments are heavily involved in regulating hospitals, doctors, and other health-service providers.[31]

The Health Security plan devised by Clinton's Task Force on Health Care Reform would have led, over time, to significantly less governmental involvement than we have now. President Clinton's approach to reform sought to further privately run and financed managed care, and would have encouraged the eventual dissolution of the Medicaid program. The Clinton plan also sought to reverse many of the public regulations and subsidies that have made the U.S. health care system a regime that has publicly facilitated lavish spending on high technologies and on generous rewards for professionals in the various health care industries.[32] Clinton was trying to move toward public encouragement of cost efficiency instead.

As for "universal coverage," the President stressed this goal in response to overwhelming public support, responding as a small-d democratic leader should have responded to concerns among the public that are both personal and ethical. Bill Clinton also aimed for inclusion because no Democratic president (or candidate for president) could avoid addressing the needs of the low-wage working families who crowd the ranks of the uninsured. Of the approximately 38 million Americans who lacked health insurance for all or part of the year when Clinton ran for president in 1992, more than 30 million were in working families. Seven of ten were adults or children in families making less than $30,000 in 1992, often by working in small businesses.[33] Such people are treated very unfairly in the current U.S. health insurance system. They work hard, often for meager incomes, but have to worry about going to the doctor or taking their children for medical attention. Uninsured working people also have to be helped—and politically inspired—if the Democratic Party is ever to achieve electoral majorities again.

Many commentators have written or spoken as if the President should have sponsored the Republican Party's preferred health care reform proposals—ideas aimed almost exclusively at making private insurance a bit more secure for the already well insured—rather than promoting policies that would meet the concerns of all Americans, including actual or potential Democratic voters. This reflects the profound upper-middle-class bias of current debates over health care financing in the United States. The debates are carried on almost exclusively by people who have no worries about affording the best possible health care for themselves and their loved ones and who are sure that, should a health crisis strike, they will be able to use social connections to reach the best doctors and hospitals. It is easy for such experts and commentators to forget ethical and political considerations about people who work for low wages and no benefits. It is equally easy for them to forget about the insecurities that worry average members of the middle class.

President Clinton and the Democrats struggled to extend health coverage to all Americans within a climate of elite opinion that is in principle unsympathetic to democratic inclusiveness. Over the last decade, self-styled "independents" in the Concord Coalition (and, more recently, Ross Perot) have propagated critiques of "middle-class entitlements" such as Social Security and Medicare. The editorial pages of the *New York Times* and the *Washington Post*, as well as the feature pages of such high-brow outlets as the *New York Review of Books*, the *New Republic*, and the *Atlantic*, all have echoed Concord Coalition arguments that security benefits for middle-class Americans are "too expensive," that they are "bankrupting" the country and depriving "our children and grandchildren" of a viable economic future.[34] Such attacks on "entitlements" have prompted many Americans to think that well-loved Social Security and Medicare benefits may not be there in the future. Arguments against entitlements have also made it very difficult for public officials to talk about new security guarantees such as health insurance coverage for everyone.

Despite the difficulties of advocating universal coverage in the climate of opinion I have just described, during 1992 and 1993 Bill Clinton came to believe that effective cost controls in health care financing were impossible without including all Americans. (Health care is not a luxury good that people do without. When people finally show up in emergency rooms, costs simply escalate and get shifted around.) For reasons that we will explore in the next two chapters, Clinton and his advisors devised a Health Security plan meant simultaneously to further universal inclusion and cost controls, through managed "competition within a budget."[35] This was no liberal scheme. Rather it was a carefully constructed compromise between previously available liberal proposals and more conservative, market-oriented ideas about health care reform.

As a candidate and then as president, Bill Clinton searched assiduously for an approach to health care reform that would allow him to bridge the contradictions he had to face by achieving a new synthesis of previously opposed views. He looked for a middle way between Republicans and Democrats and between conservative and liberal factions in the Democratic Party and the Congress. He looked for a compromise between U.S. business and other private-sector elites who wanted to control rising health care costs, and average citizens who wanted secure coverage without personally having to pay much more for it. Perhaps most important, Mr. Clinton looked for a way to reform the financing of health care for everyone in the United States without increasing the size of the federal budget deficit or creating an open-ended new public "entitlement."

During 1993, many commentators, politicians, and members of the U.S. public thought that President Clinton was appropriately pointing the way toward feasible and moderate comprehensive health care reforms. So it does no good to pretend now, in retrospect, that all along the Clinton administration was off on an obviously unrealistic "liberal," "big government" tangent.

Making Sense of an Historic Turnaround

Although I do not accept the notion that President Clinton or his health planners were "awesomely stupid" or excessively "liberal," we do need to probe into constraints and pitfalls that supporters of comprehensive health care reform did not adequately understand or cope with between 1992 and 1994. Things certainly went very wrong for the Clinton Health Security plan! It ended up furthering legislative and political outcomes that were exactly the opposite of what its promoters intended. Instead of cementing new intraparty coalitions and mobilizing renewed electoral support for the Democrats, the Clinton Health Security plan backfired on the Democrats. Instead of renewing and extending the federal government's capacity to ensure security for all Americans, the Clinton plan helped to trigger an extraordinary electoral and ideological backlash against federal social provision in general.

To make sense of obviously unintended outcomes, we need to probe beyond character flaws and surface shifts in public opinion. In this book, I analyze the societal, governmental, and partisan terrains on which Bill Clinton devised his plan to reform health care financing and on which groups and politicians maneuvered over its fate. I connect policy choices to developments in the Democratic and Republican parties since the 1960s; and I relate Health Security to earlier federal initiatives, such as Social Security and Medicare. Above all, I highlight the impact on 1990s health reform of the massive federal deficits inherited from the Reagan era. The Clinton health initiative was profoundly influenced by rigorous budgetary decision-making procedures that Congress and the executive branch have put in place in an effort to cope with the deficit and its political reverberations. Understanding what happened with Health Security, in short, takes us into the thick of the partisan and institutional forces shaping—and rapidly transforming—U.S. politics today.

A central paradox is worth keeping in mind as we proceed.[36] By 1992–93 a large majority of Americans wanted the federal government—and newly elected President Bill Clinton—to tackle a widely perceived national health care crisis.[37] At the same time, popular faith in the federal government to do things right was at a thirty-year nadir.[38] Could President Clinton and Congress produce an economically and politically viable approach to health care reform? What would happen if they botched the job? Waiting in the wings, after all, were insurgent Republicans determined to find a way to reverse the course of federal domestic policies since the New Deal. The stakes in the maneuvering over Health Security were very high.

CHAPTER ONE

A WAY THROUGH THE MIDDLE?

Looking back from the vantage point of the well-received Health Security speech of September 1993, President Clinton and his delighted advisors had every reason to think that they were acting with a rising tide in U.S. politics. For the past two years, health care reform had been an evident popular priority for governmental action; and it looked like a winning, majority-building issue for the Democratic Party. Those in the Clinton administration who had labored for months to spell out the Health Security plan believed, with reason, that they were responding effectively to the expressed needs and expectations of the vast majority of Americans. By taking a compromise route to government-sponsored yet market-based reform, they apparently had found an effective way through the middle of the various divides that had bedeviled earlier health care reform efforts.

In this chapter and chapter 2, we learn why Bill Clinton gravitated toward regulated market competion as his preferred approach to health reform. The unrelenting challenges of an electoral campaign influenced the early, conceptual stages of reform, while the budgetary and political exigencies of the early Clinton presidency shaped the formulation of the Health Security proposal.

An Issue Simmering beneath the Surface

During the decades following World War II, the United States became downright peculiar as a leading industrial-democratic nation without some sort of governmentally guaranteed health insurance for all citizens. European countries, as well as democracies in other parts of the world, had long since found ways to provide health care for all their citizens; and in 1971 even Canada took the road to national health insurance. Repeatedly across the twentieth century, reformers in the United States tried to achieve health insurance for all workers or all citizens. Such attempts were made in the late 1910s, twice during the 1930s, and again in the late 1940s with the endorsement of Democratic President Harry Truman.[1] But these movements to extend governmentally guaranteed health coverage to working-aged people all failed, and during the era after World War II many (but not all) private employers sponsored health coverage for employees and their family members.

The U.S. government entered the health care financing picture in a big way only in the 1960s. In 1965, while Lyndon Johnson was president at the height of liberal-Democratic influence in Congress and public opinion, the United States instituted Medicaid to provide insurance coverage for the very poor, especially mothers and children, along with Medicare to finance health care for all elderly Americans, sixty-five years old and over.[2] It would not be long, many U.S. reformers hoped at that point, before basic health insurance coverage was extended to everyone.

But this was not to be. During the 1970s, first Republican President Richard M. Nixon and then Democratic President Jimmy Carter pushed for health reforms that would have combined extended insurance coverage with tougher federal controls over rapidly rising health care costs.[3] Both efforts at comprehensive reforms fell short. Afterward, those policymakers and experts who remained interested in promoting health care reform decided that only very low key, incremental efforts had any chance of success. Politicians mostly avoided calls for comprehensive health reform, viewing this goal as fraught with possibilities of interest group conflict, partisan polarization, and sheer intellectual uncertainty about how best to proceed.

Problems of rising costs and receding insurance coverage nevertheless intensified in the jerry-built U.S. system for financing health care. Difficulties that were evident during the 1970s only accelerated during the 1980s. As sociologist Paul Starr explains, "in 1970 *Business Week* called health care a '$60 billion dollar crisis'; by 1991 the cost was approaching . . . $800 billion a year. Health care spending had risen from 7.3 percent to 13.2 percent of GNP. Since 1980, health care has consumed an additional 1 percent of GNP *every 35 months*."[4] Compared to other advanced industrial democracies, the United States spends a significantly greater proportion of its national income on health care. It also spends more per capita than any other nation, yet Americans are more dissatisfied than people in other democracies with the workings of the overall health system.[5]

Rapidly rising costs affected both the public and the private sectors. Public expenditures on health care for the aged and the poor rose at well above the overall rate of inflation, more than doubling (from 5.9 to over 13 percent of GNP between 1965 and 1991), while expenditures on defense receded slightly (from 7.5 to less than 6 percent), and public investments in education grew only marginally (from 6.2 to 7.2 percent).[6] In private industry, meanwhile, workers saw productivity increases not translate into higher real wages, but disappear into employer health contributions. When many U.S. employers, especially big businesses, started offering employee health insurance in the late 1940s, they were paying modest costs for relatively youthful workforces. Later, however, workforces got older and health costs shot up. "From 1965 to 1989, business spending on health benefits climbed from 2.2 percent to 8.3 percent of wages and salaries, and from 8.4 percent to 56.4 percent of pretax corporate profits."[7]

Perceiving themselves to be at an increasing disadvantage in international competition, those U.S. employers who were struggling to pay for employee health insurance responded in various ways. Many shifted costs toward employees and retirees, even if they had to fight with unions to do this. Many also imposed cost-cutting forms of "managed care" on their employees. Others either dropped coverage or offered less-generous insurance, perhaps ceasing to provide coverage for family members or else dropping altogether individual employees with potentially very expensive "preexisting" health problems. Still other employers stopped hiring full-time insured workers or "contracted out" to small companies that do not cover (often part-time or temporary) employees.

All these employer strategies happened in conjunction with ever more aggressive efforts by insurance companies to weed out individuals or groups of customers who might have unusually expensive health care needs. The U.S. insurance industry was becoming more and more competitive. Small companies engaged in "cherry picking" by looking for the cheapest groups of younger and healthier employees to insure at low rates. Bigger companies that once practiced "community rating" (in which all customers were insured for similar premiums) began to look for ways to use differential prices or exclusions to cut costs and maintain profit margins.

Amidst all these market changes, health insurance became less available and more insecure, as well as more costly, for rising numbers of Americans. "In the three decades before 1970 employer-based health plans and public plans covered an increasing proportion of Americans. But in the 1980s coverage stopped growing and the ranks of the uninsured began to expand."[8] Lack of insurance could be episodic as well as persistent. More than one in four Americans had no health insurance coverage at some point between 1987 and 1989, a time of relatively full employment.[9] In 1988 (at a single measured point), some 31.6 million Americans—or 13 percent of the population under age sixty-five—had no private or public health insurance; and most of these were in families in which at least one person was employed (usually in a firm with fewer than a hundred employees).[10] What is more, many Americans who enjoyed employer-provided health coverage had to worry about possibly losing it or seeing it cut back if they switched or lost their jobs. Observers began to discuss the negative effects on individual productivity and national economic efficiency of the "job lock" that occurred when people would not change jobs for fear of losing health insurance for themselves or family members.

Still, as political observers well know, bad or deteriorating conditions do not automatically become the subject of political debate or governmental policymaking. This was certainly true for the problems of U.S. health care financing through the late 1980s. From 1980 through 1988, a conservative Republican president, Ronald Reagan, practiced "benign neglect" of domestic social problems and pursued an agenda of sharp tax cuts and reductions in federal domestic programs. And the possibility of "national health reform" played a little discernable role in the 1988 presidential election between George Bush, the sitting Republican Vice President, and Governor Michael Dukakis of Massachusetts, the ill-fated Democratic challenger. Although Dukakis touted a health reform plan as part of his "Massachusetts miracle," he and Bush did not face off on the health care issue; and only a small minority of voters regarded health care as an important issue in the election.[11] Dukakis's effort to make "competence, not ideology" the centerpiece of his presidential bid left the

Courtesy *Minneapolis Star Tribune*

way clear for George Bush and the Republicans to paint Dukakis as an extreme, out-of-touch liberal on emotionally resonant issues such as crime and patriotism.[12]

Once elected, moreover, George Bush shied away from tackling major domestic problems, including health insurance. Bush was reluctant although by 1989–90 between 60 and 72 percent of Americans were telling pollsters that they supported some sort of national health insurance program.[13] Instead of dealing with knotty problems at home, President Bush concentrated on foreign affairs. Politically his strategy seemed to pay off splendidly. In the immediate wake of the U.S.-led military trouncing of Iraq in the Gulf War, George Bush looked like such a sure bet for reelection in 1992 that nationally well known Democrats (such as Governor Mario Cuomo of New York) decided to sit out the upcoming presidential race.

What a difference a year can make in U.S. politics! Less than twelve months after he had a 91 percent favorable poll rating in the wake of the Gulf War, President Bush looked very vulnerable in the upcoming 1992 presidential election.[14] Economic and political happenings came together to turn the tables. The nation slipped deeper into economic recession during 1991, and by November 5 of that year, a special election in Pennsylvania turned out in a most surprising way and caught the attention of all U.S. politicians. Democratic fortunes were looking up, and national health care reform had shot to near the top of the nation's political agenda.

"National Health Reform" Bursts onto the Political Scene

The recession of 1990–91 took the bloom off of George Bush's presidency, and not only among blue-collar wage earners. This downturn prodded many U.S. companies to implement or speed up strategies of downsizing to more "efficiently" meet intensifying market competition at home and abroad. More managerial and white-collar employees than usual lost their positions in this recession, and it wasn't easy for them to gain new employment in comparable positions. Lost jobs soon meant no employer health insurance for many of the affected families. The numbers of uninsured rose by a couple of million a year from 1988 onward.[15] More and more Americans became worried. Opinion analysts Robert Blendon and Karen Donelan summed up the situation in late 1991, at a time when the recession was still playing out. Many Americans, they noted, express "fear of losing all or part of their health care benefits in our employment-based system of health insurance"; "60% of Americans worry they may not be adequately insured in the future."[16]

Such fears were realistic. By 1992 the number of the uninsured had risen to 38.9 million, up 4.2 percent from 1989; and that was 17.4 percent of Americans under sixty-five. Another 40 million Americans were, moreover, underinsured, because their policies provided "little protection in the event of serious illness."[17] More than ever, the rising costs and shrinking coverage in the U.S. system for financing health care were becoming a potential issue for middle-class voters.

Still, the potential might not have been translated into electoral strategies and appeals had not some truly serendipitous events occured in Pennsylvania in the summer and fall of 1991. The story starts with a tragedy. As journalist Sidney Blumenthal recounts, one day in the spring of 1991 Pennsylvania's sitting Republican Senator John Heinz—

youthful, handsome, wealthy, and politically impregnable—left Washington in a small plane. The pilot, concerned about safety, wanted to insure that the landing gear was in good working order. He radioed for a helicopter to fly up and inspect. Suddenly, the copter veered into the hovering plane, and the aircraft descended in flames upon a suburban schoolyard. The senator and several children were killed.[18]

Pennsylvania had a Democratic Governor, Bob Casey, who now "had the chance to appoint the first Democratic senator from Pennylvania in more than a generation."[19]

But Governor Casey had trouble finding anyone to take the job, because there would be a special election within just a few months and a well-known and popular Republican, Richard Thornburgh, had quickly declared that he would run for the unexpectedly vacated Heinz seat. Thornburgh had twice been elected governor of Pennsylvania, and he stepped down as Attorney General in the Bush Administration to run for the Senate. After being refused a couple of times, Governor Casey turned to his own Secretary of Labor and Industry, a former John F. Kennedy aide, Peace Corp founder, and president of Bryn Mawr College with the unpromising name of Harris Wofford ("Wooford," Thornburgh would mockingly call him when they debated). "The 65-year-old liberal intellectual, given to bouts of high-flown rhetoric, seemed a superannuated choice. But he was distinguished enough not to embarass Casey for the few short months he would serve as senator."[20]

Democrats, of course, had to make an attempt in the 1991 special election that pitted brief-incumbent Wofford against Thornburgh, but it seemed a hopeless, uphill struggle. Gritty political consultants Paul Begala and James ("Rajin Cajun") Carville signed on to manage Wofford's campaign. They set out to fashion a populist, pro-middle-class message for Wofford to present to "the people who pay taxes, do the work, foot the bill, struggle to save and often come up a little short at the end of the month. . . ."[21] Yet the campaign's first private polls in July 1991 showed Wofford trailing Thornburgh by 47 points, 67 to 20.[22] In August, Wofford still trailed by 44 points, and most Pennsylvanians still did not recognize his name.[23]

Then the unexpected happened. Beginning in September, the Pennsylvania campaign took a startling and momentous turn. The patrician Thornburgh campaigned in an overconfident, arrogant manner as a Bush administration insider. Foolishly bragging that he knew "the corridors of power in our nation's capital from my three years as a member of the President's cabinet," the Republican candidate opened himself up to the voting public's growing unease about an incumbent administration that seemed unable to cope with (or even take adequate notice of) the economic recession.[24] Meanwhile, the improbable Wofford began to make headway with his argument that "the rich get too many breaks in America, while working families keep falling farther behind," a general message backed up by his specific advocacy of middle-class tax cuts, college loans, economic nationalism, and national health reform.[25]

Starting in September, the Wofford campaign ran an effective television ad featuring his opposition to letting U.S. jobs go overseas ("It's time to take care of our own."), along with a soon-to-be celebrated television spot about health reform. Back in August, Wofford had visited a Philadelphia opthalmologist, Dr. Robert D. Reinecke, who remarked that he could not understand why the U.S. Constitution guaranteed the right to a counsel for anyone accused of a crime, but did not provide a right to a doctor for anyone fallen ill or hurt. Wofford found this query compelling, and he persuaded his media people to turn it into a television spot featuring him standing in a hospital emergency room and telling voters: "If criminals have the right to a lawyer, I think working Americans should have the right to a doctor. . . . I'm Harris Wofford, and I believe there is nothing more fundamental than the right to see a doctor when you're sick."[26]

According to Wofford's pollster Mike Donilon, this television advertisement had an extraordinary impact, helping to cut Thornburgh's lead by half during a couple of weeks in September.[27] Thornburgh had served on a Bush administration panel that had studied health care (without making recommendations), so he claimed to know this "complex" issue from the inside. Before Wofford's ad, voters tended to accept that Thornburgh would do a better job on health care reform. But by one "week before election day [November 5], Wofford owned the issue by 27 points." In a state where elections are usually cliffhangers, Wofford won the Pennsylvania special Senate election by an astonishing 10 points. He did well among all groups and across all regions of the state, even those that normally voted Republican.

Wofford's pollster used focus groups to track strong Pennsylvania voter interest in health reform throughout the campaign and concluded that ultimately (in the words of journalist Dale Russakoff) "more than 30 percent of the voters picked Wofford on the health care issue alone."[28] An independent postelection study also concluded that "voter interest in reform of the American health care system played a central role" in this "come-from-behind victory." A representative poll of 1,000 Pennsylvania voters showed that "50 percent identified 'national health insurance' as one of two issues that mattered most in deciding how to vote" and "21 percent of voters said the issue was the 'single most important factor' in their voting decision."[29]

In some ways, this was surprising. Pennsylvania was a state with many older citizens on Medicare and many unionized workers who had coverage at work; only 10 percent of its citizens were without health insurance in 1991, a considerably smaller proportion than the approximately 15 percent then uninsured nationwide.[30] Apparently, the support of Pennsylvanians for health insurance reforms only underlined the broader popular resonance of this issue, which tapped into working families' worries "that their economic life is falling apart—no health care, no money for the kids to go to college, and an old age spent in penury."[31] "Calling for national health insurance sends a bigger message than health care," Wofford's consultant Carville concluded.[32]

While serving as Pennsylvania's Secretary of Labor and Industry, Wofford himself had seen that paying for health care was an increasing popular concern, not to mention a tension point between unions and employers. His campaign found that Pennsylvanians in general talked about access to affordable health care "with a great deal of fear and anxiety." Perhaps equally significant for a Democratic candidate, the "focus groups also found widespread belief that something could be done. 'It was a place where people believed government could actually make a positive difference,'" Donilon says. Despite the fact that Wofford never outlined any specific reform plan, many Pennsylvanians even indicated a willingness to pay higher taxes in order to have the universal security of national health insurance.[33]

The fall 1991 special Senate election in Pennsylvania was an election heard around the nation. Hope for Democrats and anxiety for Republicans was immediately read into these electoral tea leaves. Celebrating a successful "pitch to the middle class" by a candidate "who did not run as a Democratic liberal" but "won as a Democratic middle-class populist," syndicated columnist Mark Shields declared Wofford's triumph a beacon for Democrats and "unwelcome for the White

Copyright © 1991 by John Trevor. Courtesy the *Albuquerque Journal*

House."[34] Indeed the Republican White House *was* frightened. Right after watching his friend Thornburgh go down to such a surprising and ignominious defeat, President Bush canceled a planned two-week trip to the Far East and announced he would concentrate on domestic affairs. Soon he would discover that his administration was, after all, planning to propose health reforms.

For the cause of national health reform, the unexpected Wofford triumph became what political scientist John Kingdon calls a "focusing event."[35] According to Kingdon, potential policy issues do not come up for public debate and potential legislative action until problematic socioeconomic conditions are combined with proposed policy solutions *and* a widespread sense that the "time is ripe" for political action. By 1991 problems of rising costs and receding insurance coverage had been building for some time across the nation; and health policy experts had been honing possible solutions for decades. But not until the Wofford election did national health care reform become a "must issue" for politicians—for those already in office as well as those aspiring to it. After November 5, 1991, one media commentator after another declared that health care might well be (in the words of one of them) "*the* issue for 1992."[36] Similarly, the authors of the post-election voter study cited above—an investigation sponsored by the proreform Kaiser Family Foundation—did not hesitate to draw sweeping conclusions for national politics. They boldly argued that the

> results of the Pennsylvania Senate race suggest that national health insurance has arrived as a mainstream political issue. Approaches to a universal plan may vary, but politicians who fail to address this issue now do so at their peril. . . . Would health care have been the issue it was in Pennsylvania if Senator Wofford had not made it a central issue in his campaign? Our poll cannot definitively answer this question. But it does show . . . that universal health care could attract voters to those politicians who choose to make it a visible campaign issue.[37]

A Proliferation of Schemes for Reform

In the months after November 1991, the apparent message of Wofford's Pennsylvania upset—that the time was finally ripe for reform of the national system for financing health care—was taken very much to heart by America's politicians and politically engaged groups, ranging from those based in the nation's capital to those on the electoral hustings across the land. In response to rising costs and receding coverage, proposals for the reform had already multiplied during 1990 and 1991; in the aftermath of the Pennsylvania election, more proposals appeared and existing ones were refurbished or made newly visible. Dozens of bills were introduced by senators or representatives.[38] Health reform proposals, many of them sweeping, also came from business groups, trade unions, insurance companies, and assorted health policy experts.[39] Even the American Medical Association (AMA), historically the bitterest of all enemies of governmentally sponsored health reforms, came up with its own "Health Access America" plan, calling for universally guaranteed health insurance to be financed, in part, through mandatory contributions from employers.[40]

Through the first half of 1992, most plans were variants of three basic approaches to reform: market-oriented reforms aiming at incremental modifications of private health insurance markets; "single payer" tax-financed plans to cover all citizens; and a hybrid road to universal health coverage called "play or pay." Without going into the mind-numbingly technical details of every variant of each approach, we can get a sense of what each was like and notice which major actors were associated with that approach to health reform as the nation moved into the presidential election of 1992.

Incremental, market-oriented reforms were intended to promote—but not guarantee—insurance coverage. Such schemes were identified during 1991 and early 1992 with the Republicans, and were also put forward by such private groups as the Health Insurance Association of America, which spoke for many private insurers. A variety of such plans were introduced in the 102nd Congress, embodying such changes as: limits on malpractice liability, tax subsidies or credits to help low-income people buy insurance, and new rules for the insurance market (for example, to limit price variations in insurance, require companies to take all applicant groups, and eliminate exclusions of customers who suffered from preexisting medical conditions).[41]

After it became apparent that he could not avoid coming forward with a plan if he wanted to remain electorally credible in competition with the Democrats, President Bush synthesized certain ideas from previous market-incremental schemes into a proposal unveiled in early February 1992.[42] The Bush plan called for insurance purchasing pools for small business, regulations of insurance company practices and malpractice awards in order to reduce the price of coverage, and tax-financed vouchers plus tax credits to make insurance more affordable for lower-income families.[43] President Bush also wanted to encourage the spread of "managed care" forms of health-service delivery, in order to further competitive market efforts to hold down costs. When fully implemented, his plan was projected to cost about $35 billion a year. Both President Bush and Senate Republicans remained vague about where the money would come from, alluding in general terms only to reductions in existing federal outlays for Medicaid and Medicare.

Sounding staple incrementalist themes and speaking for the Republican congressional leadership, Representative Bill Gradison of Ohio told the House Ways and Means Committee on March 3 that "the President's plan will move us in the right direction—towards consumer choice, not government coercion; towards timely treatment, not waiting lists for needed care; towards ever better quality care, not arbitrary limits on the use of new technologies."[44] But market-adjusting nostrums had little appeal for supporters of universal coverage. And Democrats, including moderates, scorned the Bush plan. "Majority Leader George Mitchell of Maine said Bush flunked two important tests—cost controls and universal access. Finance Committee Chairman Lloyd Bentsen of Texas said Bush's advice to Americans . . . is to 'take two aspirins and call me after the election.' "[45] Because of its vague financing provisions and evident inability to get any handle on rising insurance costs, the Bush plan was dismissed on arrival by many media commentators and health policy experts.[46]

Apparently at the other end of the partisan spectrum from Republican-sponsored market adjustments were various sorts of Canadian-style "single payer" schemes, which called for universal health coverage for all Americans to be financed by payroll or general taxes. ("Single payer" refers to the fact that all payments for health services would be channeled through one entity, whether the federal government, a state government, or a regional quasi-public organization of some sort. Medical services would still be provided by a variety of doctors, hospitals, and clinics, most of which would be privately owned and run.) This approach to reform was passionately championed by certain health policy experts, such as Theodore Marmor and Rashi Fein.[47] Single-payer ideas were also supported by certain grassroots advocacy groups, such as Citizen Action and the Consumers' Union, and by a small, maverick group of doctors called "Physicians for a National Health Program."[48] A considerable minority in Congress endorsed a Canadian-style approach as embodied in various bills, including the "Universal Health Act of 1991," introduced by Representative Marty Russo of Illinois and endorsed by seventy cosponsors.[49]

An excellent technical case could be made that a single-payer approach would save more than enough on simplified administrative costs to cover all the uninsured. This is true because private insurers spend a high proportion of their revenues on administrative and advertising costs, not medical care. What is more, the Canadian experience after the 1970s suggested that if public financing were accompanied by the use of "global" budget limits and annually negotiated payments to physicians and hospitals, a single-payer approach might significantly reduce the rate of increase of national health care expenditures while maximizing the day-to-day autonomy of patients and health providers.[50] Some variants of the single-payer approach, moreover, called for public administration by the states rather than the federal government. As the Democratic presidential primary races were getting under way, Senator Robert Kerrey of Nebraska was attracting a good deal of interest and liberal support because of his championing of a cautiously designed state-administered single-payer plan called "Health USA."[51] This plan preserved the rights of citizens and providers to use a variety of private delivery systems including Health Management Organizations (HMOs); and the Kerrey bill was innovative in its endorsement of fixed "capitation payments" (payments prospectively covering all care to a person, with some adjustments for the needs of various types of people) as a mechanism to encourage health providers to hold down costs.

But whatever the overall advantages of the single-payer approach (or the appeals of specific variants such as Health USA), most U.S. politicians feared to endorse such plans, because they would be highly threatening to established stakeholders in health care markets. Single-payer proposals also portended upheavals for white-collar employees and would necessitate switching from employer-financed premiums toward explicit general or payroll taxation. For all these reasons, single-payer approaches to national health reform were tacitly ruled out of polite "insider" conversations among those who wanted to be "serious players" in Washington. Above all, frank talk about raising taxes was presumed to be the kiss of death for politicians—and for those advising them or aspiring to do so. Democratic presidential candidate Walter Mondale had apparently shot himself in the foot with such talk in 1984. And in 1992 George Bush was in trouble—challenged not only by Democrats, but also by Pat Buchanan in the early Republican primaries—for having broken his 1988 "read my lips" pledge never to raise taxes. Not surprisingly, therefore, most politicians facing competitive electoral challenges rejected single-payer possibilities. This included Democratic presidential aspirant Governor Bill Clinton of Arkansas, who was running a moderate campaign based on promises to help the "hard-pressed" middle class, in part by reducing taxes on everyone except the rich.[52]

The third major approach to national health care reform on the table in 1991–92 was "play or pay"—so labeled because it would require all employers either to "play" in the employer health system by offering health insurance for all employees or else "pay" a kind of quit-tax to help subsidize expanded governmental coverage for the uninsured. An expanded public program, possibly substituting for Medicaid, would cover all nonelderly Americans not employed or insured by their employers. Play-or-pay schemes for national health care reform were not elegant, for they tried to patch together universal coverage while preserving the mixed elements of America's current system for financing health care. Health policy experts had all kinds of criticisms of this approach, including worries that it might not control rising national health costs and worries that employers might start "dumping" previously insured workers into a second-rate, poorly financed public insurance program. Conservatives, meanwhile, suspected that play or pay was just a surreptitious route toward a single-payer system. Despite such criticisms from left and right alike, play or pay was the middle-of-the-road approach in the existing field of alternatives, and as such was touted by many as the most pragmatic road to national health reform.[53]

Indeed, between 1990 and 1992, play-or-pay proposals received such prestigious backing that some version of this approach seemed certain to be the legislative starting point if or when national political conditions made it feasible to enact comprehensive reform. Back in 1988, Congress had established the so-called Pepper Commission (officially the "U.S. Bipartisan Commission on Comprehensive Health Care"), which included six House members, six senators, and three presidential appointees. Charged with recommending "legislation that would ensure all Americans coverage for health care and long term care," the Pepper Commission was not able to overcome disagreements on the left or the right. There were dissents to its final report from Democrats who favored single-payer approaches and from Republican Commission Vice Chairman Bill Gradison (who, as we have seen, supported President Bush's market-incremental approach). But Senator Jay Rockefeller of West Virginia did lead a bare majority of the Pepper Commission—consisting of a core of Democratic congressional leaders—in hammering out a play-or-pay proposal for universal coverage. This was presented in the Pepper Commission's Final Report of March 1990, whose proposals in turn laid the basis for a "Health America" bill introduced by the Democratic congressional leaders in June 1991.[54]

Another version of play or pay, incorporating somewhat stronger methods of cost containment, emerged in late 1991 from an extragovernmental omnibus commission, the National Leadership Coalition for Health Care Reform. Launched in March 1990, this coalition brought together "about 60 large companies, unions, and special interest groups" to work out "a plan that would provide all Americans with health coverage and contain costs."[55] As it became obvious that an employer mandate might be endorsed, various participants dropped out, most notably such corporations as AT&T, DuPont, Arco, Eastman Kodak, 3M, and Burger King. Those remaining in the Coalition were led by such unionized companies facing staggering health care costs as Chrysler, Ford, and Bethlehem Steel, and these members accepted a final report recommending medical price controls and the principle that "all employers either provide coverage to their workers" or pay a 7 percent payroll tax. Many small businesses, meanwhile, united in opposition to the Coalition.

Democratic leaders in Congress adapted ideas from both the Pepper Commission and the National Leadership Coalition to launch a renewed drive for play-or-pay legislation during 1992, in the wake of the Wofford election. Their hope was to get a consensus Democratic bill through Congress, forcing President Bush either to bargain over reforms more comprehensive than Republican proposals or else to veto the Democrats' bill and create an issue for the November 1992 election.[56]

However, the Democratic leaders had problems in their own party ranks. Senate Finance Committee Chairman Lloyd Bentsen of Texas expressed little interest in moving forward with legislation.[57] About sixty (mostly southern) Democrats in the Conservative Democratic Forum (CDF) searched for new versions of market-based reform — something situated in between the Bush Republican position and the mainstream Democratic commitment to requiring employers either to provide insurance or to pay a tax.[58] In short, after leading Democrats in Congress spent two years tempering their own enthusiasm for single payer in favor of play or pay as a pragmatic compromise, conservative Democrats started staking out yet more market oriented and voluntarist positions on health reform. Already in the spring of 1992, CDF members were attracted to ideas about "managed competition" that would soon gain much more prominence in the national debate about alternative approaches to health care reform.

A Theme for Aspiring Presidents

Committed presidential leadership for comprehensive reform was tepid at best while George Bush remained in office, yet the American people wanted it to be forthcoming. In early 1992, as the presidential campaign was getting underway, the public told pollsters that health care reform ranked right after the economy and foreign affairs as a policy topic it wanted addressed by presidential candidates.[59] Most Americans looked to the federal government for action, and over the course of 1992 many came to believe that Democrats were more likely than Republicans to promote needed health care reforms.[60]

All the 1992 Democratic presidential hopefuls committed themselves to pursue health care reform if elected.[61] Health insurance reform was, after all, an issue that could potentially appeal (in various ways at the same time) to lower-income working people whose jobs often lacked health insurance, to middle-income employees facing higher costs and greater insecurities in their health coverage, and to private-sector leaders looking for ways to moderate rising health costs. Democrats have to hold together such cross-class coalitions in order to raise both money and votes. Along with the nation's economic woes, reforms of the health care system to promote universal coverage and cost controls were natural for Democrats to stress. President Bush had, in effect, handed Democrats possibilities in this area by being so tepid and unfocused in his own approach to reform. Democrats could use such broad, unifying themes as economic recovery and health insurance reform to try to transcend the racial and cultural divisions that had undercut their electoral strength in the 1988 election and earlier presidential contests.

One of the first contenders in the 1992 Democratic primaries was Governor Bill Clinton of Arkansas, a leader and founding member of the Democratic Leadership Council (DLC), a group largely composed of southern elected officials founded in 1985 to counter the influence of northern liberals in the national Democratic party. In its own words, the DLC aims "to reclaim for Democrats our historic role of championing the middle class and those who aspire to join it."[62] Clinton touted such staple DLC themes as limited government and personal responsibility, yet he sought to synthesize them with emphases on "investments" in social well-being and populist critiques of business.[63] These were themes Clinton had successfully deployed as the personally charismatic governor of a small and impoverished southern border state that had a history of melding populism and middle-class reformism. Arkansas was not so caught in patterns of racial and oligarchical domination as were many states of the Deep South.[64]

For such a Democratic presidential aspirant, reform of the health insurance system — understood as an aspect of economic reform — was a good campaign theme. As Clinton explained in his announcement speech in Little Rock on October 3, 1991, his would be "a campaign . . . for the forgotten, hardworking middle-class families of America who deserve a government that fights for them." He stressed "reinventing government," promoting economic growth, investing in jobs and education, and "reforming the health-care system to control costs, improve quality, expand preventive and long-term care, maintain consumer choice, and cover everybody." Clinton's promises about health reform were ambitious and populist:

> [W]e don't have to bankrupt the taxpayers to do it. We do have to take on the big insurance companies and health-care bureaucracies and get some real cost-control into the system. I pledge to the American people that in the first year of a Clinton Administration we will present a plan to Congress and the American people to provide affordable, quality health care for all Americans.[65]

This sort of discussion about health reform was destined to reappear throughout the Clinton campaign — in his acceptance speech at the Democratic Convention on July 16 in New York City and in his standard stump speeches.[66] Clinton consistently placed health care reform in the context of making government work better — to invest in people, help the middle class, and promote national economic growth. He also regularly promised reform without big new taxes and engaged in vague saber rattling against insurance company "bureaucracy."

Themes for Clinton's campaign were solidified when he recruited as campaign strategists James Carville and Paul Begala, architects of Harris Wofford's come-from-behind victory in Pennsylvania. "Clinton Wins the Carville Primary" declared the *Washington Post* when these two consultants, much sought after by various Democratic contenders, decided to go with the Clinton campaign.[67] Other members of the Clinton team were adman Frank Geer, media consultant Mandy Grunwald, and professor-turned-pollster Stanley Greenberg.[68]

Greenberg was the author of an influential 1991 article in *The Amer-*

ican Prospect calling on the Democratic Party to "reconstruct" its vision around themes of "national renewal," populist critiques of the wealthy and of irresponsible corporate power, and new public "investment" policies to help "a squeezed middle class and working families."[69] Like all of Clinton's strategists, not to mention Clinton himself, Greenberg was looking to walk a fine line: acknowledging the conservative (including DLC) critique of exhausted or outmoded "liberal," "big government" solutions to America's problems, while at the same time trying to "rebuild public confidence in the public sphere" through "thematic projects that stake broad claims to the middle class." "Indeed," concluded Greenberg, "it is the link between the broad working middle class and affirmative government that allows Democrats to define a majority politics." Reforming health care was one project that might allow Democrats—and Clinton in particular—to use government in fresh ways, to invest in America's economic future and in the enhanced security of its people.

If a commitment to reform America's health care system fit perfectly into a presidential campaign devoted to "reconstructing the Democratic vision," it did not necessarily make sense for candidate Clinton to delve deeply into the hoary details of market incrementalism, single payer, or play or pay. Clinton's campaign strategists disagreed about the desirability of outlining a specific reform approach; some wanted to remain at the thematic level. But Clinton soon found that he had to go beyond a general promise and outline in more detail what he would do to achieve national health reform.

The year 1992 was a time when media and citizens alike expected candidates to outline "plans." In the early primaries, Clinton found himself sparring with Senators Robert Kerrey and Paul Tsongas, both of whom touted detailed schemes for health reform. The Clinton campaign was especially concerned about the challenge from Kerrey, who was featuring his determination to tackle universal health coverage. As a result, amidst the heat of the 1992 presidential primaries and general election, Bill Clinton committed himself to specific ideas. Characteristically searching for a way through the middle, candidate Clinton gravitated toward "managed competition within a budget" as a modality for national health care reform that was explicitly distinct from previously defined liberal as well as conservative alternatives. This did not happen all at once, however.

Clinton Discovers a New Compromise

It was clear from early on that Bill Clinton would not accept either single payer (as advocated by some experts and Democratic liberals) or incremental market reforms (as then pushed by Bush and other Republicans). Almost by default, the candidate's first effort to outline his plan for the reform of health care financing resembled play or pay, with ideas drawn from both the congressional Democratic leadership's version and the cost control proposals of the National Leadership Coalition. While campaigning in New Hampshire and preparing to debate Kerrey and the other candidates, Clinton himself worked over many nights on his first health reform plan.[70] A press release grandly entitled "Bill Clinton's American Health Care Plan: National Insurance Reform to Cut Costs and Cover Everybody" was the result. Although this eight-page statement was big on rhetoric and vague on details, it proposed the core play-or-pay idea, specifying that "employers and employees will either purchase private insurance or opt to buy into a high-quality public program," accompanied by various suggestions for cutting costs and promoting efficiency in the health care system.[71] This early 1992 Clinton campaign statement also stressed that "[w]e don't need to lead with a tax increase that asks hardworking people who already pay too much for health care to pay even more, until every effort has been made to squeeze excess cost out of the system."[72]

Between the winter and late spring of 1992, however, Clinton changed his mind about using play or pay as the core of his approach to health care reform. Tactical campaign necessities were certainly part of the reason. Early in 1992, President Bush and other Republicans turned up the heat against approaches to health reform associated with the Democratic leaders in Congress. Bush administration people assailed play or pay as a government-takeover scheme for "socialized medicine," and as a threat to business because of the payroll taxes this approach would entail.[73] Clinton and his campaign advisors had little desire to be yoked in the public mind with Democrats in Congress — who, in any event, were proving unable to move forward with comprehensive legislation based on play-or-pay ideas.

During the spring of 1992 the Clinton campaign struggled to work out its overall campaign message, a marriage of New Democrat themes about "reinventing government" with social-democratic ideas about public "investments" in jobs, education, and health for working middle Americans.[74] At the same time the Clinton people pulled together a written manifesto, which would appear in June under the title "Putting People First."[75] There would be a section on health care reform in the manifesto, yet as it was being drafted, the Clinton campaign was not ready to abandon play or pay entirely, even though a number of its policy advisors were intrigued with approaches to health care reform that avoided payroll taxes and placed more stress on cost-reduction through regulated competition among private health plans. Some Clinton policy aides, such as Bruce Reed and Atul Gawande, had ties to market-reform-oriented conservative and moderate Democrats in the Democratic Leadership Council and the Conservative Democratic Forum, while others, such as Judy Feder, had been involved with the Pepper Commission's effort to develop play or pay as a middle road to universal health coverage.[76]

When "Putting People First" was completed in June, it was remarkably vague about the "how" of its proposals for health reform, carefully straddling notions that experts could identify as associated with play-or-pay or market-based approaches to cost containment.[77] What is more, the Clinton campaign decided *not* to spell out at that point exactly how it proposed to pay for health reform. To do so would require finalizing as yet very uncertain projections about both the cost of universal coverage and the "savings" that might be reaped from reductions of cost increases in health care, including politically touchy reductions in public expenditures on Medicare and Medicaid. It would not help candidate Clinton to discuss such matters in any detail in the midst of a contentious presidential election.

As the presidential campaign careened from summer into fall, Clinton strategists became very worried that the Bush campaign was scoring points with its claims that their candidate would, if elected, raise taxes. Clinton had experiential reasons to fear being portrayed as a "taxer," because he had once badly lost a gubernatorial race in Arkansas in the face of such a charge.[78] More pressingly, an August 9, 1992, campaign memo from Stan Greenberg warned that "voters have heard Bush charges on taxes"; and another Greenberg memo noted on August 30 that the "Bush campaign has hurt Bill Clinton on taxes. That Bill Clinton is too ready to raise taxes is now the biggest negative."[79] In August and September, various advisors juggled by Clinton's friend Ira Magaziner were trying to finalize a distinctive Clinton approach to health reform that the candidate could outline in a big September speech.

During this period, the desire to parry Bush characterizations of Clinton's health plan as a variant of play or pay, and the need to counter Bush charges that Clinton was a "tax and spend" Democrat were very much on the minds of the Governor's campaign strategists. One cannot imagine Governor Clinton choosing to endorse a play-or-pay plan at such a critical juncture—when he was facing possible erosion of voter support in competition with (at that point) antitax Republican George Bush and the obstreperous budget-cutting independent, Ross Perot. As Greenberg importuned on August 13: Voters "worry about 'all those programs,' 'all the promises to groups.' They do not believe that Bill Clinton wants to raise taxes on the middle class, but they worry 'who will pay for all of this?' They need to hear more about Clinton's spending cuts, getting health care costs under control, welfare reform, and $144 billion in across the board spending cuts."[80]

Thus the exigencies of the campaign were certainly important in Clinton's turn away from the health reform alternatives that were prominent in 1991 and early 1992. Candidate Clinton found he had to have a plan, and then further clarify it; and he had to avoid mentioning taxes at all costs. So much for play or pay (as well as single payer, which had been rejected well before the campaign started). Still, intellectual considerations were at least as important as electoral dynamics in Clinton's turn toward a fresh approach to national health care reform, which I shall label "inclusive managed competition," because I want to underline that, from the start, Clinton's version of managed competition was intended to be combined with universal coverage and publicly enforced cost controls.

Bill Clinton was, after all, a well-read and articulate Yale graduate and Rhodes Scholar. He loved to explore ideas, and his constant quest for new policy syntheses was as much a personality trait, a quality of mind, as it was the tendency of a progressive southern Democrat to search out the middle ground electorally. Even amidst the incessant bustle of his presidential campaign, Bill Clinton looked for new ideas. He was attracted to policy entrepreneurs who asserted—with conviction—that single payer, play or pay, and market incrementalism did not exhaust options for comprehensive reform of health care financ-

ing. Bill Clinton's ears perked up when he learned there might be yet
another way through the middle—a way, to boot, that was associated
with prestigious sponsors in the media and the world of academic
policy experts.

Starting in the spring of 1991, the New York Times plunged into the
nation's brewing health care debate. Not shy at all about telling the
country's leaders exactly what to do, the newspaper published a recurrent stream of what would eventually become more than two dozen
editorials by Michael Weinstein, a member of the Times Editorial
Board with a Ph.D. in economics from the Massachusetts Institute of
Technology. Weinstein endorsed "managed competition" as an alternative to the original Bush and congressional Democratic approaches
to reform, and then fought to influence the adoption and definition
of this approach by the Clinton campaign (and later the Clinton presidency).[81]

Certain core principles of "managed competition" came from the
work of Stanford University economist Alain Enthoven, whose ideas
appealed to big employers and insurance companies because they
promised to use market-competition and managed-care plans to promote efficiency and lower prices in the delivery of medical care.[82]
Enthoven and other supporters of managed competition had formed
the "Jackson Hole group"—a seminar of policy experts and health-
industry people who met from time to time at a beautiful spot in
Wyoming—to develop a proposal for a market-based road to universal
health coverage in America. This group hoped to head off stronger
doses of government financing and regulation that would be a threat
to big private insurers and private health care delivery systems.

Significantly, Enthoven and associates advocated mandatory
employer payroll contributions to health insurance premiums as a way
to finance coverage for more Americans. They also favored a step that
would have been (and still would be) quite politically explosive: institution of a cap on tax deductions for employer-provided health benefits, set at the level of the lowest-priced plan in a region. This would
force employers and employees to buy cheaper health insurance or
pay the difference in after-tax dollars. But the Jackson-Holers were
firmly opposed to any sort of direct governmental controls on insurance premiums or on medical charges. Enthoven and associates recommended some regulation of the terms on which health insurance
could be offered, and they favored the establishment of "health pur-

chasing alliances" to allow small and medium companies to purchase insurance at lower prices. To cut costs in health care, however, these reformers proposed to rely on market bargains that would encourage the spread of health maintenance organizations (HMOs) and other efficient forms for the delivery of "managed" health care by groups of providers centered on physicians offering basic, including preventive, health services.

With the crucial (and telling) exception of the call for "mandating" all employers to contribute to health insurance, bits and pieces of Enthoven's ideas found their way into President Bush's plans for health insurance reform.[83] Elements also appeared in the 1992 health reform bill developed by the Conservative Democratic Forum and in the market-oriented plan advocated by Paul Tsongas in the early Democratic primaries.[84] Many would-be health reformers, however, remained distrustful of Enthoven's ideas, fearing they might not ensure genuine universal coverage and might leave insurance companies free to discriminate among groups of Americans with varying risks of health problems.[85]

Meanwhile, certain liberal health reformers built on and modified Enthoven's approach to develop a carefully regulated and inclusive version of managed competition.[86] Among these reformers were John Garamendi, the Insurance Commissioner of California, and Walter Zelman, who had headed a commission set up by Garamendi to work out a universal, managed-competition plan for the state of California.[87] Another key player was Paul Starr, a professor from Princeton University who had become convinced during 1992 that Garamendi's California plan offered insights that could be used in designing a national plan for universal health coverage and cost containment through carefully regulated market competition among insurers and deliverers of health care.

The key to the Garamendi-Zelman-Starr approach was the establishment of encompassing "health purchasing alliances" to sponsor all health insurance plans offered to employers and citizens in a state or region. Encompassing alliances, which would have to be mandatory for most purchasers of health insurance except very large employers, would pool the buying power of many companies and individuals. The alliances would approve plans to be offered as choices to individuals. Regional alliances could therefore prompt private insurance companies to compete for business by improving quality while holding down costs. In turn, that sort of cost-conscious competition would encourage the spread of managed-care forms of health delivery by HMOs or by well-integrated networks of physicians and hospitals. The advocates of inclusive managed competition proposed government subsidies to help the unemployed and small businesses purchase health coverage through the new regional alliances. And they favored some sort of public regulatory mechanism—global budget caps or premium caps—to keep health insurance prices from rising too quickly, especially during a transitional period before market-based mechanisms of cost containment fully took hold.

Arguments from Garamendi, Zelman, Starr, and other like-minded advisors were channeled into the Clinton campaign, in part because Garamendi was the chair of Clinton's campaign organization in California and in part through brokering by Ira Magaziner. Through memos and personal meetings, the advocates of inclusive managed competition made the case to candidate Clinton that this approach could optimally reform the nation's health care system. It could do this without expanding public insurance programs such as Medicaid and without the payroll "taxes" required by play-or-pay schemes. Reform and cost containment would be based principally on structured market competition, as regulations would require insurance companies and managed-care networks to offer good care at lower prices. Most of the new financing that would be needed for covering the presently uninsured would come from employer-contributed and employer-collected payments. Candidate Clinton could, in short, advocate using new federal regulations and mandates on employers—but not big new "taxes"—to move the U.S. health care system simultaneously toward cost-efficiency and universal coverage.

An inclusive version of managed competition was just what Bill Clinton was looking for. So it is little wonder that this is what he finally embraced in the showcase campaign speech he gave on national health care reform at Merck Pharmaceuticals in Rahway, New Jersey, on September 24, 1992. Speaking to an enthusiastic crowd at a company he repeatedly hailed for its progressive employment and sales practices, Clinton was surrounded that day by New Jersey's Democratic Governor Jim Florio and by Democratic Senators Bill Bradley and Frank Lautenberg of New Jersey, Harris Wofford of Pennsylvania, and Jay Rockefeller of West Virginia. Wofford, of course, was the veritable symbol of the health care reform issue, and Rockefeller was the leader of mainstream Democratic health care reformers in Congress. Rockefeller had previously championed play-or-pay legislation, yet now stood by the side of his party's presidential candidate Bill Clinton as he unveiled an alternative middle-of-the-road approach to comprehensive reform. The symbolism was obvious: the Democratic Congress and a new Democratic president would be able to work together on health care reform.

In his Merck speech, Clinton introduced health care "in the context of the overall American health scene," as "part of our efforts to restore growth, improve education, and manage change in a tough global economy. It's part of a plan to create a high-wage, high-growth, high-opportunity society in America, to educate and train our people, . . . to promote both personal responsibility and family security."[88] Governor Clinton stressed that Americans "are not getting the system we are paying for and nobody is paying as much as we are for health care," and he told a series of "heartbreaking stories" about individual Americans, all seemingly middle class, who were having troubles affording or keeping health insurance just at the moment when their own illnesses or those of family members required it.

Having underlined the nation's economic and personal problems with the current system for financing health care, Bill Clinton discussed solutions and claimed the middle ground "beyond partisan political debate" for himself. Counterintuitively, but cleverly, he criticized then-President Bush for wanting to spend too much: "the Bush plan would put another $100 billion in tax credits through the same system between now and 1997, pouring good money after bad, with no plan for cost control" and without guaranteeing universal coverage. As for his own approach to health care reform, Clinton stressed that it "is a private system. It is not pay or play. It does not require new taxes." Clinton summed up his vision as "personal choice, private care, private insurance, private management, but a national system to put a lid on costs, to require insurance reforms, to facilitate partnerships between business, government, and health care providers." He stressed his commitment to "a national budget ceiling" and secure coverage for all. Throughout Clinton's speech, the most consistent themes were savings and the beneficial economic effects of reform. "If we can cover everybody and bring costs within inflation, we will save hundreds of billions of dollars per year by the end of the decade to the private sector—money which can be reinvested in growth, in productivity, in wages, in benefits, in making America a stronger country. . . . This is a matter that is critical for the future of this country's survival."

Squaring Many Circles

Why wouldn't this regulatory, yet market-based approach to comprehensive health reform look good to Bill Clinton? Aside from apparently avoiding taxes and an up-front governmental role, it promised to satisfy the public's desire for affordable universal coverage while simultaneously furthering the cost "efficiencies" so favored by powerful elites (favored in principle, that is, as long as each elite's particular source of profits or income was not cut by much). As opinion analyst Bob Blendon has documented, ordinary Americans care most about attaining secure protection and keeping their own insurance payments low, while experts and institutional leaders such as employers and politicians are obsessed with spending less overall, having each major organizational sector cover less of health care costs.[89] Inclusive managed competition within a budget, Clinton must have hoped, had some chance to give everyone what they wanted, citizens and elites alike.

This approach presumably would please big employers and large insurance companies and so allow the would-be president to court and work with these powerful interests, just as moderate southern Democratic governors have always done. Inclusive managed competition also promised to solve Clinton's problems within the fractious Democratic party. At first, of course, many of his fellow Democrats would not understand the new scheme vaguely outlined in New Jersey on September 24—and that might be just as well for the remaining weeks before the election. Still, inclusive managed competition must have looked like something that could, over time, be sold both to those in the Democratic coalition who cared primarily about universal coverage and to those "New Democrats" in the Democratic Leadership Council and the Conservative Democratic Forum who wanted market-oriented reforms that minimized taxes and public spending.

Finally, Clinton was especially attracted to the public finance features of managed competition within a budget. If he were to be elected president after a campaign promising deficit reduction and avoidance of taxes, he was going to have to devise a health care reform plan that did not include huge new taxes. An inclusive version of managed competition within a budget might enable a new Clinton administration to do all this, while still promising universal health security to the electorate. The apparent budgetary logic of this approach was irresistable to a moderate Democrat who wanted to cut the federal deficit and free up resources for new public investments.

On November 3, 1992, Bill Clinton was elected President of the United States with 43 percent of the popular vote (and a much more commanding margin in the electoral college). More voters turned out than usual, and Clinton triumphed after a proficiently run campaign, benefiting from the split among those who did not vote for him in a three-way race. The hapless George Bush never did convince the American people that he had a plan to deal with domestic economic problems, while the wacky and inconsistent Ross Perot was, by the end of the campaign, unable to serve as more than a vehicle for protest against party politics as usual.

Hopes for Clinton were high, even among Americans who had not voted for him. People wanted the new President to break the logjam in the nation's capital by quickly devising and putting through comprehensive plans for improving the economy and reforming the national health care system.[90] After all, the incoming President was a reformist Democrat, and he ostensibly enjoyed Democratic majorities in both houses of Congress. All William Jefferson Clinton had to do was make his way to Washington and accomplish what he had promised during the 1992 campaign.

CHAPTER TWO

DESIGNING HEALTH SECURITY

"A New Beginning" was the slogan that appeared on pins, cups, and other inaugural momentos marking January 20, 1993, the day that President Bill Clinton and Vice President Al Gore took their oaths of office. Change was indeed in the air. The long Republican grip on the presidency was broken. Democrats and their sympathizers sensed opportunities they had not enjoyed, even briefly, for over a dozen years. They would, at long last, "get the nation moving again" in directions they believed were progressive and democratic.

Euphoria lasted only a matter of days, because the fledgling administration got off to a rocky start. There were slipups in cabinet appointments, an imbroglio about the White House travel office, and a huge (ultimately very politically damaging) brouhaha about gays in the military. In due course, though, the new administration settled down to concentrate on economic and fiscal policies. At the same time, some of the President's people undertook to spell out a detailed legislative proposal for readjusting the one-seventh of the U.S. economy now devoted to health care. The appearance of the Clinton plan for comprehensive health care reform would take considerably longer than the hundred days the candidate had rashly promised during the heat of the 1992 presidential contest. Yet before 1993 was out, there was to be a fully articulated legislative draft of the Health Security Act, described in its preamble as a bill "To ensure individual and family security through health care coverage for all Americans in a manner that contains the rate of growth in health care costs and promotes responsible health insurance practices, to promote choice in health care, and to insure and protect the health care of all Americans."[1]

Inaugural Button

Grand ideals met obdurate fiscal reality during the first year of the Clinton presidency. Many fateful decisions had to be made about the precise design of an intricate set of federal regulations—rules meant to nudge America's incomplete, employer-based system of health insurance simultaneously toward contained costs for powerful private and public actors and universal protection for America's working-aged citizens and their children. The new administration had to decide how these decisions were to be made, and then make them.

Policy Planning through a Task Force?

For many players in and around the Clinton White House, the first eight months of 1993, from January through August, were devoted to devising and enacting the President's first budget submission to Congress.[2] Candidate Clinton had promised to make "growing the economy" his top priority, and tight congressional deadlines forced budget politics to the fore anyway. Deficit hawks at Treasury and the Federal Reserve persuaded the President to use the budget as a vehicle to reduce significantly the huge federal deficit that the nation had inherited from the Reagan-Bush years. At the same time, many Clinton administration people hoped to promote economic growth and shift federal spending toward job creation and "investments" in America's future. During this period the new President and his advisors learned how little fiscal room in which they had to maneuver if they were serious about cutting the federal deficit. Clinton had made promises about controlling the deficit during the campaign, and during the transition period between the 1992 election and his January 1993 inauguration he decided to attempt even more in the way of deficit reduction.

Candidate Clinton had also promised comprehensive health reform, and he moved at once to make good on that pledge. A team of advisors had worked on health financing reform during the transition; their deliberations revealed the stark choices the health planners would have to make in tight fiscal circumstances.[3] Within days of the inauguration, moreover, Ira Magaziner finalized a twenty-three-page "Preliminary Work Plan for Interagency Health Care Task Force" that would work out "the structure for the new American health care system proposed in the campaign—Managed Competition Within a Budget." As Magaziner explained, "the model . . . proposed for health care in the United States does not exist anywhere in practice. The campaign proposal, while sensible conceptually, needs significant definition."[4] He set forth an organizational blueprint for a multi-pronged task force, suggested ways to pull together participants mostly from within the government, and outlined an ambitious timetable for drafting a health reform plan by May 1993. The task force envisaged in the "Work Plan" would be embodied in "working groups" assigned to tackle parts of major "areas of analysis" including:

Phasing in universal health insurance;
Defining the options by which health care cost increases can be controlled during the next few years as the system phases in;
Developing ways for the federal government to finance the new system, capturing private health care savings to cover universal access and possibly contribute to deficit reduction.
Programs for preventive care and care for underserved populations.
Defining programs for improved long-term care.
Analyzing the economic impact of current health care policy versus our proposed policies.[5]

Specific policy options as well as practical plans were outlined for each area of analysis. There was much that needed to be explored and spelled out by people knowledgeable about the myriad highways and byways of public and private arrangements in U.S. health care. Magaziner's memorandum also anticipated likely criticisms and political obstacles, and offered specific tactics for dealing with them. He proposed consultations with "the enormous number of groups interested in health care" as well as regular communications with staffers of key congressional committees, governors, and mayors "so we don't proceed too far down paths which are 'non-starters' for them" and so we "build support for the eventual program."[6] There should likewise be a major "communications effort" Magaziner argued, because "reforming the health care system will involve government-led changes on a scale not attempted since Social Security. People are calling for massive change, yet their support for individual plans is very weak. We should . . . begin the process of educating the public about the nature of the problem and the kinds of changes required."[7]

Accepting the approach outlined in the "Work Plan" memo, President Clinton created the President's Task Force on Health Care Reform to be chaired by First Lady Hillary Rodham Clinton and coordinated by Magaziner. Later, after the Clinton Health Security bill collapsed, critics argued that the President should have proceeded in one of two alternative ways back in early 1993. Some say he should have used a small group to outline broad principles for health care reform, and then let Congress work out the details.[8] Others say the President should have convened a prestigious national commission to hammer out the details of a health reform plan that could have garnered backing from key interest groups, including business, as well as bipartisan support in Congress.[9]

After-the-fact critics may be right that another process for developing reform legislation might have worked better than an intraadministration task force. Yet it is easy to see why alternatives must not have looked desirable in early 1993; and there are important reasons why other ways of proceeding might not have worked as well as their advocates retrospectively imagine. Could Congress really have been expected to work out a technically and politically viable plan for reforming one-seventh of the national economy? Congressional staffs could not match the executive branch's command of the analytical resources and expert advice needed to spell out detailed legislation of the kind that was necessary to meet existing congressional budget rules.[10] Key leaders of Congress originally *wanted* the Clinton administration to present its own bill, and then let Congress modify it. This approach had the appeal of allowing congressional representatives to take credit for "compromises," for example with business interests. A detailed proposal from the administration was also essential if the Congressional Budget Office was to be able to "cost out" provisions and "score" the overall impact on the federal budget deficit.

There were political problems, too, with the option of throwing the initiative to Congress. Democratic leaders had failed to work out an enactable health reform compromise during the 102nd Congress. And as we shall see in the next chapter, sharp divisions remained in the 103rd Congress—divisions across five congressional committees with jurisdication over health legislation, divisions among conservative, moderate, and liberal Democrats and among Republicans, as well as between Democrats and Republicans. Apparently, the Clinton administration needed to work out a new synthesis, which is what its task force set out to do.

As for appointing a bipartisan commission, exactly which people should the President have invited to join—and which should he have left off? If a national commission were to move forward promptly and coherently, it would have had to be of modest size, while still assembling all the key players it would take to facilitate congressional enactment of reform. But was this possible? Republicans might well have refused to join, preferring to keep their powder dry for maneuvers in Congress.[11] Dozens of groups with a stake in health care financing and delivery would have wanted "representatives" on the commission; yet many would have had to be left off, and thus perhaps been spurred to undercut any attempted compromises. There were numerous self-styled health reform experts in Congress, and key congressional players from both parties would have felt slighted if left off such a nationally visible body.

Finally, and perhaps most decisive, the recent history of omnibus reform commissions on health care—including the Pepper Commission and the National Leadership Coalition—hardly suggested that such bodies were a royal road to consensus. As we saw in the previous chapter, the Pepper Commission did not achieve bipartisan support or even bring along all its Democratic members, and the National

Leadership Coalition saw many initial business participants defect as it moved toward a final report endorsing employer mandates to help pay for universal health care. The Clinton administration could easily have appointed a commission only to see it devolve after many months into acrimony or indecision or vague evasions. A failed commission's high-profile wranglings could well have embittered proponents of alternative reform measures and prematurely politicized specific issues, making it harder rather than easier for the President to keep his promises about health reform to the American people.

In contrast to many of the parliamentary systems of Europe, the U.S. political system does not lend itself to making binding bargains among nationally disciplined interest groups. Social scientists use the term "corporatism" to refer to a system in which such bargains can be made among government officials able to command parliamentary majorities and the authoritative leaders of "peak associations," each of which can speak with a single voice for a major national interest, such as business, labor, or physicians.[12] But there are virtually no disciplined, unitary "peak associations" in America. Instead, multiple associations form and reform and compete to speak for each major interest in society. For example, various associations compete to represent business, including the Chamber of Commerce (a nationwide business federation), the National Association of Manufacturers, the Business Roundtable, the National Federation of Independent Businesses, and countless associations specialized by industry or policy area. Even U.S. physicians these days do not speak with one voice, because the American Medical Association encompasses only about 41 percent of the country's doctors and faces competition from a variety of other medical associations (including the American College of Physicians, the American Academy of Family Physicians, the American Society of Internal Medicine, and the American College of Surgeons).[13]

Even more important, the divisions of authority across U.S. governmental institutions ensure that organizations claiming to speak for different sectors or subsectors of any one interest can undercut one another in policy deliberations. There are many opportunities for undercutting and end runs, because in the United States the road to successful legislation is long—winding through two houses of Congress and multiple committees, before a bill reaches the president for signing (or vetoing).[14] Even if one group gets its preferences embodied in a legislative proposal—such as one hammered out by a commission—competitor groups still have chances to go to one or another congressional committee to get the proposal fundamentally modified or defeated. Because every group in the system knows that there will be opportunities down the line for modifications of any initial bargain, complex compromises are difficult to work out in the first place. Groups that might want to sign onto bargains fear being undercut by legislative end runs or by appeals to their constituencies by competitor associations. Policymaking commissions in the United States thus do not have the authority and consensus-building prowess that they do in some other industrial democracies.

Given the obvious drawbacks of alternative routes to devising health reform legislation, it is not surprising that President Clinton chose to work out a plan from within his administration. He believed that he had recently discovered a workable middle way to national health care reform, and he must have wanted to keep hold of the process by which the details, including specific compromises, would be worked out. Understandably, the new President—who would face a tough contest for reelection in four years—also wanted to be able to claim credit for a reform victory. By putting the prestige of his office behind a plan that appeared to respond to widespread public concerns, President Clinton surely hoped that he could rally public and congressional support for change. The appointment of the First Lady to head the task force was a highly visible way to put the President personally on the line behind this big reform effort. Mrs. Clinton had already proved her mettle during a high-profile 1983–84 drive for comprehensive educational reform in Arkansas.[15]

Perhaps administration people should have anticipated that the First Lady would later become a lightening rod for attacks on Health Security (more on this in chapter 5). But at the start they were more focused on the personal, "caring" touch that her leadership could bring to the planning process.[16] As Health Security was devised and launched, the First Lady held many meetings with citizens (as well as with stakeholder groups) and received hundreds of thousands of letters from individual Americans concerned about health care issues.[17]

We need to keep in mind that, early in the Clinton administration, pundits and members of the American public alike had faith—perhaps too much faith—that the new President could pull off comprehensive health reform. In his well-received first State of the Union address delivered in February 1993, Clinton discussed health care reform in the context of the economy and the budget:

> All of our efforts to strengthen the economy will fail unless we also take this year—not next year, not five years from now, but this year—bold steps to reform our health care system. . . .
>
> Reducing health care costs can liberate literally hundreds of billions of dollars for new investment in growth and jobs. . . .
>
> Later this spring, after the First Lady and the many good people who are helping her all across their country complete their work, I will deliver to Congress a comprehensive plan for health care reform that finally will bring costs under control and provide security to all of our families, so that no one will be denied the coverage they need, but so that our economic future will not be compromised either.[18]

Around the time of this address, most Americans believed that comprehensive health care reform certainly would occur in 1993. A March 1993 Kaiser-Harris poll revealed that hefty majorities approved of the specific reform provisions being contemplated by the administration—employer mandates, limits on insurance premium increases, purchasing cooperatives "to bargain for lower insurance rates," and an extension of "government subsidized coverage to the uninsured."[19] And in April, over 70 percent of Americans told Roper pollsters that they liked what they had heard so far about the emerging Clinton proposals.[20] At this stage, too, national interest groups were falling all over themselves to signal public and private willingness to cooperate with the President and the First Lady on significant reform.[21] With all of this happening, we should not be surprised that President Clinton and his key advisors also thought in early 1993 that they could take direct leadership of a comprehensive health care reform effort—an undertaking whose time, it seemed, had finally come.[22]

Policy Planning in Operation

Although the full working out of the Clinton Health Security plan would end up taking nine months rather than three or four, a gargantuan policy planning effort *was* achieved in a remarkably short span of time. Most of the work of the administration's task force took place in four frantic months, from January to May 1993 (although its report could not be finalized until after President Clinton got his first budget through the contentious Congress at the end of the summer of 1993). We get a vivid description of how the planning proceeded from task-force participant Paul Starr, who served as a temporary consultant while "on loan" from Princeton University, where he is a professor of sociology. As Starr explains, "clusters" of sets of working groups proceeded in parallel within a model taken from Magaziner's prior "experience as a business consultant. The paradigm was a corporate restructuring or technological innovation that required thinking through innumerable options and suboptions and meshing together previously uncoordinated activities and groups into a coherent plan. . . . The scale of the project was astonishing even to some of us who had long advocated a comprehensive plan," Starr comments, "and rather than being scaled back, it expanded" as new planning groups were added to deal with issues not encompassed in the original grand design.[23]

Members of the various working groups knew that the President had made a general commitment to managed competition within a budget. But there were hundreds of specific technical issues and alternative possibilities to be explored, first through broad-ranging overviews of "all relevant issues and options" and then through efforts to "reduce the alternatives to a manageable set for decision-making." Groups worked up memos and options, and presented them to the task-force leaders in protracted sessions called "tollgates."[24] As Starr recounts, the

> tollgates will long be engraved in the memory of the hundreds who took part in them. They generally took place in the ornate Indian Treaty Room at the top of the Old Executive Office Building overlooking the White House and stretched on for entire days, even through one weekend. The members of each cluster, the largest of which included well over a hundred people, would file into the room, and Magaziner and several others of us who worked for him sat on folding chairs at tables arranged in a large rectangle to hear the presentations and ask questions. The tollgates were marathon seminars, often technical and inconclusive, but the grandeur of the setting and the size of the meetings gave them a theatrical quality.[25]

During its life, the President's Task Force on Health Care Reform mobilized at least part-time participation of some 511 people, mostly executive branch employees drawn in "from the various Cabinet departments concerned with health care" or its financing, principally the Departments of Health and Human Services, Labor, Treasury, Veterans' Affairs, and the Office of Management and Budget. Also involved were health policy experts, academics, and physicians who were "on loan" as temporary government employees or consultants.[26] In addition, and somewhat unusually for this sort of executive branch policy formulation, dozens of Democratic congressional staffers participated in task-force working groups, as did officials sent by Democratic and Republican governors of various states. Their expertise was relevant to planning legislation that would affect the states and had to make its way through Congress. Although things often did not work out this way (because congressional and state staffers did not necessarily feel that their views were significantly taken into account), task-force leaders hoped that key congressional committees and state-level officials would gain an understanding of, and a stake in, the President's proposed legislation.

"Stakeholder" groups—those with financial interests or occupational roles in the current U.S. health care system—were *not* officially represented on the Task Force on Health Care Reform (it was, after all, not a commission). But the Task Force did hold many hearings, and its leaders consulted with hundreds of representatives of stakeholder groups. Pushing and pulling from contradictory directions, groups told the Clinton planners what they wanted them to do about specific aspects of reform. Ostensibly, the purpose of such consultations was not political bargaining. Rather, leaders of the task force tried to discover ideas and concerns that they could take into account as an overall plan was fashioned. As the January 1993 "Work Plan" explained, the Task Force would receive "inputs" from stakeholder groups "on a systematic basis. Many may be useful. These people will also help us as sounding boards for ideas and they will help give us information on the 'political' lay of the land."[27]

As this last remark suggests, there were rich possibilities for misunderstanding in the many consultations held between task-force leaders and stakeholder groups. When groups ranging from the Chamber of Commerce to the American Association of Retired Persons were "sounded out" about acceptable reform options, their leaders might suppose they were getting implicit commitments. At the very least, group leaders might think that they had made compelling arguments,

Courtesy the *Des Moines Register*

establishing points that certainly should be heeded in the final Clinton proposal (even though that was bound to be impossible in many cases). While group leaders naturally wanted their ideas to be accepted and were prepared to be offended if they weren't, leaders of the Task Force on Health Care Reform might suppose that groups would appreciate being heard, even when not heeded. And if a given stakeholder's ideas *were* accepted and incorporated into the Health Security proposal, task-force leaders might anticipate that the group would get strongly "on board" to lobby and agitate in support of the President's proposal. From each stakeholder's point of view, however, it might seem wiser to take whatever early "concessions" it could get from Magaziner, and then keep pushing for still more, with an eye to future battles in Congress.

After September 1993, indeed, many parties to task-force consultations would find causes for bitterness when their expectations were frustrated. Some "interest groups would come to feel that White House aides, and Magaziner in particular, had falsely assured them that their concerns would be tended to. . . . The lapels of various disillusioned lobbyists soon sported a button that read 'But Ira promised.' "[28] Likewise, Magaziner was surprised and chagrined by what he would come to see as betrayals of implicit deals or, in some cases, explicit promises of support made by representatives of stakeholder groups as well as by members of Congress.[29]

There was also bound to be an asymmetry of perception of the Task Force's product, even though the Clintons and Magaziner would always say that the Health Security proposal was just a "starting point" for legislation. Because the Task Force on Health Care Reform made such a gargantuan effort to come up with a truly comprehensive plan for reform—a plan thought at the time to be both technically and politically workable—there was a natural tendency for administration planners to see their proposal as a logical achievement to be "explained." But others would take it from the start as a building to be remodeled—or demolished. Many participants in the 1993–94 reform struggle did not want to "understand" the Health Security proposal. Yet that proposal's devisers were proud of it, and felt that if properly grasped, the proposal would seem compelling.[30]

After the full Task Force on Health Care Reform was officially disbanded in May, further planning for Health Security was pulled into the hands of several small teams, including one in the White House charged with thinking about political strategy and communication, an interagency team charged with working up budgetary estimates, and a drafting group responsible for putting final decisions into legislative language. Over the summer, these groups operated under tight secrecy. As the President's budget proposal became mired in partisan battles in Congress, it became clear that leaks of even very preliminary options from the reform planning process could cost the administration preciously needed votes in Congress. For example, California's representatives in Congress threatened to vote against the budget when they heard that wine taxes were under consideration to pay for a part of health care reform.

As a result of the Clinton administration's concern to maintain confidentiality and keep a focus solely on getting a budget through Congress, health planners had to stop writing decision memos. High-level meetings ceased between May 21 and August, and elaborate efforts were made to maintain confidentiality.[31] The entire planning process, which had barreled forward so rapidly from January through April, was abruptly put on hold—causing many in the press and the Washington community to speculate that health care reform had run into trouble or been derailed inside the Clinton White House.

The President could not (or, in any event, would not) make final decisions about the financially relevant aspects of health reform, until his much-modified budget finally squeaked through the Senate by one vote in early August. Presidential decisions on a number of crucial issues about reform design and financing were finally completed in the end of August and early September. On September 7, a few copies of the "Working Group Draft" of the Health Security plan were sent to Congress for consultations. Although the plan was still being finalized, not surprisingly it leaked at that point.[32] In the evocative words of *National Journal* reporter Julie Kosterlitz, copies "began, like escaped pet gerbils, to multiply." For "a brief moment, after weeks of frenzied efforts to pry out stray details of the plan, quiet settled over the city [of Washington, D.C.]. The only sound was the turning of pages . . . as congressional aides, academics, journalists and lobbyists of all stripes tried to grasp the details and the essence of the proposal."[33]

Going Forward with a Bold Reform

Eager readers of the Health Security plan (either the September draft or the slightly modified full bill, which appeared in late October) could not have been very surprised at its overall thrust. The Clinton administration put forward a plan featuring universal coverage paid for mainly through employer mandates, along with government regulation of privately competing health plans for the purpose of containing future increases in health care costs to individuals, employers, and public budgets. In general, this was exactly what Democratic candidate Bill Clinton had promised a year before at Merck Pharmaceuticals. His Task Force on Health Care Reform had fashioned a middle-of-the-road vehicle for comprehensive reform, one that tried mightily to bridge divides between those who wanted to foster market competition in the financing and delivery of health care and those who wanted public guarantees of universal inclusion and fairness.[34]

Still, during 1993 the Task Force on Health Care Reform and the White House had made many critical specific decisions, and of course these specifics were what all the inside players were looking for as they read through the leaked Health Security draft in September (and pored over revisions made by the administration during the fall). What had the appealing general promises of Clinton's campaign speeches meant? Exactly where would the money for expanded health insurance coverage come from if substantial new tax revenues were not available and if health reform had to contribute to reducing the federal budget deficit? How exactly had the administration put together its compromise between market-oriented and government-oriented proponents of health care reform? "Managed competition" was, after all, a vague and, to many, an unfamiliar approach, which could mean various things. Would the Clintonites go forward with little more than Republican market incrementalism in disguise, or would they meld market regulations with generous governmental guarantees and tough public regulations?[35]

As the President's Task Force did its work in the spring of 1993, certain advocates of market-oriented managed competition — notably including conservative Democrats attracted to a bill being drafted under the leadership of Tennessee Congressman Jim Cooper — had reached the fateful conclusion that they would devise an alternative to the emerging Clinton plan that would *not* assure universal health coverage. Much like the Republicans under George Bush in 1992, supporters of the Cooper plan wanted to encourage small businesses to purchase basic coverage for their employees through voluntary "regional health plan purchasing cooperatives" of modest scope, while also giving some public subsidies for the purchase of private insurance policies by very low wage workers.

In contrast even to (the 1991–92 positions of) Alain Enthoven and the Democratic Leadership Council, the Cooperites would *not* accept a mandate for all employers to contribute to health insurance (yet they agreed with Enthoven on other politically controversial tenets, including a call for the removal of tax advantages for the good employee health benefits that many big companies already offered).[36] Supporters of the Cooper plan wanted no public-sector budgetary or price controls on rising health costs. They proposed to rely only on market competition and changes in tax rules to encourage enrollments in Health Maintenance Organizations (HMOs) and thus, supposedly, reduce costs. Medicaid would be dismantled in favor of modest public subsidies to help the poor individually contribute to insurance premiums for bare-bones coverage. Universal coverage and generous standard benefits would *not* be assured to all Americans, proponents of this minimalist version of managed competition acknowledged. The Cooperites proposed to wait some years to discover whether voluntary methods and market forces would reduce costs and extend coverage on their own, before undertaking any stronger governmental measures to spread health coverage or control costs.[37]

Whatever forces might have pushed the mid-1993 Clinton administration in the direction of very partial (and possibly self-defeating) approaches to health care reform, there were stronger forces reminding the President that he should carry through on his popular campaign promises to extend health coverage to all Americans while using public as well as market means to control costs. The President didn't need much reminding, anyway. As we saw in chapter 1, during the 1992 campaign Clinton leaned away from more voluntary understandings of managed competition, favoring instead more inclusive and regulatory ideas from the likes of John Garamendi, Walter Zelman, and Paul Starr. During the 1993 policy planning process there was never much chance that the President, the First Lady, and these advisors—all of whom were centrally involved with the task force—would back away from their vision of inclusive managed competition.

During the summer of 1993, health care reform might have been killed within the Clinton administration by an (open or de facto) decision to put off this ambitious effort indefinitely. Some of the President's economic advisors more or less openly wanted such a delay.[38] Failing that, there was little chance that presidentially sponsored health care reform could go forward in 1993 along minimalist lines. The public and the punditocracy had much higher expectations, which the Bill Clinton himself had stoked (and appealed to) during 1992.

The very fact that Cooper and his congressional allies refused to compromise by accepting some sort of employer mandate to fund universal coverage had the paradoxical effect of making their preferences less compelling to the planners of Clinton's Health Security legislation. The Clinton presidency was irretrievably "on the line" when it came to ensuring universal coverage, yet market-oriented minimalists in the ranks of conservative Democrats seemed to be asking Clinton to launch the health reform process by abandoning this very popular promise to the American people. To court a few votes associated with Cooper and his congressional allies, the Clinton administration would have had to alienate many more Democrats in Congress, including crucial committee and subcommittee leaders and dozens of liberals who favored single-payer approaches.

Such a retreat would surely have turned off most nonconservative Democrats in Congress, and virtually all organized Democratic party constituencies in labor and citizens' movements, because even those not preferring single-payer approaches *were* determined to set the United States on the road to universal health coverage. Loyal Democratic constituencies had been patient while the Clinton administration obsessed about deficit reduction throughout the spring and summer. They had seen most new "investments" trimmed out of the Clinton budget in order to get it through Congress. The one thing the President could do for his Democratic party allies—as well as for the large majority of the American people who want universal health security—was to proceed with an inclusive version of comprehensive health insurance reform. There is no evidence that I have found that he ever intended to do anything but that.

Critical Decisions about the Design of Health Security

When the President and his aides made final decisions about the Health Security plan, there were special concerns and fateful choices about employer mandates, the size and nature of employer contributions, the generosity of the standard benefit package, the scope of health alliances, and regulatory controls to control rising costs in health care. Over the course of 1993–94, choices made in each area were to prove politically critical, often in unanticipated ways. That story will be told in subsequent chapters. Here we should get straight what President Clinton decided and why.

In the end, the President made socially responsive or proregulatory decisions on a number of major issues. In some areas presidential decisions went against what advocates of less-inclusive versions of managed competition might have preferred, yet the President repeatedly built on precedents that had appeared earlier in health reform bills introduced by moderate Republicans and conservative or moderate Democrats. Contrary to what many commentators have suggested, President Clinton did not just make knee-jerk "liberal" decisions. A complex mixture of political and fiscal considerations went into the presidential-level decisions, and we must sort out these considerations to avoid stereotyped and mistaken explanations about the design of Health Security.

As we have already seen, the "employer mandate" (that is, a legal requirement that all employers contribute to health coverage for their employees) was the only way that President Clinton could spread insurance coverage without a big new public program and huge taxes. For the sake of federal deficit reduction, some tax increases had already been included in President Clinton's first budget—which had barely passed Congress with only Democrats voting for it. The last thing the President could or would decide to do right after that squeaker was to call for new general taxation to pay for health care reform. If there had ever been any room for maneuver on general taxation for health reform, it had finally disappeared during the budget struggle of the summer. The only "taxes" to be included in the Health Security proposal would be "sin taxes" on tobacco, along with many carefully crafted charges on businesses and health care providers designed to "recapture" for the federal government projected "savings" from reductions in the growth of health care costs.[39]

An employer mandate had to be in the Health Security bill, yet decisions remained about whether employers should contribute percentages of payrolls or percentages of health premiums and at what level payments should be set for various sorts of companies. Employers with higher-paid workers, the Chamber of Commerce, and moderates in Congress from both parties, all strongly preferred the percentage-of-premium approach.[40] That is what the Clinton administration fundamentally chose to do—even though this was a much less straightforward way to proceed than percentage-of-payroll payments would have been. According to Ira Magaziner, the detailed regulations required to put into effect the premium approach added hundreds of pages to the fully spelled out Health Security bill.[41] What is more, to buffer small businesses, a complex set of not easily understood subsidies was deemed necessary to offset the relatively high cost of health premiums for low-wage workers. Here was a clear instance in which the Clinton administration's efforts to please congressional moderates and key

Courtesy of David Donar

business associations led toward much greater regulatory complexity. In the end, the administration put together a very complicated combination of percentage-of-premium assessments combined with subsidies for smaller employers.

Would all Americans be guaranteed decent health benefits or just a bare-bones package? As the Health Security plan came together in August, President Clinton came down on the side of relatively good standard benefits. He and many of his advisors hoped that a governmentally guaranteed baseline package—comparable to what is now offered by many of America's biggest corporations—would appeal to security-conscious middle-class Americans. Citizens would be assured of good benefits if they should find themselves divorced or pushed out of jobs with health insurance. Popular fears about exactly such misfortunes lay behind the national desire for reform of health care financing. Moreover, the administration's choice to guarantee comprehensive benefits fit closely with Bill Clinton's carefully fashioned political image: He was not a "traditional Democrat" offering "welfare" to the "poor." He was, instead, a reformed Democrat offering "security" to the "middle class."

The Clinton health planners presumed that whatever benefits package they started out with might have to be cut back somewhat as the Health Security bill wended its way through Congress.[42] By starting at a fairly good level, even a somewhat reduced final package would, they reasoned, still be attractive to the employed middle class. Similarly presuming that Congress might later reduce the level, the President also chose to start with an apparently hefty employer contribution to premiums: 80 percent for larger businesses, with generous subsidies and limits on contributions for small businesses. (There were adjustments in the Clinton plan to take account of the fact that many employers were already subsidizing family members who worked for noninsuring businesses, so the actual level of required employer contribution would have averaged about 57 percent).[43] In lieu of general taxation, substantial employer contributions were very much needed if the Health Security reforms were to guarantee a decent level of health benefits for all Americans.

For health alliances, the critical issues had to do with whether to require medium-sized and larger companies to use these purchasing agencies as mechanisms for buying health insurance and offering approved plans to their employees. The Clinton planners considered cutoffs for the level at which business enterprises could "opt out" and choose to handle the purchase of health insurance themselves; the levels considered ranged from one hundred employees up to a requirement that all companies, regardless of size, be legally required to purchase insurance through alliances. In the end, the President chose what he considered a high-middle-range starting cutoff. He decided to propose that all employers except those with 5,000 employees or more should be required to purchase insurance via state-approved regional alliances. This level was expected to come down during congressional deliberations, perhaps as far as to one hundred employees. Yet the Clinton administration clearly wanted the new regional alliances to be as encompassing as possible.

The rationale for relatively encompassing mandatory alliances went to the very heart of the President's commitment to reduce health care costs and complexity for both the public and private sectors of the economy.[44] If bigger employers were required to purchase coverage through the alliances, it would be easier to standardize insurance practices and keep insurance prices down for small businesses and for governments paying subsidies for poor people (including low-wage workers). Big, inclusive health purchasing alliances seemed to be a key mechanism for harnessing competitive market forces to produce true price reductions in health care, as well as for inducing insurers to compete over quality and efficiency of delivery, rather than through the exclusion of actually or potentially sicker people.

As the Clinton administration finalized decisions about Health Security, it was not only under pressure from the assorted conservative minimalists, moderates, and liberal advocates of inclusive universalism. Simultaneously, budget officials in the White House and the Treasury Department, as well as officials of the Congressional Budget Office, were pressing for tough cost controls and guarantees that health care reform would not explode the federal deficit. As the President and his allies discovered, they could not even propose health reform legislation without meeting tight so-called "paygo" budget rules that had been institutionalized during the 1980s and early 1990s.[45] All aspects of their new Health Security legislation needed to be "costed out," and if the legislation was to go forward through normal congressional processes, the Congressional Budget Office (CBO) had to certify that projected new revenues or savings offset projected new expenditures. Attempts to anticipate such budgetary and "costing" procedures had much more influence on the specifics of the Clinton Health Security proposal than did contending conservative, moderate, and liberal political factions.

The CBO, it is worth underlining, has by now become virtually a sovereign branch of the U.S. federal government, comparable in its clout in relation to the executive and the Congress to the courts back in the Progressive Era and the New Deal. Back then, proponents of new public social policies used to spend a lot of time trying to guess what the courts, and especially the Supreme Court, would accept as constitutional. Legislative proposals were carefully crafted with future court review in mind, as policymakers tried to anticipate—not always successfully—what the judges would allow. Years of work could go into drafting legislation and struggling for it politically, only to see it struck down by a few unelected judges.[46] Today, a comparable process occurs with the CBO, an expert-run agency that the Founding Fathers certainly never imagined when they wrote the Constitution! Today's drafters of legislation live in fear that the CBO will, ultimately, reject their proposals as not "costed out."[47]

They also fear matters so simple as how the CBO will label components of their proposals. For example, during the late summer of 1993, Ira Magaziner and other White House planners thought they had an understanding that the CBO under Robert Reischauer would not label the Health Security employer-mandated contributions to premiums as "taxes." But in February 1994, at a very delicate political watershed for the Clinton Health Security plan, the CBO would finally issue a report that called these employer-mandated premiums the equivalent of taxes.[48] Of course, this was true in any meaningful substantive sense. But it also gave incendiary material to forces opposed to significant reform at a crucial juncture.

To have any hope of passing muster with deficit hawks and the Congressional Budget Office, the Clinton plan had to be credible about paying for new federal benefits or subsidies through hefty employer mandates and compensating cuts in existing federal programs (such as Medicaid and Medicare). The Clinton plan also had to convince the CBO that it had cost-control mechanisms with teeth if it wanted to project lower health care inflation for the future. Such projections of lower cost increases were, in turn, critical to justify claims that the Health Security plan would, after a few years, help to reduce rather than sharply increase the federal deficit.

At first glance, it might seem that the President and his health planners could have mollified budget hawks and the CBO by backing off on universal coverage and proposing only the sorts of market adjustments and modest subsidies for the poor that the conservative Democrats and some Republicans wanted. But in fact a minimalist managed-competition plan such as Congressman Cooper's could end up looking very costly for the federal budget. There is an irony here. The CBO had already decided that potential health care cost reductions from market competition alone would be "scored" only at modest levels in its budget calculations.[49] The reason the CBO took this position was that there was (and is) little empirical evidence, from real-world trends, that market competition among managed-care plans in and of itself saves a lot of money in health care. Thus, any legislation reviewed by the CBO had to include public budget cuts or regulatory controls of some sort, if its "savings" to the federal government were to be "scorable." Advocates of minimalist managed competition wanted the market alone to do virtually all the work of controlling health costs, but the CBO would not give much credence to such projected savings. Yet the CBO would count the minimalists' subsidies to the poor as cost increases against the federal budget. (In the end, the Cooper bill was destined to run aground on these rocks, among others.[50])

The Clinton planners tried to anticipate and mollify CBO scorers both by rearranging public financing in America's health care system and by injecting tight government regulations into reconfigured market relationships. On the public finance side, the President projected large cuts in Medicare and Medicaid, using some of those ostensibly freed-up funds to pay for subsidies to extend coverage to the uninsured and to pay for new benefits (prescription drugs and long-term care) promised to Americans over sixty-five years old. On the regulatory side, the President's plan furthered cost-reducing market competition by establishing mandatory large alliances to bargain for low prices. The plan also featured contingent "premium caps" on future price increases for private insurance policies.

The choice to require all employers of fewer than 5,000 workers to purchase health insurance through encompassing regional alliances, a key decision endorsed by President Clinton at the end of the summer, was of course pleasing to supporters of inclusive managed competition. People such as Walter Zelman and Paul Starr favored (as the latter put it) "breaking the job linkage" in America's employer-based health insurance system for working-aged adults.[51] Supporters of inclusive managed competition wanted to retain employers as contributors to the cost of health insurance, but (for the most part) not as purchasers of insurance for their employees. Big, mandatory regional alliances, these liberals believed, would transfer "choices" among plans to individuals rather than their employers and would promote social justice by ensuring huge "community rating" pools to allow similar coverage at similar prices for rich and poor, well and sick alike. In addition, encompassing alliances would also promote cost consciousness in health markets, because health plans and insurers would have to offer quality care while keeping prices down.

Tellingly, on this point the Congressional Budget Office tended to agree with the advocates of inclusive managed competition.[52] The requirement for all but the very largest businesses to purchase insurance through alliances was very pleasing to the CBO, because this created large purchasing pools for private health insurance. Such pools, the CBO people believed, would act as a backup to market competition among health plans in slowing the increase of health costs in the future. For different if overlapping reasons, therefore, liberals and budget hawks agreed on pushing all but the very largest companies into regional health alliances.

Liberals and deficit hawks also agreed on the regionally adjusted contingent premium caps that President Clinton and his health planners finally chose to include in their proposed legislation. The CBO wanted an unmovable backup mechanism of last resort just in case market forces and big alliances were unable to hold down health costs. Advocates of inclusive managed competition were happy for such a backup, too, because they did not want the phasing in of universal coverage to be associated with an explosion of health costs (and profits for private insurers). Rapidly rising costs had occurred in the wake of the enactment of Medicare and Medicaid in 1965, and the Clintonites did not want to repeat such an experience, which might undermine the U.S. economy and gut the federal budget in the future, and thus delegitimate governmentally sponsored universal coverage.

The inclusion of the contingent premium-cap mechanism in the President's plan would be, it was hoped, less offensive to opponents of big government than the global national limits on health spending that Bill Clinton had alluded to during the 1992 campaign. As of the summer of 1993, moderate Democrats and Republicans in Congress signaled to Ira Magaziner that contingent premium caps were an acceptable cost containment mechanism. And the President was attracted to them, because versions of such caps had previously appeared in health bills introduced or endorsed by moderate Republicans Nancy Kassebaum and John Danforth, as well as by conservative Democrats Dave McCurdy of Oklahoma and Dan Glickman of Kansas.[53] Moderates in Congress, not to mention many stakeholder groups in the U.S. health system, definitely did not want direct price controls on medical services or "global" budgets enforced by a national government board. If some sort of cost containment mechanism of last resort had to be there to satisfy the CBO—and it did—then premium caps were apparently the least objectionable. Such caps might not come into force if other mechanisms for cost reduction, working through market competition, did their job.

In sum, when the final, presidential-level decisions were made about key features of the Health Security plan—about the employer mandate, premiums, the benefit package, alliance size, and premium caps—it wasn't just a question of liberals versus conservatives, or populists versus deficit hawks. Journalists may have tried to tell the story mainly in terms of such warring factions and the personalities attached to them. But this approach overlooks the often ironic alignments of forces and considerations that shaped key decisions about the Health Security plan.

The very sorts of federal fiscal exigencies that might, under some circumstances, reinforce the policy arguments of conservatives or minimalists had the opposite effect in the case of the formulation of the Clinton Health Security plan. Requirements to keep down costs for the federal government, along with the need to convince the Congressional Budget Office and other fiscal watchdogs that health care reform could ultimately help to cut the federal deficit, strengthened the hands of those Clinton administration people who favored inclusive and regulatory features for the Health Security plan. While the choices to go with employer premiums and a decent standard benefit package may have been primarily "political"—in the sense of trying to address the expressed needs of most Americans—such other features as the employer mandate, encompassing alliances, and contingent premium caps were prompted by a *combination* of institutionalized fiscal constraints and progressive preferences for social fairness.

As he made his final decisions about the Health Security plan, President Clinton considered the promises of security and universal coverage he had made to all the American people. Of course he was spurred on by liberal advisors, while other advisors pushed in counteracting directions. But President Clinton also had his eye on the federal budget. Accordingly, he sponsored an intricate, interlocking set of regulatory mechanisms that were cleverly designed to push all actors in U.S. health care toward cost consciousness—and, not incidentally, to cut costs for the federal government in the process.

The Health Security proposal that President Clinton ultimately signed off on would have meant some straightforward things for Americans—most of which, I suspect, the vast majority of citizens would have found quite appealing or at least comfortable had they come to pass. In due course, all Americans, regardless of income, employment status, or family ties, would have been continuously covered by decent health insurance. The older citizens would have stayed in Medicare as that system was pushed toward greater cost-efficiency, and they would also have gotten some new coverage for prescription drugs and long-term care. All employers (and employees) would have had to contribute to health coverage for working Americans and their family members, while federal and state governments would have subsidized coverage for the unemployed.

In a reformed health insurance marketplace, most employers would have ceded many of their present functions in choosing insurance to state-sponsored regional purchasing alliances, and as a result most individual employees would have been guaranteed more choices among insurance plans of comparable quality than in the past. Employees would have had to pay higher shares from personal income if they wanted extra perks or absolute free choice of physicians. Insurance companies would have faced premium controls and weighty downward pressures on prices from alliances bargaining on behalf of purchasers of health policies. Yet there would still have been a prominent place for private insurance companies (especially big ones), as well as for private hospitals and physicians. In the reformed system that the Clinton plan aimed to further, health care providers would have had to look for increasingly cost-effective ways to deliver care. Yet because all Americans would have been included in the system, insurance companies and care providers would not have easily been able to save money simply by trying to avoid costlier patients.

The End of the Beginning

By September 1993, President Clinton had made good on his campaign promise to devise a comprehensive plan for reforming the U.S. health financing system. He and his Task Force on Health Care Reform had parried pressures to give up in advance on the goals of universal coverage and security. As Bill Clinton had believed in September 1992, he still thought in September 1993: he had found a good way through the middle of America's never ending and always before inconclusive debates about health care reform. His new Health Security plan, the President was sure, was an excellent basis for public and congressional deliberations.

Yet for this vision of reform to come true, Congress and the American people had to understand and accept the new federal measures that President Clinton was proposing. At first, there was considerable public approval, but it was accompanied by virtually no understanding of the "thousand interlocking parts" that composed the often well-disguised regulations and resource transfers that made up the Health Security plan.[54] Ostensibly absent from the plan were big tax increases, just as Bill Clinton had always promised. Meanwhile, employers and insurance companies, health care providers and con-

Courtesy Tribune Media Services

sumers, all were called on to accept new public "rules of the game" — rules designed to encourage lower costs and more standard practices in a huge sector of the U.S. economy. How would these work, and what would they mean for people? As of early fall 1993, it remained to be seen whether President Clinton, for all his intelligence and ability to give a compelling speech, could convince Congress and his fellow citizens that the nuts and bolts of his Health Security plan would be good for America and good for them.

CHAPTER THREE

DEMOCRATS IN DISARRAY

What went wrong and when for the Clinton Health Security proposal? Observers have placed the fatal illness of comprehensive health care reform at various points in time, ranging from the earliest months of the Clinton administration when the President's Task Force on Health Care Reform did its work to the end of the summer of 1994 when Congress at last gave up trying to fashion a "mainstream" compromise symbolically preserving bits and pieces of what the President had aimed to achieve. A year and four days after the birth of Health Security was announced to much fanfare, death for the comprehensive reform effort was officially pronounced by then Senate Majority Leader George Mitchell. But the patient was grievously ill long before Senator Mitchell intoned the end. The questions are when the reform initiative took sick and when it sunk so low as to be beyond resuscitation.

The critical loss of political momentum occurred within three to five months after the Health Security initiative was launched, during the period from the fall of 1993 through midwinter of 1994.[1] As Table 1 shows, overall public support for the Clinton plan registered at nearly 60 percent right after the President's September 23 speech; thereafter, support declined, but recovered somewhat in December and January. During February and March 1994, however, public support declined below 50 percent, and it never again rebounded. By that time (as we shall see in detail in chapter 5) concerted ideological campaigns against universal health reform had locked into place. The support of elite and middle-class Americans for ambitious reforms had begun to

TABLE ONE. Evaluation of President Clinton's Plan

"From everything you have heard or read about the plan so far,
do you favor or oppose President Clinton's plan to reform health care?"
(Gallup Organization)

RESPONSE	DATE	DATE	DATE	DATE
	9/24/93	10/28/93	11/15/93	11/19/93
Favor (%)	59	45	52	52
Oppose (%)	33	45	40	41
Don't know / refused (%)	8	10	8	7
Number	1,003	1,017	1,003	1,003
	1/17/94	1/28/94	2/26/94	3/28/94
Favor (%)	56	57	46	44
Oppose (%)	39	38	48	47
Don't know / refused (%)	6	5	5	9
Have not heard about the plan (%)			1	
Number	1,010	1,013	1,015	1,014
	4/20/94	5/20/94	6/11/94	6/25/94
Favor (%)	43	46	42	44
Oppose (%)	47	49	50	49
Don't know / refused (%)	10	5	8	8
Number	1,002	1,005	756	1,019

Data from Roper Center for Public Opinion Research, Storrs, Conn. Table from Lawrence R. Jacobs and Robert Y. Shapiro, "Don't Blame the Public for Failed Health Care Reform," *Journal of Health Politics, Policy and Law* 20, no. 2 (Summer 1995): 418.

slide inexorably downhill, and momentum toward inclusive reform was irretrievably lost.[2]

This identification of the critical period as falling between October 1993 and February 1994 presumes that major stakeholders in the present health system would not keep bargaining over changes in the rules of the game unless they saw that a strong proreform coalition existed and that the public continued to want such changes. Nor would Congress, with all its internal fissures and procedural obstacles, fashion a difficult compromise, unless it was clear that a broad coalition and at least a majority of Americans were supportive of change in the status quo.

If they were to prevail in 1993 and 1994, proponents of President Clinton's Health Security proposal needed to do a huge amount of mobilization and education, at a level surpassing the efforts that had gone into designing their proposed legislation. Supporters of reform had to be fast off the mark, and they had to work together with clarity and consistency of purpose. But nothing at all like that occurred— certainly not during the critical several months following the launching of the Clinton Health Security plan. The President and his allies in and around the administration did not fully gear up to campaign for Health Security until the spring of 1994, which was certainly too late.[3] By then public openness had turned toward skepticism, and determined ideological opponents of *any* sort of comprehensive health care reform were fully aroused and making considerable headway in their all-out effort to totally defeat the President's initiative. When congressional committees seriously undertook the process of marking up legislation during the spring and summer of 1994, they did so in a situation of waning faith that comprehensive, governmentally mediated change was either possible or desirable. An historic window of opportunity for comprehensive health reform in the United States was already nearly closed.

As this chapter and the following ones explore, there are significant reasons why the Clinton administration and its (actual or potential) allies did not work effectively together to build a coalition and deepen public support for the intricately designed approach to health care reform that the president advocated. The reasons reveal telling things about how U.S. government and politics work today. Or perhaps I should say that the reasons reveal important things about how U.S. government and Democratic party politics do *not* work, especially when challenged to address complex problems that require thorough democratic discussion and the fashioning and readjustment of compromises among leaders, citizens, and powerful groups.

Access to the President's Agenda

Right after the President gave his stirring Health Security speech in late September 1993, there were a handful of well-staged media events—featuring the President talking to carefully selected citizens in Florida and New York about their personal fears and health care problems. The President assured these featured citizens that his plan would end their worries. First Lady Hillary Rodham Clinton also made her much-touted visits to Congress.[4] Things looked very promising for the Clinton reform effort during the period right after its official launching.[5] And reform planners were counting on about six weeks of presidential time to push forward a nationwide campaign during October and early November.[6]

Once introduced, however, Health Security virtually disappeared from the White House schedule. As far as the President himself was concerned, little was done about Health Security for months—except when the effort was, at intervals, "relaunched." One relaunching came on October 27, when the final text of the 1,342-page Health Security bill at last appeared.[7] Another highly visible relaunching came during the State of the Union Address on January 25, 1994. In that speech, President Clinton quoted from some of the "millions of letters" Hillary Rodham Clinton had received from citizens anxious about their health coverage, and defended his reform proposals against accusations that they would entail too much government or would hurt Medicare. Then he dramatically waved a pen and declared to the assembled members of Congress:

> I want to make this very clear. . . . If you send me legislation that does not guarantee every American private health insurance that can never be taken away, you will force me to take this pen, veto the legislation, and we'll come right back here and start all over again.[8]

Even as he delivered this dramatic flourish, however, President Clinton had virtually nothing to say about the contents of his own proposed legislation. Instead, he signaled great flexibility in his dealings with Congress: "I am open, as I have said repeatedly, to the best ideas of concerned members of both parties. I have no special brief for any specific approach, even in our own bill," except the commitment to guarantee "health security" to "every hardworking, tax-paying American."[9] Not until a couple of months later did Clinton begin to travel extensively around the United States and give presentations that included some attempts to explain important substantive features of his reform plan.[10]

A basic reason for the President's relatively slight involvement during late 1993 and early 1994 flows from something political scientists know well: Despite never ending rounds of planning by their advisors, presidents of the United States do not really control their own calendars.[11] Crises can, and frequently do, interrupt previous plans. Matters rarely unfold according to preconceived schedules. For the Clinton administration, both unanticipatable foreign eruptions and a protracted legislative imbroglio intervened to undercut the foward momentum on health care reform that seemed to be there in late September and early October.

Not long after his September 22 speech, the President flew off to California for Health Security events. But he abruptly returned to Washington when word came that members of the American armed forces had been killed in Somalia, where they were stationed on a humanitarian mission (one that had not been initiated by Clinton, but by his Republican predecessor, George Bush). For much of October, the President and his foreign policy advisors were preoccupied with repeated incidents in Somalia and their congressional fallout at home, even as other foreign crises bubbled over.[12] Violent interelite conflicts broke out in Moscow, threatening to undermine the presidency of President Boris Yeltsin. Dramatic problems also reappeared about Haiti, as seaborne refugees poured out of that benighted land and the Haitian military leaders refused to follow through on an agreement to step down at the end of October.

Then President Clinton got involved in a protracted struggle to sell the North American Free Trade Agreement (NAFTA) to a reluctant public and Democratic Party. Much cajoling with individuals and small groups had to be done to assemble a bipartisan coalition to shoehorn the legislation through the House of Representatives.[13] NAFTA was an international agreement that had been passed down to the Clinton administration from previous presidents; the treaty had to be approved by Congress before the end of 1993, or else years of previous international and domestic negotiations would go down the drain. Most Republicans supported this pact furthering unfettered international trade, and so did many "New Democrats" from the moderate and southern wings of the party with which Clinton partially identified. Clinton himself always supported the principles of NAFTA. But the treaty was hated by many liberal Democrats and by most of the trade unions that composed what little was left of the organized labor movement, a key aspect of the party's shriveled infrastructure. Many ordinary Americans told pollsters that they feared implementation of the treaty would cost them their jobs, as companies transferred low-wage work to Mexico.

"BOY... DID I DO SOME HORSE TRADING OR WHAT?"

Copyright © 1993 The Florida Times-Union. Courtesy King Features Syndicate

People advising the Clinton administration had argued during the summer about whether the President should go all out for NAFTA in the fall.[14] I do not think it surprising that President Clinton decided to push for NAFTA when he did, however, in part because he must have imagined it would take much less time and presidential political capital than it ultimately did. Given the reliance of Clinton's overall approach to "economic recovery" on free trade and the creative adaptation of the U.S. economy and workforce to international economic competition, Clinton could hardly avoid advocating NAFTA, and if he delayed beyond the end of 1993, Congress would have new opportunities to amend the treaty. Still, the impending fall 1993 NAFTA decision in Congress forced the President to wage an all-out campaign of public persuasion and Congressional arm-twisting just when he should have been devoting his time to explaining his health reform plan to the American people. The pro-NAFTA effort proved to be a protracted cliff-hanger, soaking up presidential energy and media attention. Finally, on "November 17, after a marathon of Clinton lobbying, the House approved NAFTA, 234 to 200. The winning coalition included 132 Republicans and only 102 Democrats."[15]

In retrospect, President Clinton may have given away his last chance to mobilize Democratic support for his crucial Health Security initiative by devoting to NAFTA so much time, energy, and arm-twisting of people in Congress. Progressive critics of the Clinton White House argue that, however well-intentioned he may have been, Bill Clinton squandered a rare opportunity to build support for inclusive social policy in order to pursue an essentially Republican, promarket economic program. Of course, at the time, the Clinton White House (urged on by advisors such as former Reagan administration communications aide David Gergen) probably thought it would win bipartisan "credit" in the NAFTA struggle—credit that could be transferred to the looming Health Security battle. Yet that is not how U.S. politics works. Organized interests, especially among conservatives and the business community, are happy to take what they can get from Democrats. But they will not reciprocate, even on issues of fundamental national concern such as health care reform.

NAFTA apart, it is obvious that the Clinton administration's launching of the Health Security effort got badly squeezed on both ends by apparently uncontrollable exigencies in the presidential agenda. The NAFTA distraction would have been less of a blow if Health Security had been unveiled in the late spring or early summer of 1993. Ira Magaziner, Mrs. Clinton, and others devoted to comprehensive reform foresaw right at the start of the Clinton presidency that it would become harder to enact health care legislation the longer the President waited to introduce a plan. During February and March 1993, when public support for impending health reform was at what turned out to be its peak, task-force leaders tried to short-circuit the delays they dreaded by getting the President and congressional Democratic leaders to include health reform in negotiations for the budget.[16] Not only would this approach have speeded up the introduction and consideration of health reform legislation. Given congressional rules, it would have allowed health care reform to pass with only a majority vote in the Senate, because a (threatened or actual) filibuster would not have been possible on budget reconciliation legislation. This would have gotten around a problem that ultimately killed off comprehensive reform—the fact that Democrats plus moderate Republican supporters of reform did not add up to sixty votes in the Senate, the number necessary to break (or preclude the credible threat of) a filibuster. House Majority Leader Richard Gephardt and Senate Majority Leader George Mitchell were prepared to try this budget reconciliation route to health reform.

But as a traditionalist protector of congressional prerogatives, Senator Robert Byrd would not accept the idea of slipping health care reform through Congress in this way. In any event, there probably would have been a huge public hue and cry if it had been attempted. With some justification, people would have opposed enacting a reform affecting one-seventh of the national economy without substantial discussions focused on health care as such, apart from necessarily compressed deliberations on the annual federal budget.

Not only was health reform forced to wait until after the budget passed Congress; the delay greatly reduced prospects for congressional, press, and public understanding of the emerging Clinton health plan. While Congress wrangled over the summer about the budget, the President struggled to broker and rebroker detailed compromises—stroking the egos of key senators like Robert Kerrey one by one. Meanwhile, from May onward, the White House put health care reform on hold and—more important—pulled it back into secrecy. For fear that leaks about financing decisions might alienate a vote or two in Congress, meetings ceased and Clinton planners refused to talk in any detail to the media or Congress or advocacy groups; they thus missed chances to explain the emerging health reform plan.[17] Explanatory and promotional materials could not even be finalized, let alone deployed, because crucial presidential-level decisions about the design of Health Security were not to be made until August.[18] Furthermore, during this period of suspended animation, little hard thinking was going on at top levels of the Clinton administration about what sort of legislation *really* had a chance to get through Congress.

During the protracted maneuvers over the budget, both health reform and the President himself lost credibility with the public and Congress. At the time, Ira Magaziner observed in an internal White House memo that

> the "stop and start and stop again" nature of the health care decision process, the pernicious leaks and the constantly changing deadlines—early May, late May, late June, late July, September—have seriously slowed our momentum, undermining our credibility with Congress, interest groups, the media, and the American people. . . . Interest groups who were offering support and a willingness to compromise on long held positions are now backing away. Congres-

sional leaders eager to support health reform are questioning whether we are serious and are getting nervous that we will leave them "high and dry."[19]

During the same period the President's public ratings went down, as Americans began to suspect that Clinton could not control Congress—that he might not, after all, be able to break the gridlock in Washington as many had hoped a new Democratic president might be able to do in dealing with the Democratic-led Congress. The President lost clout with key senators and representatives. Some in Congress concluded that Bill Clinton, a newcomer to Washington from Arkansas, could be pushed around. Others came to believe that they should not commit themselves to politically risky votes at presidential behest, for fear that Clinton might later back off from his initial position. (For example, House members felt they got burned during the budget battle when they supported the President on a tough vote for a tax on energy, only to see him back off this provision in his dealings with the Senate Finance Committee).[20]

The effect of all this on Health Security was more than delay and the lost opportunity for education. Another aftereffect of the summer 1993 budget mess was to make President Clinton's advisors reluctant for him to take detailed positions on the mechanisms of health care reform, for if the President took such positions and later had to compromise or back off from initial stands, he could again be accused of "waffling" by Congress—and the media. Better, some advisors argued, to have the President endorse the goals of reform and leave detailed bargains to Congress.

When he did occasionally speak out about Health Security during late 1993 and on into 1994, President Clinton did not explain or solidly defend the operational guts of his reform plan. The plan was finally launched in September without much educational basis having been laid in Congress, with the media, or among Democratic constituencies. Even so, President Clinton stuck to talking about overall goals: the commitments to "reducing costs" and providing "security" and "choice" for all Americans. When queried about the details of his plan, the President remained "above it all" and signaled flexibility about the particular mechanisms and provisions in his bill. As Paul Starr would later lament, after "the submission of the bill, the White House focused entirely on the principles of reform and made little effort to defend parts of the proposal. The administration had gone to the trouble of writing a bill and then left it like a foundling on the doorstep of Congress"[21] — and, I might add, on the public's doorstep as well.

The Changing Landscape of U.S. Politics

Looking at the situation more broadly, we can take the focus off the presidency in isolation. What happened to the Clinton Health Security plan was profoundly influenced by the limited institutionally available means of political mobilization and communication open to a U.S. president and allied policy promoters in the 1990s, especially if they are Democrats. Why was it, we should wonder, that so much seemed to ride on presidential speeches and presidentially attended media events? President Clinton may not have given enough speeches or covered all that was necessary in his speeches. Yet the sputtering and ultimately futile campaign for the Clinton Health Security plan was also profoundly influenced by the lack of other good options for communication and organization on behalf of Health Security.

Striking transformations are altering the landscape of American politics, changing the terrain on which groups form, politicians maneuver, and policy proposals rise and fall.[22] Voter participation has declined markedly in the last couple of decades, with the falloff of participation occurring disproportionately among lower-income Americans. Elections have at the very same time become much more expensive, as huge amounts of money must be raised for television advertising and to pay for the services of pollsters and consultants. Politicians are necessarily obsessed with fund-raising, dependent on political action committees (PACs) and other sources of funds that disproportionately channel contributions from business interests and wealthy or upper-middle-class citizens. Such factors as these are often cited, singly or together, as responsible for the increasing bias of U.S. public policymaking in the direction of privileged interests and socioeconomic groups.[23] This analysis is accurate enough, as far as it goes. It helps to explain why an initiative involving the extension of health insurance to lower-income working people might not easily make headway in Washington, D.C.

Probing more deeply, we also need to consider how the changing organizational and resource patterns in U.S. politics and society make certain kinds of political communication, mobilization, and alliance formation more or less feasible. President Clinton's options for explaining his health care reform plan to his fellow citizens, and the administration's capacities to mobilize broad support on behalf of the plan were sharply limited by the groups and technologies at work in contemporary U.S. civic life.

In the post-World War II period, from the mid-1940s through the mid-1960s, U.S. politics was patterned by relatively stable electoral competition between two dominant parties, the Democrats and Republicans. The two dominant parties coexisted with—indeed operated through or in alliance with—a limited number of nationally widespread yet locally present socioeconomic interest groups. Although critics of this postwar "pluralist" polity (as it was often called) pointed out that it was biased toward business and the middle class, there were important groups and resources on both sides of the partisan divide. Usually on the Republican side were widespread federated interest groups such as the Chamber of Commerce, the National Association of Manufacturers, the American Medical Association, and the American Farm Bureau Federation (which brought together commercial farmers especially in the West and South). On the Democratic side, meanwhile, labor unions and other farmers' groups were hefty players. At their peak in the mid-1950s the labor unions of the American Federation of Labor and the Congress of Industrial Organizations (AFL-CIO) represented about 40 percent of the private-sector labor force (along with about 5 percent of the public-sector workers).[24] Most AFL-CIO unions supported the Democrats and offered crucial funding and electoral support to the party's candidates.[25] Both Democrats and Republicans have always been very open to business funding and influence; and the Democrats were never a working-class-based, social-democratic party in the European sense. Still, the postwar "New Deal" Democrats did have a capacity to mobilize both organizational and voter support from working-class and middle-income majorities.[26]

From the New Deal onward, conservative alliances of such major federations as the Chamber of Commerce, the AMA, and the Farm Bureau consistently allied with one another and with Republicans and southern Democrats to block or blunt attempted national social policy initiatives such as universal health insurance and federal full-employment programs.[27] Even so, popularly rooted and widespread groups on the liberal-Democratic side of the spectrum could and did support some federal policy breakthroughs. For example, the enactment of Medicare in 1965 under Democratic Party auspices was strongly supported by labor unions and certain associations of older citizens, while the American Medical Association and assorted business groups were defeated in that policy battle.[28] On certain issues at key junctures, the Democratic Party and its constituent or allied interest groups, including the AFL-CIO and advocates for older citizens, could muster enough electoral and institutional leverage to expand or sustain America's federal social and economic programs.

Starting in the 1960s American society and politics were rocked by protest movements and momentous transformations: the Civil Rights struggle and the enfranchisement of African Americans in the South; disputes over the Vietnam War, the emergence of feminist and environmental movements, and the birth of grassroots citizen action movements.[29] Under both liberal Democrats and moderate Republican President Richard Nixon, the federal government considerably expanded its social expenditures and regulatory activities. Courts, Congress, and the executive branch became increasingly active in regulating corporate practices on behalf of workplace safety or environmental concerns; and the various branches of the federal government were also drawn into promoting or protecting the "rights" of various groups of citizens, such as minorities, women, and the handicapped. In order to monitor and lobby all these enhanced federal activities, think tanks and policy research institutes sprouted, and all sorts of advocacy organizations set up shop in Washington, D.C. Bypassing more general-purpose associations, so did individual corporations and specialized industry or occupational associations. A veritable organizational explosion occurred, as John Judis explains:

> In the 1950s, no more than a dozen very large pressure groups dominated Washington politics. . . . [But] what distinguishes Washington politics today is the sheer proliferation of citizen organizations, trade associations, think tanks, and policy research groups. In its Spring 1991 directory of the most prominent Washington organizations, the *National Journal* listed 328 interest groups, 98 think tanks, 288 trade and professional associations, and 682 corporate headquarters.[30]

On the face of things, citizen participation in U.S. democracy soared amidst the proliferation of advocacy and interest groups. While the new corporate lobbying groups that proliferated after the 1960s could be considered narrow and privileged, many of the recently created or vastly expanded advocacy organizations seem much more citizen oriented. Some are networks of groups engaged in community-based activism—examples here would include Citizen Action and the Association of Community Organizations for Reform Now (ACORN)—while many others are national issue-focused or particular-constituency organizations—such as Common Cause, the National Abortion Rights Action League (NARAL), Greenpeace, the National Organization of Women (NOW), or Handgun Control. Citizens' associations or public-interest groups range from small local operations to national associations claiming huge memberships. Using a relatively narrow definition, political scientist Karen Paget suggests that such groups involve perhaps 15 million people.[31] A broader definitional net might yield a much higher estimate of group adherents, especially if we include the biggest advocacy group of all, which works on behalf of Americans fifty years of age and older. As Judis points out, "dwarfing even the AFL-CIO, the American Association of Retired Persons (AARP) has 28 million members, a legislative staff of 125, and 20 registered lobbyists."[32] Judis used figures referring to the situation before 1992. By 1993–94, the AARP had about 33 million members, or half the U.S. population over the age of forty-nine; and its annual budget was $300 million.[33]

In truth, however, most contemporary U.S. advocacy and interest organizations are not very participatory or popularly rooted at all, not even as much as the imperfectly participatory AFL-CIO unions and the locally rooted federations of commercial farmers, physicians, and businesses that once stood out more prominently among all politically active U.S. interest groups. Setting aside tiny local groups that have little presence in state or national politics, today's issue-advocacy and constituency groups are likely to be "professionalized," that is, run "by their staff and by a board of directors that is often dominated by the staff."[34] Professional advocacy leaders are highly sensitive to the concerns of outside donors, whether these be wealthy individuals, corporate sponsors, or foundations.

The more citizen-oriented groups may also raise resources from mass mailings, telephone solicitations, or even door-to-door canvasses by paid solicitors. But the thousands or (at times) millions of members claimed by such groups are more atomized subjects than socially

interconnected participants. Most members of today's citizens' or public-interest associations do not get to know one another, because they
are *not* regular participants in local affiliated groups, such as clubs,
union locals, churches, local medical societies, or neighborhood associations.[35] In most cases, the citizen members merely receive mailings—of fund-raising appeals accompanied by newsletters, magazines,
or carefully crafted questionnaires. Their involvement consists almost
entirely of sending a check to help keep the national staff afloat and
at work in Washington, D.C.

The proliferation of professional staff-led advocacy and interest
organizations in U.S. politics has outflanked or internally divided the
political parties, especially the Democratic Party. As we will later see,
the conservative right in and around the Republican Party has partially
overcome the fragmentation and rootlessness that proliferating corporate and advocacy groups have also brought on that side of the spectrum. But on the progressive side, groups that raise funds through
national direct-mail appeals (or even through canvassing door to door
across many localities and states) have discovered that upper-middle-
income citizens are the best financial supporters. Dramatic appeals
featuring the "rights" of specific constituencies, or hot-button issues
(such as saving endangered species or protecting access to abortion)
work best to reach such people. General appeals on behalf of political
parties or comprehensive socioeconomic policies do not work so well,
especially not for liberal advocacy groups trying to raise money from
relatively privileged Americans. As Karen Paget explains:

> A major consequence of the necessity to compete for an always
> scarce dollar is that a "market niche" mentality has come to domi-
> nate many organizations and funders alike. To succeed in raising
> money, the leaders of each organization are forced to argue that
> their consituency, geographical domain, issue, or approach to the
> issue warrants support because it differs from all other competing
> groups [or issues]. . . . This need to define a niche to survive finan-
> cially means that the world of citizen organizations has come to
> mirror the dominant tendency in America's political culture of frag-
> mentation and specialization. . . . There are few incentives . . . for
> organizations to coalesce with each other or with other constituen-
> cies, to work together on issues other than their own, or to develop
> a broader (common) vision.[36]

I think Paget's conclusion can be slightly modified, in that advocacy groups typically do form temporary coalitions to fight for, or against, specific pieces of legislation in Congress. But she is basically right, in that groups are likely to focus especially on aspects of legislation that matter most to them.

Citizen-oriented advocacy groups tend not only to be minutely differentiated from one another and oriented to single issues or particular constituencies. Most are also officially nonpartisan, and thus by definition at arm's length in their relationships to the Democratic Party and to Democratic candidates or officeholders. Professional, staff-led organizations in America have a long history of tension with party politics; ever since the Progressive Era it has been fashionable for such groups to take a nonpartisan, "expert" stance, "above politics." For new reasons, the social movements of the 1960s also spawned activists accustomed to taking an oppositional stance toward the dominant parties. Finally, and perhaps most important for sustaining nonpartisan organizations over time, current U.S. Internal Revenue Service rules offer tax-exempt status only to groups that can claim to be devoted to nonpartisan educational or advocacy purposes.[37] So there is a significant fund-raising advantage for groups that emphasize loyalty to causes rather than to a party, candidates, or officeholders pushing policies with partisan appeal. Along with the market-niche incentives for successful fund-raising, the IRS rules reinforce the fragmentation and upper-middle-class focus of contemporary U.S. policy advocacy.

Along with major changes in the U.S. economy since the 1950s, the changes we have surveyed add up to a very difficult "brave new world" for the Democratic Party. The 1990s Democratic Party no longer has a locally rooted infrastructure of loyal local ("machine") organizations and allied broadly focused groups, especially labor unions, through which concerted grassroots campaigns can be run. Unions now encompass only about 11 percent of private-sector workers.[38] The labor movement and the Democrats have become more reliant on public-sector unions, such as teachers' unions and unions of state and local governmental employees; but these have not made up for much of the loss of private-sector union strength. During elections as well as afterward, Democratic politicians depend almost exclusively on pollsters, media consultants, and television to get messages out to the citizenry. And Democratic politicians are in constant competion for money and attention with the newly predominant staff-led advocacy organizations.

Those groups, as we have seen, are ostensibly nonpartisan and focused on single issues or constituencies. Their leaderships and (mass-mailing) memberships tend to be upper-income people, and thus typically animated by rather different concerns than the low-income Americans to whom the Democratic Party must try to appeal to win elections. What is more, while certain middle-class or wealthy people who send money to Common Cause, the Sierra Club, or the National Organization of Women may normally vote Democratic, many are Independents who vote for certain Republicans or an occasional maverick like Ross Perot. Many adherents of citizens' groups or advocacy associations do not consider themselves loyal to the Democratic Party, still less to the full range of issues pushed by Democrats through Congress or the presidency. Advocacy organizations thus find it very much in their interest to take a cautious stand in relation to policies promoted by candidates or officeholders.

When policies are not exactly the ones each group advocates, it may ignore any given legislative battle or take a tepid stance or focus on seeking minute adjustments in a bill making its way through Congress. If a group claims to represent a slice of the overall American population—such as older citizens, or children, or women, or Latinos—that group may devote *all* its energy to bargaining on behalf of very specific legislative provisions to benefit that group. The forest gets lost for the trees, because successes in narrowly focused endeavors can be trumpeted as "victories" in the next mass mailing, while a victory for a very broad piece of legislation designed to help the national economy or benefit many different sorts of Americans would not be very useful for such a purpose.

What do the weaknesses of the Democratic Party and associated political forces have to do with the fate of the Clinton proposal for health care reform? As we shall see in the remainder of this chapter and the next, the transformed features of the U.S. political universe which I have surveyed had considerable relevance as Health Security was unveiled and nationally debated during 1993 and 1994.

Mobilizing a Coalition for Health Security?

The Clinton administration and its friends tried to construct intergroup coalitions and grassroots campaigns on behalf of their vision of national health care reform. Such attempts started in the summer of 1993 and continued through the first half of 1994. But there were organizational pitfalls, and even at their most effective, these efforts had pitifully scanty resources and faced great difficulties in mobilizing support for the President's reform plan as such.

Ira Magaziner and Hillary Rodham Clinton coordinated extensive resources to devise the technical details that went into the Clinton Health Security proposal. But no comparable organizational effort was made on the *political* side, because for many months there was a remarkable vacuum of top-level White House leadership for the politics of health care reform. Here was the biggest, most distinctive initiative of Clinton's presidency. Yet from the summer of 1993 through the beginning of 1994, key White House people who were supposed to take charge of the politics of health reform got distracted by the budget battle and then the NAFTA struggle, and then left. Not until early 1994 did the skilled New York political operative Harold Ickes take over as health politics "czar." And even then, Ickes could devote only part of his time to health care reform, because he simultaneously had to deal with the so-called Whitewater affair, which became a big issue in the media in late 1993 and early 1994.

In the spring and summer of 1993, detailed strategies for political mobilization had been sketched out by the leaders of the policy task force. There were communication plans for Congress, the media, experts, and the general public, as well as scenarios for alternative patterns of bargaining over legislative modifications during 1993–94.[39] But most of these plans never got beyond the pages of lengthy memos. Until the very belated arrival of Ickes, high-level White House operatives were not reliably in place to manage political efforts on behalf of health reform. In large part because they had only junior White House aides to talk with, people in Congress did not find White House political leadership credible. And many opportunities were lost in dealings with stakeholder groups and the broader public as well.

To be sure, the Democratic National Committee (DNC) under Chairman David Wilhelm did get involved in fighting for health care reform (a courageous move on Wilhelm's part, because of course not all Democrats endorsed the Clinton plan).[40] However, DNC efforts at first aborted, and then regrouped ineffectually. In the spring and summer of 1993, while the Health Security plan was being spelled out inside the administration, an attempt was made to use a seed grant from the Democratic National Committee to set up a nominally nonpartisan National Health Care Campaign (NHCC), which hopefully would raise from $20 to $37 million "from corporations, labor unions, and wealthy individuals" and use such funds to target messages to twenty to twenty-seven states identified as keys to the ultimate passage of legislation.[41] Nonpartisan status would afford important tax advantages and allow the NHCC to operate outside finance disclosure laws. But almost at once this project came under legal attack from the right, and media critics agreed it was not nonpartisan. That form of the NHCC was quickly abandoned.

With Wilhelm's agreement, the White House moved the NHCC back under the auspices of the Democratic National Committee. Yet this "doomed any hope of tapping into vast new financing resources."[42] Because the campaign was now directly sponsored by a party entity, it was less able than had been originally hoped to energize a coalition that included advocacy groups that had to maintain "nonpartisan" tax status. In its second manifestation as well as its first, the NHCC never got very far off the ground. A temporary first leader left in mid-October, only to be followed by former Ohio Democratic Governor Dick Celeste, whose job never became clearly defined in his own eyes or in those of others in and around the DNC.[43]

NHCC efforts on behalf of Health Security fell short for another important reason. During the fall of 1993, the Democratic Party's usual sure donor and grassroots supporter, the AFL-CIO, diverted resources and attention to the battle against NAFTA. Many activists were greatly embittered by the Clinton administration's support of NAFTA, and union leaders "turned off the spigot" for the NHCC during the very period when opponents of the fledgling Clinton Health Security plan were channeling large resources into oppositional advertising and organizing.[44]

In the middle of March 1994, the "DNC's sputtering grassroots campaign for health care reform" was put "out of its misery."[45] By then an alternative was doing better, although belatedly. After the Clinton plan had been unveiled in the fall and it was clear that the NHCC was faltering, West Virginia Democratic Senator Jay Rockefeller expanded the Health Care Reform Project (HCRP), an officially nonpartisan promotional coalition. Led by John Rother of the American Association of Retired Persons, this effort was better organized than the DNC undertaking.

The HCRP had insufficient funds for a big national media campaign, yet it focused on mobilizing support for "universal health care" in swing congressional districts. According to *National Journal* reporter Julie Kosterlitz, "after a shaky beginning, in which groups unaccustomed to working with one another had to iron out conflicting and competing agendas, the Health Care Reform Project seems to have come into its own, launching a series of sophisticated TV commercials and setting up a far-flung grassroots organization."[46] Even so, the HCRP could not specifically promote—or explain—the President's bill as such, because member groups, including Rother's AARP, had not endorsed the Clinton plan, only broad goals for reform that resembled that plan.

The AARP and the Clinton Health Reform

The story of the AARP's relationship to the Health Security legislation is emblematic of the Clinton administration's limited opportunities for alliance formation and popular communication within an environment dominated by advocacy groups, particularly groups that had grown lazy during years of Democratic ascendency in Congress, accustomed to insider lobbying rather than popular political mobilization.

The formulators of the Health Security legislation were very careful to attend to the possible concerns of older citizens, because they wanted to attract strong support from the AARP as the principal association claiming to represent more than 30 million citizens fifty years and older. If the President's overall deficit-cutting requirements were to be met, some of the funding for the Health Security effort had to come from cuts in otherwise projected federal expenditures on Medicare (the universal health insurance program for Americans sixty-five and older) and on Medicaid (which covers nursing home expenses for many older citizens).

To counteract the impact of those cuts, the final Clinton Health Security proposal included a prescription drug benefit for older citizens (who often pay huge amounts for medication), as well as the promise of eventual contributions to home-based long-term care, also of great concern to older citizens and their families. The leadership of the AARP liked these features of the Clinton Health Security bill, which had been worked out in close consultation with them. And the AARP was already on record in support of universal health coverage for all Americans. Not surprisingly, people in the Clinton administration hoped that the AARP would get enthusiastically on board and unequivocally push for the passage of administration-sponsored health reforms.

Eventually, after virtually all hope for comprehensive health care reform was gone, the AARP would indeed endorse Clinton-type legislation in the summer of 1994.[47] But early in the reform campaign when strong support might have mattered, the AARP held back, refusing to endorse the Clinton Health Security plan. The AARP Board passed up opportunities officially to endorse Health Security at meetings in both November 1993 and February 1994.[48] The February 23 gathering of the AARP leadership was held right after President Clinton had openly appealed for an AARP endorsement. During the week prior to the AARP Board meeting, the President and the First Lady had staged nationally televised health care events designed to dramatize the advantages of his plan for senior citizens. "Clinton Fails to Get Endorsement of Elderly Group on Health Plan" was the *New York Times* headline on February 24, announcing to the country the results of the President's pleading. This media framing overshadowed the fact that the AARP leadership had called the Clinton proposal "the strongest and most realistic blueprint to date for achieving our goals."[49]

Why did the AARP leadership hang back, especially given that many officials of the association wanted the Clinton plan (or its virtual twin) to pass? Part of the reason for the AARP's conduct lay in recent history. In 1988, the AARP's leadership had endorsed and strenuously lobbied for the Medicare Catastrophic Coverage Act, only to discover after it passed that hundreds of thousands of well-to-do older citizens were very angry at Congress and at the AARP leadership because of the progressive premiums that were to have been collected to finance the catastrophic illness coverage.[50] The AARP leadership had taken a drubbing during the catastrophic-coverage episode at the hands of a competitor older-citizen advocacy organization, the National Committee to Preserve Social Security and Medicare.[51]

During 1993–94, AARP leaders knew that many older citizens were confused about the Clinton health plan and very worried about its proposed cuts for Medicare. Unfortunately, certain people inside the Clinton administration who were opposed to substantial Medicare cuts leaked information about options being considered by the President just before the 1993 Labor Day weekend. A flurry of unanswered media coverage occurred while President Clinton and other administration leaders were out of town; this caused many older citizens— and their congressional representatives home on recess—to become worried about what was in the Clinton health care plan. The premature leaks about Medicare cuts were very harmful, because they undercut possibilities for the Clinton administration and the AARP leadership to explain the cuts and the offsetting new benefits at the same time.[52]

Older citizen support for the emerging Clinton plan began dropping. By the turn of 1993–94, older citizens were markedly less supportive of the Clinton proposal than the general population, and their overall support declined more than any other group between September 1993 and April 1994.[53] This was truly disastrous for the fortunes of comprehensive health care reform, because the administration needed enthusiasm from elderly organizations of older citizens to get legislation through Congress.

From the time of the pre-Labor Day leaks, AARP leaders became very cautious about fully supporting the Clinton administration's proposal. They were hearing from elderly people about their fears of Medicare cuts, and the last thing the AARP wanted was a repeat of the catastrophic-coverage debacle. For their own organizational reasons, therefore, AARP leaders decided in the fall of 1993 to endorse broad goals for national health care reform, conduct educational forums comparing the Clinton plan to others, and keep their options open for bargaining in congressional committees. As the New York Times reported, the AARP

> like many groups, seems to have decided that it can maximize its influence by preserving a degree of independence and by stressing its concerns, without giving a blanket endorsement to one proposal. Such independence gives lobbyists more room to maneuver on Capitol Hill, where the politics of health care are continually in flux.[54]

The AARP had large resources available for advertising about health reform. Instead of using them to endorse the Clinton plan, it ran ads calling for provisions such as a prescription drug benefit and help to pay for long-term care to be included in "any" legislation enacted by Congress. Ironically, the AARP ads had the effect of confusing Americans, making them think that the President's plan omitted the desired provisions (when it actually included them).[55]

AARP leaders were not intentionally trying to undermine comprehensive health care reform, for they rightly saw the extension of health coverage to all Americans and the institution of some overall cost controls as vital to protecting Medicare for older citizens in the future. AARP leaders wanted something like Health Security to pass. But the association's tepidness over many months inevitably helped to undercut the Clinton administration's plan—which was, like it or not, the point effort for any prospect of universal health coverage once the 1993–94 battle was joined.

Few Wholehearted Supporters

The AARP was not untypical among reform-minded advocacy groups. Every once and a while, groups participating in the health care debate straightforwardly endorsed the Clinton plan. The American Nurses Association was consistently very supportive.[56] And on December 16, 1993 leaders of ten groups claiming to represent more than 300,000 physicians appeared with President Clinton at the Old Executive Office Building. These "obstetricians, pediatricians, family doctors, internists, specialists in preventive medicine, and spokesmen for groups representing black doctors and Hispanic doctors" outright endorsed the Clinton plan, in an effort to counter criticisms registered by the 296,000-strong American Medical Association a week before.[57] But this was not the usual story. Like the AARP, many sympathetic groups registered criticisms of this or that provision of the Clinton plan and maintained an arm's length stance in order to bargain for changes (or protect advantages) in Congress.

In mid-December 1993, Mike Lux, a young White House aide working on health reform prepared a telling overview of "Interest Group Positioning" in relation to the Clinton proposal. Writing to President Clinton, Lux did his best to sound cheerful, suggesting that a "winning coalition is essentially in place. All of the labor, senior, children's advocate, general practice physician, non-physician provider, consumer, and single-payer groups that we thought we had a realistic chance of getting . . . are basically on board, even if for internal political reasons they have held back on completely embracing us."[58] But the overall contents of Lux's very detailed memo presented a much more pessimistic picture—not least in the "bad news" it honestly presented about the groups supposedly most supportive of the Clinton Health Security proposal.

It would take most AFL-CIO unions "a while to cool off and then gear up again for health care reform," the memo reported, because of "the residue of anger and bitterness—both at the leadership and the rank-and-file level—that NAFTA leaves us."[59] More generally, there were "continued problems with allied organizations' activism," because

> we still have to contend with all the problems we've faced these last few months: the nit-picking over the 10% they didn't get; the national staff and leadership always seeking to cover themselves in case things go sour; passivity and lack of sophistication about how to engage in successful campaigns.[60]

Groups on "our side" also lacked financial resources equal to the opposition, Lux's memo stressed. Perhaps most discouraging, given the stage of the game at that date, the memo acknowledged that

> because of the complexity of our bill and the huge levels of mis-information and mis-understanding about it, supportive groups are having to devote enormous amounts of resources to educating their *activists*, let alone their members. This huge educational process is slowing down the groups' ability to move people into action. Until they get ahead of the curve on this process, grassroots pressures on our side will be relatively sparse.[61]

In short, the Clinton administration's failure to inform and prepare its potential supporters *before* the Health Security plan was publicly launched was still hurting badly several months later—even as opponents of the Clinton plan were already engaged in their campaigns of lobbying, advertising, and grassroots mobilization. Opponents were fully in the field in late 1993 and early 1994. Meanwhile the administration and its putative supporters were either dithering or just gearing up; and potential supporters were still trying to understand the bewildering complexities of the President's bill!

One last point is worth making about the efforts of groups in the core of whatever supportive coalition there was for comprehensive health care reform in late 1993 and early 1994. An "educational" rather than unabashedly pro-Clinton stance was characteristic of most of the public advertising deployed by such groups. The Henry J. Kaiser Family Foundation, for example, was essentially a close ally of the Clinton administration during the entire health reform effort (and its staff certainly fully understood the Health Security bill).[62] Yet given the tax rules for foundations and nonpartisan groups, the pro-reform ads run by the Kaiser Foundation in conjuction with the League of Women Voters Education Fund were about "Straight Facts on Health Reform." At the top each ad asked a question and indicated an answer:

WHO ARE THE UNINSURED?
Most are working people and their families.

WHO ARE THE UNINSURED?
Most are adults of modest means and their family members.

WHAT HAPPENS WHEN PEOPLE DON'T HAVE HEALTH INSURANCE?
They get less care.[63]

A page of densely packed facts followed to document the answer. Each ad concluded in an exhortation to readers to "Get the facts. Get involved."

For people in the know, these ads sponsored by the Kaiser Foundation and the League of Women Voters none too subtly pointed toward the need for exactly the sort of comprehensive reform that President Clinton was proposing. Yet to maintain their nonpartisan, educational style, the ads stated: "We know there are legitimate differences on how to achieve national health reform. This public information campaign does not advocate any specific program or legislation." What were people to do with the new "factual" information these ads were dispensing?

Other core supporters ran ads endorsing general reform principles—often exactly those that appeared in the Clinton plan—but without mentioning that plan as such. An excellent example of such an almost endorsement was "A Message from America's Health Care

Workers Coalition," an alliance of eighteen health groups of health workers and social-service professionals, that appeared in the *New York Times* on March 30, 1994[64] This ad virtually outlined the Clinton Health Security proposal, yet never named it. Although the groups sponsoring the ad were obviously Democratic, they declared "We don't think of ourselves as Democrats or Republicans when it comes to delivering health care." The ad focused on Congress, asking readers to "Send a Clear Message to Congress. . . . Ask your Representative to support guaranteed, comprehensive quality care for your family. . . . Join the campaign for real health care security." The only difficulty was that readers were not asked to tell congressional representatives to *do* anything very precise, and certainly nothing as specific as to vote for President Clinton's Health Security bill.

The vague educational-style messages on behalf of Clinton-style health care reform may have been responsible—along with the fierce, not at all vague attacks on Health Security that we shall encounter in chapter 5—for a remarkable finding reported in March 1994 by the *Wall Street Journal* in an article entitled "Many Don't Realize It's the Clinton Plan They Like."[65] This article reported results of a *Wall Street Journal*–NBC News poll conducted jointly by Republican and Democratic investigators. Overall, the poll revealed that 45 percent of Americans said they opposed "the Clinton plan," while only 37 percent favored it. Yet the same poll asked people about an *unlabeled* "plan that would guarantee a standard private health benefits package to all Americans, try to promote competition in the medical industry, include some government regulation to keep prices under control and require employers to buy insurance for their workers with the promise of government subsidies to help the smallest companies." In response to that description—of the essential provisions of the Clinton plan—a whopping 76 percent of those polled said the unlabeled plan had either "a great deal of appeal" or "some appeal." The unnamed Clinton plan, moreover, did a lot better than similar unlabeled descriptions of four other plans also under consideration in Congress (including the Cooper plan, the single-payer plan, a system of individual mandates supported by Senator John Chafee, and an ultra-free-market "medical savings account" approach being pushed by Senator Phil Gramm of Texas).

"Mr. Clinton is losing the battle to define his own health-care bill," concluded the *Wall Street Journal*. This was five months after President Clinton had so propitiously launched Health Security. Obviously the administration and its allies, such as they were, had failed to get a coherent political message across to millions of citizens who were potentially receptive. Politics, after all, is very much about labels, and Americans needed to know that tenets of reform many of them liked were best embodied in the Health Security bill. But that is exactly what they didn't know, as a majority turned against "the Clinton plan."

Congress Makes It Worse

Despite the absence of a passionate coalition of supportive groups, the Democratic-led 103rd Congress might have seized the health reform bull by the horns. Although the votes were never there to pass the Clinton Health Security bill unmodified, leaders in Congress could have tried to work out and put through a reasonably comprehensive substitute.[66] Even if such an effort had fallen short, it would have brought the 1993–94 debate to a much more politically clarifying conclusion than the morass of indecision into which it ultimately sank. Such a congressional leadership initiative did not happen in a timely fashion, however—not during the winter or spring of 1994. By late summer, when the top Democratic congressional leaders desperately tried to paste last-minute compromises together, it was too late.

Nor can all the blame for Congress's failure to work out a modified (or substitute) approach to substantial health care reform be placed on the usual suspects: Republican obstructionism and pressures from lobbyists and interest groups against health care reforms. To be sure, as we will see in chapter 5, there were such culprits, up to no good about Clinton-style reform of the health system. Nevertheless, the institutional routines of Congress, activated by short-sighted congressional Democrats, were also very much involved in the failure of health care reform in 1994.

Without going into great detail about all the ups and downs in Congress over many months, the thing to explain is why this Democratic-led institution furthered fragmentation and confusion, rather than moving toward systematic modification of the Clinton plan or the substitution of another feasible approach to significant reform. While nominally members of the same political party as the President, Democrats in Congress never did agree with their titular leader, or among themselves, about exactly what kind of health reform they wanted.[67]

In the end, congressional Democrats—perhaps in the majority for the last time for years or decades—did not even bring health care reform legislation, of any kind, to floor votes. They maneuvered over committee drafts and leadership bills for interminable months, and then scurried away in disarray.

There were various reasons for persistent disarray and lack of direction. True, Democrats of the 103rd Congress were more coherent in outlook than were their counterparts back in the 1940s and 1950s, when a strong southern Democratic bloc supported by a racially exclusionary electorate faced off against northern liberal Democrats rooted in significantly unionized regions of the Northeast and Midwest. However, contemporary congressional Democrats still range from probusiness conservatives to assorted varieties of liberals (with many of the latter oriented toward scattered middle-class advocacy interests rather than toward organized labor). The rise of interest-group and advocacy "hyperpluralism" in Washington, D.C., has encouraged differentiation among representatives.[68] Most Democrats in the 103rd Congress were long-time incumbents who had worked out carefully negotiated relationships with particular constellations of business and advocacy groups, on whose regular contributions and support they depended to run reelection campaigns.

Equally pertinent, quite a few Democratic representatives and senators considered themselves (along with people on their sizable staffs)

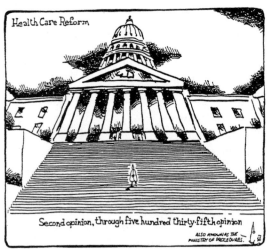

Courtesy Universal Press Syndicate

to be experts on relevant policy matters. California Representative Pete Stark and Massachusetts Senator Edward Kennedy were long-time warhorses on health issues. And the Senate's roving domestic policy "expert" was the obstreperous former Harvard professor New York Senator Daniel Patrick Moynihan, who repeatedly told reporters how much he wished that President Clinton had recommended welfare reform prior to (rather than along with) health care reform! Moynihan is one of the least disciplined of Democrats, yet he was the chairman of the critical Senate Finance Committee, which had to sign off on enactable legislation. No one in either house of Congress could ever be sure that Senate Finance would act, and that had a profoundly undercutting effect on the entire process of working out health reform legislation.

Whether self-understood experts or not, dozens of Democrats sat on the three House and two Senate committees that had come in recent years routinely to handle health issues. By the early 1990s, Congress had an unusually large number of committees (and subcommittees) claiming health jurisdiction.[69] Each and every one of those expected to have "a piece of the action" during 1994. Congresspeople on those committees and subcommittees wanted to be the ones to make deals and "concessions" to business and health interests. The wanted to do this as various health bills—not just the President's, but alternatives to it, including many from Democrats—were drafted and redrafted, combined and recombined in the various committees.

Ironically, the election of Democratic President Clinton had a galvanizing effect on Republicans in Congress. They pulled together and started digging in to fight against legislation sponsored by Democrats. But congressional Democrats did not follow suit, even though they had but narrow margins for passing legislation. House Democrats were set in their habits and ties to committees, subcommittees, and constituency groups. They had been in the majority for four decades, and collectively considered themselves a more permanent fixture of Washington policymaking than a president from a small state elected with a mere 43 percent of the 1992 votes. The Senate, meanwhile, is an institution that, by nature, furthers individualistic prima-donna-ism on both sides of the aisle. During 1993–94, moreover, the Senate was loaded with Democrats who personally compared themselves very favorably to Bill Clinton. A number of Senate Democrats, including Senator Robert Kerrey of Nebraska, had run for President. No doubt, others also thought they could do better at the job than Bill Clinton.

To deal in a prompt and focused way with the gargantuan deliberations required for processing the Clinton Health Security submission, Senate Majority Leader George Mitchell and the House leaders (Speaker Thomas Foley and Majority Leader Richard Gephardt) might have tried to set up special omnibus committees of carefully selected members. But Democrats in both bodies had little enthusiasm for such extraordinary procedures; and by 1993 Mitchell, Foley, and Gephardt did not have the kind of interpersonal or institutional clout that great leaders of the past had enjoyed. So the Democratic leaders deferred for many months to five committees, allowing health care bills to make their way painstakingly through the Labor and Human Resources Committee and the Finance Committee in the Senate and through the Energy and Commerce Committee, the Education and Labor Committee, and the Ways and Means Committee in the House. Routine mechanisms were invoked to deal with an extraordinary policy decision.

As Brookings Institution scholar Allen Schick explains, this approach might have paid off if, as often happens, the assorted congressional committees had been able to maneuver freely toward well-compromised bills that had a hope of getting majorities on the floor of the House and Senate.[70] But it wasn't easy for congressional coalitions to manipulate alternative provisions, because (as I discussed in chapter 2) CBO rules were so rigid about "costing out" options in advance and proving that each was "deficit neutral." This time-consuming process had to occur before each new legislative variant could make much headway toward enactment. Health care reform during 1993–94 was, moreover, an extremely visible undertaking, with very high gains or losses for stakeholder groups and for Democrats versus Republicans — not to mention for individual politicians who were worried about reelection or were pursuing new offices in their home states.

Around the time that President Clinton launched his Health Security plan, *National Journal* writer Julie Kosterlitz reported a telling anecdote about two friends, both Democrats on the crucial House Ways and Means Committee through which any comprehensive reform legislation would have to pass. One friend was Representative James A. McDermott of Washington state and the other was Representative Michael A. Andrews of Texas. As Andrews recounted to Kosterlitz: "My good buddy Jim McDermott and I went to a ball game not too long ago. . . . We both agreed during that baseball game that neither one of us would vote for the other's proposal."[71] They didn't mention agreeing on President Clinton's attempted compromise, either.

Representative Jim McDermott was working in partnership with Democratic Senator Paul Wellstone of Minnesota to push for single-payer health reform legislation. The Wellstone-McDermott bill had gained up to ninety congressional cosponsors during the time when Clinton's Health Security bill was formulated and debated. This legislation enjoyed

> support from a number of key national groups: more than a dozen unions, including the American Federation of State, County and Municipal Employees, the Communications Workers of America and the United Mine Workers of America; mental health and public health organizations . . . ; consumer groups, including the Consumers Union of the United States Inc. and the Consumer Federation of America; some elderly advocates, including the National Council of Senior Citizens and the Gray Panthers. . . .[72]

The Clinton policy planners took account of the very considerable support for Canadian-style health financing reform by promising to reach the same goal of universal coverage and by writing their legislation to allow individual states to experiment with single payer if they wanted to.

In Congress, single-payer advocates were certainly prepared to vote for the Clinton approach as an acceptable compromise. So the problem the President faced with them was never sheer obstruction. Nevertheless, many grassroots groups continued through the spring of 1994 to publicly agitate for single-payer ideas in contrast to those in the Health Security bill, sometimes going so far as to argue that the President had sold out to insurance companies.[73] Continuing single-payer agitation, not just for their own ideas but against the Health Security proposal as well, was just one more element among many that undercut public understanding and acceptance of the Clinton compromise. (Single-payer advocates imagined themselves to be in a bargaining position pushing for all they could get from the President, when in fact they were part of a tenuous and inadequate coalition for universal coverage. That coalition needed all hands enthusiastically on deck and prepared for difficult maneuvers if the ship of inclusive health care reform was to make it—perhaps with heavy damage—through very stormy seas.)

Meanwhile, Jim McDermott's baseball-watching friend, Representative Michael Andrews, was a leading person among some sixty members of the Conservative Democratic Forum. Andrews was loyal to the so-called Cooper plan for market-oriented managed competition without a guarantee of universal coverage. Often from the South and West, conservative Democrats came from districts or regions where small businesses were unusually predominant or mobilized, and also where employer-provided health insurance was less prevalent. Consequently, they were highly sensitive to fierce small-business opposition against any requirement for all employers to contribute to employees' health insurance. Pressures from small businesses could be particularly troublesome for Democrats who expected to face tight reelection struggles in 1994 or who were gearing up to run anew for public offices. Thus, for example, a key member of the House Energy and Commerce Committee, Jim Slattery of Kansas, refused to provide the final vote needed to report out a bill that modified the Clinton Health Security bill, because Slattery was running for governor of Kansas and wanted to avoid intense small-business opposition.[74] (His caution didn't work, for Slatterly lost his 1994 gubernatorial bid anyway.)

Aspiration for higher office was also operating in Jim Cooper's case.[75] A Rhodes scholar like Bill Clinton, Cooper coveted national visibility, and he was running for a Senate seat in Tennessee, a state with a lot of for-profit hospitals. Nationwide contributions from the health care industry flowed into Cooper's campaign coffers, as he made a big fuss about being a "New Democrat" who could not accept alleged "old Democrat" elements in the Clinton Health Security plan.[76] Celebrated at times by the New York Times Editorial Board, Cooper's noisy posturing, repeated throughout the 1993–94 process, had the effect of undercutting President Clinton's credibility as a fashioner of a true compromise or centrist approach to health care reform.

By late 1993 and early 1994, Cooper and his so-called Clinton-lite bill had become magnets for business, insurance, and health-industry interests that wanted to signal mild continuing interest in national health care reform, but without having to endorse legislation with effective cost controls or adequate funding to ensure universal coverage. (Ironically, in the end, Cooper's bill did not do very well when analyzed by the Congressional Budget Office; and despite his receipt of huge donations from insurance and health industry PACs Cooper was ultimately defeated for the Senate by conservative Republican Fred Thompson. This occurred even as Tennessee's incumbent Democratic Senator, Jim Sasser, was defeated by Bill Frist, a heart surgeon and millionaire businessman from the for-profit health sector.[77])

As discussed in chapter 2, President Clinton never had the option of simply accepting Cooper's bill. Cooper's budget numbers did not add up very well, and his plan did not envisage even the gradual achievement of health insurance for all Americans, the one goal to which Clinton had been irrevocably committed from 1992 onward. The goal of universal coverage was shared by most Democrats as well as a few moderate Republicans and by many groups, such as unions, the AARP, and some physicians' groups, that were potentially supporters of comprehensive health care reforms. Consequently, "universal coverage" was the slogan that received the most lip service as the President's plan was politically launched and promoted, and as the assorted congressional committees deliberated.

But even the congressional supporters of universality had many different notions about how to achieve it (or move toward it over time). These ideas included single-payer plans such as the one sponsored by Representative McDermott and Senator Wellstone, as well as Representative Pete Stark's preference for an expansion of Medicare as a residual program for those not covered through employment. Other key players such as Rhode Island Republican Senator Chafee, Massachusetts Senator Edward Kennedy, and Senate Majority Leader Mitchell floated many possible combinations of governmental subsidies with either employer or individual mandates requiring the purchase of private insurance policies.

How could congressional Democrats (and a few moderate Republicans) explain to the public the governmental mechanisms that would be used to attain universal health coverage when they were so divided about them? Democrats and the cacaphonous array of advocacy groups and interests swirling around them never did unite around President Clinton's Health Security bill—or around any other compromise approach to comprehensive reform. Democrats in the 103rd Congress treated the President's bill and various alternatives to it as grist for protracted bargaining over this or that provision and as fodder for infinitely complicated legislative maneuverings in five different House and Senate committees. Four committees eventually reported

Courtesy Los Angeles Times Syndicate

out bills, but none of them had any hope of gaining majorities on the floor of the House and Senate. So new variants continued to be brokered and discussed under the auspices of the congressional leaders. Congressional discussions wore on and on.

In sum, when the battle over comprehensive health care reform took place during 1993 and 1994, many groups in and around the Democratic Party favored some sort of universally inclusive reform. Yet they pushed and pulled in irreconcilable directions, as each group sought to bargain on behalf of its own constituency. Multiple committees and ambitious politicians in Congress gave points of access for the full range of conflicting groups and positions. All these maneuverings dominated press coverage for months and further undercut public understanding of how the federal government might, credibly and effectively, improve the health care system. Continuing disagreements—as much those among reformers and Democrats as those between Democrats and Republicans—ensured that the watching American public would become more and more perplexed about exactly what was at stake. Confusion and division only deepened over time.

CHAPTER FOUR

MARKETING AN AMBIVALENT
MESSAGE

The Clinton administration and its potential supporters were slow to mobilize on behalf of Health Security after its introduction in the fall of 1993. Even if policy planning was handled with intelligence, the coalitional politics of the reform effort were in many ways bungled. This is what we learned in the previous chapter. Yet the politics of health care reform had an additional connotation in the White House. "Politics" above all meant "getting the message right." Simple and resonant themes needed to be devised to present the President's formula for comprehensive health reform to the American people.

"Politics" in this sense was handled proficiently. There was no dearth of top-flight expertise to devise the Health Security message, because the same team of media and political consultants that Bill Clinton used during the 1992 presidential campaign also devoted its talents to the health care reform effort. Operating under severe constraints, the Clinton consultants did a timely and technically sophisticated job. The messages they helped the Clinton administration to devise—especially for the President's own showcase speeches on health reform—were brilliant appeals to the personal hopes and worries of ordinary citizens. Most Americans very much liked what they heard President Clinton say on September 22, 1993 (and in other featured speeches) about the ultimate goals of national health care reform. The goals compellingly articulated by the President were: security ("Health care that's always there"), along with simplicity, savings, choice, quality, and responsibility.

But in other ways messages about Health Security proved thin and unconvincing. Messages were especially anemic when it came to explaining *how* the President proposed to achieve the appealing goals he had set forth for health reform. Little was said about employer mandates, finances, and regional health alliances. The American people were never told much about what was *in* the Health Security bill that President Clinton asked Congress to debate and use as a basis for comprehensive legislation.

Bill Clinton certainly succeeded in arousing public interest. From the beginning of his presidency, Americans had high hopes that their new president would deliver on national health care reform. And in the fall of 1993, substantial majorities of Americans thought that the President might have a workable proposal to offer, at least as the basis for congressional deliberations. Although few people thought they knew much about the President's proposal as it was introduced, they were certainly open to learning more.[1]

President Clinton and other advocates of his plan had to hold the public's interest and respect as the details of their approach were spelled out. They had to do this not because the Health Security bill had to be enacted unchanged, but simply in order to ensure that members of Congress and leading societal groups would remain willing to bargain over the final terms of enactable legislation. Public opinion could not be expected to dictate the details of the legislation. Nevertheless, sustained presidential inspiration and education of public opinion were essential to render some Republicans willing to flesh out the insufficient Democratic majority for passage of legislation in the filibuster-prone Senate, and also to give Democratic House and Senate leaders the leverage they needed to ride herd on competing committees and self-promoting senators and representatives.

As Figure 1 shows, in the early 1990s the faith of Americans in the federal government to "do what is right" (either "always" or "most of the time") was at an extremely low point. Less than one-fifth of Americans had that level of trust in their national government by the time Bill Clinton came to the presidency. Polling research done for the administration in the spring of 1993 showed that, despite holding positive expectations for the forthcoming Clinton health care reforms, more people (53 percent) considered it "the greater danger" that "the government will try to change things but will create new problems," than those (41 percent) who saw the greater danger to be "that the system won't be changed and that costs will continue to rise and people will continue to have problems with insurance."[2]

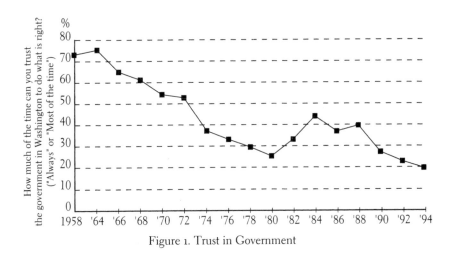

Figure 1. Trust in Government

Against this backdrop, it is remarkable that President Clinton's September 1993 Health Security speech was received as well as it was — remarkable that Americans seemed, for a time, so open to the idea that the federal government might be able to reform the national health system and ensure health security for everyone. Still, Americans' openness to the idea of comprehensive health care reform was not the same thing as solid support for specific legislation along the lines proposed by the Clinton administration. Opinion studies showed that people had a strong sense that the national system of health care and insurance financing was in crisis and needed fixing with the help of government. But studies also showed that there was no consensus about any particular approach to national health care reform.[3] And Americans were very skeptical that government could do anything in an efficient, cost-effective manner.[4]

Given Americans' general skepticism about the contemporary federal government's capabilities, the President and his allies needed to provide a convincing vision of *how* the new federal regulations and state-level purchasing alliances they were proposing would actually work in conjunction with nongovernmental arrangements to deliver on the appealing overall goals the President had articulated. As Stan Greenberg noted in a memo written right after the September 1993 presidential speech, "voters want more details about the plan."[5] There had to be a sustained campaign to influence public understanding of the workings of the intricately structured Health Security proposal.

Americans needed to be treated like sophisticated citizens, with legitimate concerns about whether and in exactly what ways the laudable goals of the Health Security effort could be accomplished through the combination of market forces and public regulations that the Clinton plan envisaged. The very real concerns of Americans, especially those about government bureaucracy and inefficiency, needed to be addressed immediately, before opponents of the President's approach to reform had the chance to define his plan in their own unfriendly terms.

The necessary explanations to the American people were not forthcoming. In his September 1993 Health Security speech, President Clinton said little about the new governmental regulations and activities his reform plan envisaged. For instance, the mandate on all employers to contribute to health coverage for all workers was alluded to, but the President did not make an explicit case for this as a desirable kind of law for Congress to enact. Throughout the 1993–94 debate, most Americans remained open to the idea of requiring contributions from all employers, and it seems likely that President Clinton could have counteracted some small-business pressure against his proposed employer mandate by making a frank case for its workability. He could have pointed to the state of Hawaii as a place in America where a mandate for all employers to contribute to health insurance had already been successfully implemented without doing visible harm to the economy or small businesses.[6]

In the September 1993 speech, President Clinton spoke briefly about how Health Security would be financed, but mostly just to stress that there would be no new taxes except on tobacco.[7] Ironically, this downplaying of taxes may have undermined public faith in his proposal, because "Americans could not understand how more people could be covered, more benefits added, and more bureaucracies established without costing them more money." As Robert Blendon and his associates elaborate, the

> public believed that considerable savings could be achieved from the existing system, which could be used to expand coverage. However, 75 percent of Americans also expected that the savings would not be enough and that some tax increase would be required. They even showed some willingness to pay a modest amount in order to achieve universal coverage. When the president proposed no new

taxes, aside from a higher cigarette tax, Americans thought that there was something wrong with the financing of his plan. In October 1993 eight in ten Americans (80 percent) thought that the reform plan would cost more than the president had estimated it would; 54 percent expected it to cost much more.[8]

Blendon and associates also speculate that the drop in support for Health Security among older citizens may have been prompted by fear that savings from Medicare would be substituted for a tax increase to finance the extension of coverage to the uninsured of working age. Such concern was not confined to older citizens; 69 percent of all Americans "said that they would be less likely to support health care reform if it involved a threat to Medicare."[9] Consequently, if older Americans became anxious about the financing of Health Security—which was likely, given how little the President said about where the money for universal coverage was to come from—then their children and grandchildren might well come to share the same worry.

Also not discussed in the original Health Security speech were the regional purchasing alliances and intricate public regulations that were to be at the heart of President Clinton's version of inclusive managed competition. Encompassing regional health alliances were crucial for reducing the costs of private insurance for everyone, guaranteeing quality care at comparable prices for all, and assuring that individuals could choose freely among various kinds of health plans. The President could have said so. He might have said that health alliances would be public commissions set up by the voters, governors, and legislators of each state to devise fair "rules of the game" to be followed by all companies that either sell health insurance or help to buy it for employees.

But Mr. Clinton didn't say anything about alliances in the September 1993 speech. Nor was there any follow up—on health alliances or the other issues I have just discussed—in the critical period after the unveiling of the Clinton proposal. The President did not, for example, give another nationally televised speech on the how of his health plan. Nor was a nationally televised "infomercial" sponsored by the Democratic party or a coalition of Health Security supporters. The regulations and finances that would go into Health Security remained vague—and hence anxiety producing.

As the 1993–94 debate wore on, presidential avoidance of governmental specifics became still more pronounced. The Clinton administration responded to accusations of "big government" by rechristening its health reform plan "guaranteed private insurance." The President used this terminology in his 1994 State of the Union Address. And a picture taken during one of his 1994 appearances on behalf of health care reform showed him earnestly standing in front of a poster that read:[10]

AMERICA'S CHOICE:

Government Insurance
Guaranteed Private Insurance
No Guarantee of Coverage

As usual, President Clinton was positioned in the middle of the array of alternatives displayed. But how informative was this? "Guaranteed" by whom or what? Such reticence about governmental mechanisms in Health Security was characteristic of the entire 1993–94 effort. As one observer acerbicly put it, the administration's message turned out to be "Health Care That's Always There (But Leave the Details to Us)"![11]

Courtesy *Colorado Springs Gazette Telegraph*

Thin communications about the how of Clinton's Health Security proposal did not happen by chance. Several factors were at work, including those discussed in chapter 3: an absence of resources to buy media time, the reluctance of advocacy groups to endorse Health Security and describe it favorably to their members, and the difficulties of finding time on the president's agenda to campaign for health care reform. Beyond such difficulties, the Health Security proposal itself was not easy to explain, because it was intricately designed and in some respects called for daring leaps of innovative organization building. The means of political communication available to President Clinton and his advisors did not lend themselves to formulating or propagating messages about the how of public policies. And this was something they were extremely reluctant to do, anyway. Having stressed antigovernment themes on their way to Washington, the Clintonites were not very comfortable featuring explanations of governmental structures or processes in their public messages about Health Security.

Crafting the Message

The Clinton administration understandably worked hard to devise a compelling message about its proposed health reforms. Leaders of the Task Force on Health Care Reform, as well as White House communications people working on the administration's health care effort, turned for insights about messages to the very same campaign consultants who had helped to get Bill Clinton elected president in the first place.[12]

Candidate Clinton, we should recall from chapter 1, benefited during 1992 from a much sought-after team of electoral consultants: James Carville and Paul Begala, Mandy Grunwald and Stan Greenberg. This team had guided him toward a populist and reformist electoral strategy, one that downplayed race, poverty, and "big government" in favor of initiatives to help the middle class that could be portrayed as relatively free of bureaucracy and taxes. After the inauguration, the same consultants—especially Greenberg as pollster and Grunwald as media consultant—were still tapped for constant advice about how best to present the President and his major policies. Health care reform promised to be the signature initiative of (at least the first term of) Clinton's presidency. As advisors directly to the President, the consultants were bound to be brought into the launching of this initiative.

What exactly did the consultants do, and what impact did they have on the emerging health reform legislation? Some have suggested that the consultants "worked behind the scenes to shape policy" and that "polling results concerning health care" from Greenberg Associates were used "as a weathervane to guide . . . the formulation of policy."[13] But I do not believe this is correct. True, Greenberg's reports to the White House did include poll and focus-group results about particular features that were possibly going into the emerging health care plan.[14] His opinion research showed voters to hold divided views on some policy design issues (such as premium contributions versus payroll contributions from employers), even as they were overwhelmingly in favor of other features such as employer mandates. Yet employer mandates were already decided on long before Greenberg's results came in, as were other elements in the emerging health care plan. After all, the basic outline of the President's approach was set before 1993.

As we learned in chapter 2, final choices about legislative design were made by the President at the end of the summer, after the task force had outlined the technical pros and cons of alternative options. With one exception, Greenberg's polling and the advice of the consultants had little influence on such specifics of policy design. The exception had to do with how generous the "standard benefits" package should be. On this matter, the political consultants arguably did have an impact, because they reported that "When voters think the package is 'standard' or 'basic,' they lose interest and show less willingness to risk change. When voters see the package as comprehensive, they think this is about their lives, not somebody else."[15] The consultants pushed for reasonably good mandated benefits that would capture the imagination of many Americans. Otherwise, though, they had little to do with policy design. On such arcane but crucial matters as the employee cutoff for required membership in health alliances, global budgets versus backup premium caps, or payroll charges versus employer contributions input came mostly from business groups, congressional moderates, and budget officials, not from pollsters or other political advisors.

One could reach the opposite conclusion from the conventional wisdom: instead of having too much influence on the design of Health Security, perhaps political advisors to the Clinton administration had too little influence. After the fact of the 1993–94 debacle, opinion analysts (both consultants tied to the White House and independent scholars) have argued that certain core features of Clinton's proposal—especially the regional health alliances—were so inherently unpopular that they could not have been explained in a favorable light to most Americans.[16] I do not necessarily agree with this assessment. But if one does believe it, a poignant question arises: Why design an approach to health care reform with a key mechanism deemed so unpopular that it cannot be explained and justified to the American people? Given the media-driven nature of U.S. politics today, the worst course of action would seem to be to put provisions into a legislative proposal that one feels one cannot openly discuss.

In early 1993, as Health Security was being designed, perhaps there should have been much more back-and-forth between those in the Clinton administration charged with designing Health Security and political advisors in and around the administration who would have to mobilize all sorts of support for it. Policy design and politics should have been more closely coordinated—arguably just as closely or more so than policy design and budgetary considerations (which *were* tightly meshed). Had policy and politics been better coordinated, the designers of Health Security might have proposed less-encompassing and more-voluntary health alliances. Or else there could have been a better strategy devised for explaining and mobilizing support for the proposal calling for encompassing regional alliances mandatory for all companies with fewer than 5,000 employees.

Instead of giving political advisors too much influence, the Clinton White House did what all U.S. institutional managers in the private and public sectors increasingly seem to do in the late twentieth century. It created a divide between, on the one hand, experts who designed a technically compelling policy and, on the other hand, operatives who were supposed to sell the finished program to those who would have to live with it.

Policy design aside, polling and focus-group data powerfully influenced decisions about *how to present* the finished Health Security plan to the American public in speeches, pamphlets, videos, and media events. "Message" was the concern of the consultants. Their advice focused especially on how to word things and how to portray the administration's proposal in a clear, humanly accessible way. The nationwide audience the consultants had in mind was working, middle-class Americans, including those with no more than a high school education. Keep it simple, personally vivid, and free of insider jargon, the consultants repeatedly urged. Research and arguments from the consultants went in confidential memos to an inner circle of White House leaders. In addition, media consultant Mandy Grunwald worked with White House communications people not only on publicly disseminated materials but also on "message statements" that were periodically distributed inside the administration to guide ways of presenting and talking about health care reform.

Labels were certainly modified—indeed repeatedly—in the light of what consultants had to say.[17] Early in the task-force process, consultants reported that Americans did not respond warmly to the phrase "managed competition." It reminded people of "managed care," about which there was considerable popular ambivalence.[18] Yet the Clinton administration had to have *some* name for its proposal. By late spring 1993, "Health Security" had become the chosen appelation, and "comprehensive reform" was also acceptable. An intraadministration memo on "Talking About Health Care" discouraged "plan" as sounding "too definite" and banned "program" on the grounds that it seemed "too bureaucratic."[19] We have also seen that in 1994 the preferred terminology shifted toward "guaranteed private insurance," as people in the Clinton administration apparently hoped to parry conservative attacks on the health reform proposal by changing its name.

Beyond labels, other decisions about public presentation were also made with the aid of advice from the consultants. Should controlling costs or ensuring secure coverage become the main theme for the Clinton reforms? Should emphasis be placed on extended coverage or heightened protections for the already-insured middle class?

On costs versus security, Greenberg's May 1993 issue poll included the following query:

> What is the most important thing for the government to do in changing the health care system?
>> Get the rising costs under control so people won't have to pay more and more out of their own pockets for insurance, doctor bills, and drugs.
> OR
>> Make sure health is secure for everybody so that nobody loses insurance because they change or lose a job, or because of a preexisting condition.

Interestingly, nearly half the respondents (49 percent) picked the first alternative, as compared to 38 percent who chose the second, 10 percent who indicated "Both," and 3 percent who said "Don't Know."[20] For some time, the Clinton reformers were unsure whether to feature controlling costs or "health care that's always there" as the central feature of their emerging plan. The plan aimed to do both, of course.[21] Yet the consultants reported that people were not sure the federal government "can deliver on cost control." Americans believed government could ensure health security, but not necessarily keep costs down.

"We must set out a simple, core idea that captures the whole complicated exercise," argued the entire group of consultants in a September 14, 1993, memorandum offering suggestions to help with the preparation of the President's upcoming speech to the American people and the joint session of Congress. By a large margin, research showed that when presented with descriptions of the emerging plan, people best recalled that *"Every citizen will receive a Health Security Card that guarantees them a comprehensive package of benefits."* Thus the consultants recommended:

> *The dominant goal should be health security:* that people will have health insurance and they will never lose it, never; whether people get sick, change or lose a job, or move; whether people live in Mississippi or California, they will have comprehensive insurance. Health care security has much more power than the cost argument, and it is much more believable. . . . There is also an emotion in security (lacking in cost) that empowers our rationale for bold change. . . . That costs are out of control is very important, but we should emphasize how rising costs threaten the security of every family.[22]

Those to be most clearly featured in public discussions of the Health Security plan were working middle-class families, most of whom already had some sort of health coverage. The consultants certainly urged an inclusive course that paralled the American people's desire for universal coverage: "We must establish thematically that we are reshaping the health system to serve ordinary people," the consultants wrote in September. Yet carried over from the 1992 presidential campaign was a concern to reassure the middle class that this was not just another Democratic welfare program. The Health Security message was aimed "at the vast majority of middle-class Americans who have insurance but live in fear of having it taken away." "This is not an argument about 'access' . . . or 'extending coverage' or 'the uninsured,' " stressed an intraadministration message memo. "Since most Americans have insurance, they think of the uninsured as 'them'—this creates an 'us versus them' mentality. We should not even talk about '37 million uninsured' because that is not who the proposal is designed to protect."[23]

This last statement was a truly amazing thing for anyone in a Democratic administration to say, and one suspects that it was not widely believed in the Clintonite ranks. But it is an indication of the anxiety many crafters of the Health Security message felt to make the new proposal appealing to already-insured middle-class Americans, in a nation where electoral politics and public discussions are profoundly biased upward in the class scale.

Throughout the 1993–94 campaign for health care reform, talk about the governmental contents of the Clinton plan tended to be discouraged by those who fashioned the Health Security message. Americans were thought to be wary of bureaucracy and taxes, so better not to mention such things. The consultants doubted that most Americans would be able to understand the inner workings of a 1,342-page bill that, if truth be told, they themselves barely grasped. " 'With any policy of this kind,' the President's pollster Stan Greenberg told the New York Times, 'it's hard to explain the mechanism. . . . It's more helpful to focus on goals.' "[24] "Whatever you do," warned the authors of an internal message memo, "don't get caught up in the details of the policy. . . . If pressed on approaches, talk about the National Health Security Act as a blend of different approaches—a uniquely American solution to an American problem. And then move on to explain how the proposal will solve the problems that consumers . . . are now facing."[25]

As this last exhortation indicates, the crafters and purveyors of the Health Security message spoke about ordinary Americans as consumers of health services rather than as fellow citizens involved in a national decision. Thus the consultants advised sticking to broad themes about the desirable personal outcomes of reform. "Humanize everything," was a primary tactical exhortation. "Using your own story or individual stories is the best way to communicate about health care."[26] Letters and personal testimonials could be used to show personal dilemmas about health insurance that the President's plan

Checklist

*Before deciding if a health reform plan will provide
you with the health security you deserve, ask yourself:*

Does it guarantee that you and your family will
<u>never</u> lose your health insurance, no matter
what? Can you change jobs or move to another
state without losing your benefits? ✓

Does it allow you to choose your own doctor? ✓

Does it guarantee comprehensive benefits
including hospital care, doctor care, and a
broad range of preventive services? ✓

Does it guarantee you and your family
affordable health care? ✓

Does it offer a prescription drug benefit for all
Americans? Does it help older and disabled
Americans get long term care at home and in
their communities? ✓

Does it prohibit plans from charging you more
for being sick or having a sick child? Does it
ban lifetime limits on your health coverage? ✓

Does it demand less of your time filling out
forms and reading fine print? ✓

Does it take aggressive steps to get
skyrocketing health costs under control? ✓

Does it help protect small businesses from
insurance company discrimination and provide
discounts to make insurance more affordable? ✓

Back cover of *Health Security: The President's Health Care Plan*, October 1993

would ideally solve. Then the provisions of the plan could be
explained in terms of what they would do for "you and your family."
As an intraadministration memo put it, the description to be offered
of Health Security "walks through the system from a consumer's perspective—it's not a structural analysis of the system."[27]

Very concretely, Americans were encouraged to think about the impact of the Clinton plan on their own personal situations. "Health Security: The President's Health Care Plan" was a pamphlet disseminated by the Democratic National Committee, members of Congress, and administration representatives, starting in the fall of 1993.[28] The pamphlet's back cover offered a "Checklist" for readers to use in "deciding if a health reform plan will provide you with the health security you deserve." There were nine key items on the checklist— all of which referred to goals for reform, rather than structural ways of achieving it. Seven checklist points asked about guarantees or benefits for individual people and families. Of the two more systemic items on the list, one was about small business ("Does it help to protect small businesses from insurance company discrimination and provide discounts to make insurance more affordable?"), and the other was ambiguous in its referent ("Does it take aggressive steps to get skyrocketing health costs under control?"). The latter was a question that apparently referred to the nation as a whole, but could also refer to costs for ordinary families.

Not just on its back cover, but in its entire contents as well, the "Health Security" pamphlet carefully carried out the chief advice of the message consultants: to focus on the personal, human impact of Health Security, not on its governmental means or legislative contents. As summed up by Mandy Grunwald, the overall message was:

> The President's reform works for you. . . . Opponents will try to confuse the issue by making it seem more complicated, but it's really pretty simple: If the President's reform passes, you'll know this: You'll get a Health Security card which guarantees you that you can pick any doctor you want, fill out one form, and you're covered.[29]

What to Say about Health Alliances?

Of course it really was more complicated than that, as soon as one took a systemic rather than a consumer perspective. A central mechanism in the new Health Security plan was the mandatory regional purchasing cooperative, something the Clintonites decided to label the "health care alliance." One or more of these new quasi-governmental institutions would have been established in each state, and they would have undertaken all sorts of revenue-collecting, data-collecting, information-dispersing, and legal tasks in relation to employers, insurance companies, and individual citizens.

According to the original legislation submitted by the Clinton administration, all employers with 5,000 or fewer employees would have been required to channel contributions to health premiums through these encompassing regional purchasing alliances. Self-employed people and nonemployed people would also have obtained insurance through the alliances. And various subsidies would have flowed through them. As the Congressional Budget Office awkwardly tried to sum up in its February 1994 report on the Clinton plan, the "regional alliances—as the frontline agencies responsible for orchestrating the flow of funds through the health care system—would . . . combine the functions of purchasing agents, contract negotiators, welfare agencies, financial intermediaries, collectors of premiums, developers and managers of information systems and coordinators of the flow of information and money between themselves and other alliances."[30]

Faced with such complexity and given their basic approach to selling Health Security, it is not surprising that the Clinton administration's message consultants shied away from the subject of health alliances. " 'That's not where the debate goes,' " James Carville "snapped back" when New York Times reporter Robin Toner asked about the alliances. " 'I don't understand exactly how the Social Security system works, but I'm for it.' "[31]

But Carville did not have his lessons from history in order. The retirement insurance provision of Social Security was neither popular nor very visible when it was first enacted. When Franklin Roosevelt's landmark legislation was created back in 1934 and 1935, handfuls of experts designed the national contributory retirement insurance program that would later become popularly known as "Social Security."[32] Except for some controversy about whether certain big businesses could "opt out," there was little congressional or public discussion of contributory retirement insurance, even less of its payroll tax mechanism. The 1934–35 debates mostly dealt with unemployment insurance and public assistance programs, both of which had precedents in prior state-level programs. Public understanding of, and strong popular support for, "Social Security" (in the sense of retirement insurance) came only much later, especially after 1950. Americans eventually learned to like an expert-designed public program the likes of which they had not experienced before. Perhaps the same thing would have happened eventually if the Clinton Health Security proposal had been passed by Congress. But we will never know.

A much closer analogue to the 1993–94 politics of Clinton's Health Security plan was the 1963–65 politics of Medicare, in which Americans' prior understanding of, and affection for, Social Security *was* important. Both the 1960s and the 1990s episodes involved much media coverage, open clashes of interest groups, and responses by politicians to public opinion as measured in polls. Tellingly, however, when the Medicare program of health insurance for older citizens was debated and enacted in the mid-1960s, its sponsors had the advantage of being able to build on widespread public understanding of, and affection for, the Social Security program of contributory retirement insurance.[33] By the 1960s, Social Security was very well established as a virtually universal pension program covering middle-class Americans. Medicare was complex, and its founding legislation had various parts.

The core of public support for Medicare was built on an analogy to Social Security as a well-regarded, previously established federal government program. Older citizens and many others in American society appreciated the universal and non-means-tested nature of Social Security's contributory retirement insurance. Americans also had an operational image of how earmarked payroll taxes worked to fund federally administered benefits for older retired people. The U.S. public responded warmly to the possibility of Medicare in large part because both the scope and the mechanisms of this proposed new health insurance program for older citizens seemed to be modeled on the already familiar and popular Social Security program.

Three decades later, when he introduced his 1993 Health Security bill, President Clinton tried to invoke the Social Security precedent once again. But this time the analogy was thin. It held only for the *goal* of universal, secure coverage. There was no relevant similarity to Social Security with regard to *how* governmental mechanisms in the proposed Clinton Health Security system would work. Medicare uses (in part) payroll taxes to finance fee-for-service medical care for older citizens. Clinton's health policy planners deliberately rejected Medicare as a model for what they were doing. Instead of relying on payroll taxes, as in Social Security and Medicare, Clinton's Health Security proposal aimed to use administrative and regulatory mechanisms—employer mandates, premium caps, and health alliances—to encourage Americans to buy lower-cost private health insurance policies. Arguably, most people had some understanding of what premium caps and requirements on employers might mean. But what in the world were health alliances?

Supporters seeking to explain the proposed Clinton health plan never found any consistent examples of preexisting organizations that health alliances could be said to resemble. Sometimes alliances were likened to health insurance purchasing cooperatives (such as the large California Public Employee Retirement System, known as "Cal-PERS"), and sometimes they were said to resemble food coops or grain coops for farmers. Although one or another of these analogies may have resonated for particular audiences, there was no clear, convincing, well-understood, and popular federal program precedent—nothing that could serve as Social Security had for Medicare. What is more, citizens were left to imagine the health alliances arising out of nowhere. Little was said about where the officials or organizational forms of the health alliances would come from (and food or farmers' coops could hardly serve as convincing models in this regard).

Because health alliances would have been very new, it was hard to make sense of them in terms of analogous or already-existing public institutions. Alliances would have constituted a distinctive level of government within the federal system, and they would have had considerable authority.[34] Yet promoters of the Clinton Health Security plan tried to avoid discussing the alliances as new sorts of governmental organizations. Instead of telling Americans as simply and clearly as possible why this kind governmental endeavor would be effective and desirable, their accomodation to the public's distrust of government was to pretend that President Clinton was proposing a virtually government-free national health security plan.

Consider pages 8 and 9 from "Health Security: The President's Health Care Plan," the explanatory pamphlet whose back cover was discussed above. Most of this twenty-four-page pamphlet focused on explaining benefits and choices from the point of view of individual citizens; yet pages 8 and 9 offered an overview of "The System After Reform." The reader can see that every effort is made to portray government, particularly the national government, as marginal to reform. The President, we are assured, "specifically rejected a government-run

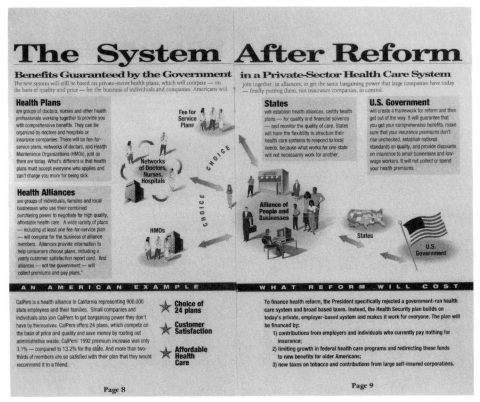

The System After Reform

Benefits Guaranteed by the Government in a Private-Sector Health Care System

The new system will still be based on private-sector health plans, which will compete — on the basis of quality and price — for the business of individuals and companies. Americans will join together, in alliances, to get the same bargaining power that large companies have today — finally putting them, not insurance companies, in control.

Health Plans
are groups of doctors, nurses and other health professionals working together to provide you with comprehensive benefits. They can be organized by doctors and hospitals or insurance companies. There will be fee-for-service plans, networks of doctors, and Health Maintenance Organizations (HMOs), just as there are today. What's different is that health plans must accept everyone who applies and can't charge you more for being sick.

Health Alliances
are groups of individuals, families and local businesses who use their combined purchasing power to negotiate for high quality, affordable health care. A wide variety of plans — including at least one fee-for-service plan — will compete for the business of alliance members. Alliances provide information to help consumers choose plans, including a yearly customer satisfaction report card. And alliances — not the government — will collect premiums and pay plans."

Fee for Service Plans

Networks of Doctors, Nurses, Hospitals

HMOs

CHOICE

CHOICE

CHOICE

Alliance of People and Businesses

States

U.S. Government

States
will establish health alliances, certify health plans — for quality and financial solvency — and monitor the quality of care. States will have the flexibility to structure their health care systems to respond to local needs, because what works for one state will not necessarily work for another.

U.S. Government
will create a framework for reform and then get out of the way. It will guarantee that you get your comprehensive benefits, make sure that your insurance premiums don't rise unchecked, establish national standards on quality, and provide discounts on insurance to small businesses and low-wage workers. It will not collect or spend your health premiums.

AN AMERICAN EXAMPLE

CalPers is a health alliance in California representing 900,000 state employees and their families. Small companies and individuals also join CalPers to get bargaining power they don't have by themselves. CalPers offers 24 plans, which compete on the basis of price and quality and save money by rooting out administrative waste. CalPers' 1992 premium increase was only 3.1% — compared to 13.2% for the state. And more than two-thirds of members are so satisfied with their plan that they would recommend it to a friend.

★ **Choice of 24 plans**

★ **Customer Satisfaction**

★ **Affordable Health Care**

WHAT REFORM WILL COST

To finance health reform, the President specifically rejected a government-run health care system and broad based taxes. Instead, the Health Security plan builds on today's private, employer-based system and makes it work for everyone. The plan will be financed by:

1) contributions from employers and individuals who currently pay nothing for insurance;
2) limiting growth in federal health care programs and redirecting those funds to new benefits for older Americans;
3) new taxes on tobacco and contributions from large self-insured corporations.

Page 8

Page 9

"The System After Reform" from *Health Security: The President's Health Care Plan*, October 1993

health care system," and the "U.S. government will create a framework for reform and then get out of the way" of the private sector, businesses, and people. The U.S. government is portrayed as assuring "you," the individual citizen, all sorts of good things: comprehensive benefits, stable insurance premiums, and quality health care. But apart from being told that the states will have great "flexibility," we get little sense of how all this will happen through law and governance.

Health alliances are clearly to be critical, for "alliances—not the government—will collect premiums and pay plans." Yet alliances are implicitly portrayed as if they were giant voluntary associations: "Americans will join together, in alliances, to get the same bargaining power that large companies have today—finally putting them, not insurance companies, in control." The word "choice" is repeated like a mantra all over pages 8 and 9 (and indeed throughout the pamphlet). A person reading the "Health Security" pamphlet could easily end up quite unsure about what a health alliance would look like, organizationally speaking, not to mention who would work for one, doing what. The reader would also be quite unprepared to hear the fact that, under the Clinton plan, most employers would, by law, be *compelled* to buy health insurance through a regionally designated official alliance.

Not surprisingly, in a poll taken in February 1994, only one in four Americans claimed to know what a health alliance might be, and only 22 percent supported the idea after being told that "the creation of multiple government agencies" might be involved.[35] At that point in time, just as the majority of the American public was turning sour on what people understood about the Clinton approach to comprehensive health reform—yet well before President Clinton went on the road for his most extensive and persistent efforts to sell his Health Security plan[36]—the plan's central governmental mechanism was already being substantially weakened in Congress. Between September and January, the President and his allies had failed to explain why their approach to reformed health care financing needed relatively encompassing regional alliances to work well. The alliance remained "a large and potentially frightening unknown, and thus a vulnerable target for opponents of the Clinton plan."[37]

Elections, Policy Campaigns, and the Media

Message politics in the Clinton Health Security effort was not a set of mistakes by misguided pollsters; it was a manifestation of the way things tend to be done today in U.S. public life. Governance is increasingly assimilated into the marketing styles that have already come to dominate elections. As we have already learned, U.S. electoral politics has undergone major change since the 1950s and 1960s.[38] The focus is now on raising huge sums of money to pay for campaign consultants, specially tailored polls and mailings, and television advertising. Candidates compete to hire the hottest pollsters and campaign consultants. These specialists, in turn, identify themes and issues for television ads (and other communications) that would especially appeal to whichever voters are considered to be swing voters for that contest.

In contrast to the way elections were run in the pretelevision age, there is less need—or opportunity—to reach out for blocs of voters through their already-established interest-group or local-group leaders. Instead, pollster-consultants try to discern the opinions and issue preferences of voters en masse, and especially of the swing voters among them. Then these operatives use television advertising (or perhaps targeted mailings or canvasses) to project a consonant image and policy themes for their candidate. After turning up through polls or focus groups, the concerns of potential voters are projected back to them in sound bites.

Once an election is over, the successful candidates find that very little enduring loyalty—or understanding—may have been built up among those citizens who voted amidst the heat of warring television commercials. Elected officials have to keep selling themselves and the policies on which visible stands are taken. If they can afford it, officials continue to use the services of pollsters and consultants, just as they did during the campaign itself.

Pollsters and political consultants tend to think in terms of central themes (Health Security) and appealing slogans ("Health Care That's Always There" or "Guaranteed Private Insurance"), rather than in terms of explanatory discussions, especially of complicated legislation. This is not because consultants are unsophisticated or manipulative people. Rather, consultants think in terms of themes and slogans because of their skills and occupational outlooks, and the methods of data gathering they have at their disposal. Perhaps most important, they approach electoral and policy campaigns this way because of the very limited means of political communication currently available to them and their politician clients. Ironically, Democratic Party consultants today may be even more restricted in the tactics they can use than Republican consultants, because the Democratic Party (as we have seen) no longer has much of a local base or a very reliable set of group allies.

Consultants learn what is going on in the polity through polls and focus groups. Then they make recommendations about speeches and media events. They naturally look for aggregate public attitudes and try to devise phrases and slogans to make their candidate (and his or her issue positions) thematically appealing. Consultants try to avoid knotty or complicated issues, particularly where they suspect public opinion cannot be quickly influenced by the (relatively limited) communication channels at hand. During the Health Security campaign, for example, the message consultants felt constrained to find one or two basic themes to highlight. The consultants had relatively little money at their disposal and hardly any political infrastructure to work with, and they could use only bits and pieces of presidential time for nationally visible events. They had to devise a message that could get across under those restricted conditions—hoping to arouse and sustain enough positive attitudes toward Health Security to counter interest-group opposition and keep Congress working toward legislation. Given the draconian constraints they faced, those who shaped the Health Security message did remarkably well.

For Bill Clinton from 1992 through 1994, however, the media-oriented, thematic approach to politics worked much better during the election campaign than it did when he was trying as president to push forward a complicated reform. The consultant-run, media-crafted approach to political selling necessarily works much better for a candidate than for a positive policy proposal. The kinds of struggles involved are fundamentally different. And the media interacts very differently with an election than it does with a policy debate.

In an election, after all, a day on the calendar is bound to come when the voters will make a decision among the surviving alternatives. (In the United States of the late twentieth century, only a minority of eligible voters may show up at the polls, but a decision still will be made.) A thematic approach to selling candidates works in part because voters don't need many details; they need to see broad, contrasting strokes. Visual and print media cover each major candidate every day, clarifying their profiles in relation to one another over time. In contrast, when a policy proposal enters public and congressional debate, there may never be a definite outcome, no definite winner as in an election.[39] Stalemate and an eventual "nondecision" are very possible in policy debates. And stalemate may be encouraged by the operations of the media, because its normal routines do not serve to clarify policy proposals or alternatives over time.

For example, given the way the national for-profit media operates today, even the President of the United States cannot be sure of getting television coverage to speak directly and at length to the American people. The U.S. television networks almost certainly would have refused to cover another major health care speech by Mr. Clinton should he have tried to offer more information on the how of his reform plan soon after the September 22, 1993, Health Security address. The networks would have had to give up a lot of advertising revenue to cover an additional presidential address, and the chances are that their executives would have decided that more detail from the President was not sufficiently newsworthy or entertaining to preempt their regular commercial programming. More generally, when Bill Clinton was promoting Health Security rather than himself as a presidential candidate, he could no longer expect assiduous, relatively unmediated television coverage day after day. Even his most elaborate health care events were likely to be covered only regionally, not nationally. And television news, in particular, usually conveyed only snippets of what the President had to say about health care reform, except during the September 1993 speech and the 1994 State of the Union Address.

There is also the matter of how reporters generally cover complicated and controversional issues such as national health care reform on a day-to-day basis. Reporters tend not to repeat stories—for instance, discussions of how policies might affect people, comparisons of different policy proposals, or analyses of the effectiveness of proposals—but instead always look for a new angle. Ordinary citizens may need repetition if they are to gain an understanding of a proposal such as Clinton's Health Security plan (or alternatives to it). But reporters seek novelty.

Reporters also gravitate toward conflict, because it is inherently dramatic. Thus, as various observers have argued—and as a careful study by Kathleen Jamieson and her associates has documented for the 1993–94 health care debate—the media tend to focus not on the substance and adequacy of proposals, but on dramatic struggles among conflicting politicians and interest groups.[40] During the 1993–94 health reform debate, previous health policy reporters, some of whom had been plugging away for years on relatively unglamorous issues, were often displaced by higher-profile political reporters. Political reporters tend to move from one policy area to another, so they are not extremely interested in the substance or likely human impact of any given type of policy. More important, political reporters normally highlight who is arguing with whom, giving perhaps the most weight (and certainly equal weight) to outrageous or extreme claims, while doing very little to help the public see the details of proposals or the validity of claims about them.

From late 1993 through 1994, coverage of the health reform debate was heavily of this "horse race" variety. Opinion studies tell us that

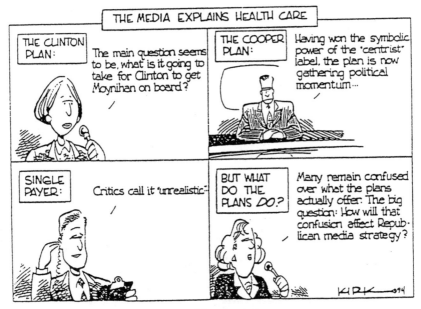

Reprinted by permission

voters still did not claim to understand the Clinton plan (or alternatives to it) as Congress settled down to business in the spring of 1994. But at that point, political and congressional reporters were the ones likely to be in charge of coverage, and they were unlikely to sort out plans and issues for the public. They were following day-to-day maneuvers, arguments, and ups and downs between Congress and the president, within and among congressional committees, and between Republicans and Democrats as the parties headed for the midterm 1994 elections. The American public gave the media lower marks for its coverage as the health care debate wore on, probably because people were not gaining the understanding of the issues that they were seeking.[41]

Once policy battles are fully joined, in short, reporters concentrate on the "horse race" itself. Yet in policy debates, unlike in elections, new horses can keep joining the race. The characteristics of the horses are hard to discern. And no horses at all may cross the finish line. This is what happened during the 1993–94 U.S. health reform debate. New proposals and "compromises" kept appearing. Not all were seriously intended by their sponsors, but each was complicated to grasp. In the end, Congress simply bogged down in befuddlement; and so did the American people.

Long before this happened, President Clinton's Health Security plan had lost focus and become muddied. Americans did not even realize that the plan contained many elements they rather liked.[42] Key elements of the Clinton plan, such as the health alliances, had been more successfully defined by the outright opponents of any kind of comprehensive health care reform than by the Clinton administration. Over time, the terms of public discussion were taken over by the President's most ruthless enemies—the worst-case scenario that Stan Greenberg had projected even before the Health Security plan was publicly launched. "There is much to recommend reform and people can understand its benefits," wrote Greenberg. But the "health care issue can be turned against us if we do not successfully control the terms of debate."[43]

The Limits of Ambivalent Salesmanship

Those presenting the Clinton Health Security plan to the American public thought like advertisers. They would promise appealing benefits to make reform popular with ordinary consumers of health care. They would use images about voluntarism and words about choice to prevent or calm Americans' fears about government "takeovers" or "bungling."

The consultants who helped to craft the Health Security message along these lines honestly did not think it would hurt to downplay the how of the reform plan: "The best analogy," declared Paul Begala to the *New York Times*, is that "President Kennedy committed this country to going to the moon. He did not say we'll use a three-stage Saturn V rocket with a tracking station in New Guinea, New Mexico and New Zealand."[44] But of course this was a very faulty analogy! Back in the 1960s, Americans had faith in the federal government, whereas in the 1990s they don't. And there is a huge difference between the technical undertaking of sending rockets to the moon and a necessarily politically contentious effort to reform institutional and social relationships affecting one-seventh of the U.S. economy. Comprehensive health care reform along the lines proposed by President Clinton would have touched every aspect of American life at least to some degree, whereas going to the moon directly involved only a small number of people and was a spectator sport for the rest.

This is not to say that the Clinton Health Security plan failed because pollsters, media consultants, and other such campaign-style advisors had too much influence in the White House. The Clinton consultants did a very good job at their assigned tasks, given the limited resources and means of data collection and political communication to which they, and the President, had access. Without the efforts of the consultants, moreover, there would have been less input to the White House about the hopes and fears of millions of ordinary Americans. In the absence of other democratic arrangements in U.S. politics, polling and focus groups are better than mere discussions among elites and Washington insiders.

Nevertheless, there were two grave shortcomings in the message politics of Health Security. In the first place, presidential speeches, media events, and shifting labels were weak political reeds for proponents of comprehensive health care reform to rely upon. No matter how cleverly crafted, mass media messages about Health Security rarely got through, except through occasional nationally televised presidential speeches. Message politics needed to be much better coordinated with other kinds of political mobilization on behalf of Health Security (which, of course, implies that there needed to be much more mobilization than there was). In the next chapter, we will see that the enemies of comprehensive health care reform did a significantly better job of getting their messages through. This happened not only because oppositional interest groups and conservative Republicans had more money and emotional fervor, though they certainly did. The opponents were also more astute at activating natural social and institutional networks. Media efforts crafted by their own pollsters and consultants were well coordinated with political efforts reaching into communities across the nation.

Secondly, and more fundamentally, I believe a mistake was made by the Clinton administration and its consultants when they chose not to talk frankly and clearly about the governmental mechanisms—including encompassing health alliances—that were at the operational heart of the Health Security proposal. In the aftermath of Ross Perot's "infomercials," the President and his advisors should have realized that Americans were hungry for a credible understanding of how health care reforms would work for the national polity and economy, not just for individual "consumers." Ironically, this was especially true

of the middle-class Americans that the Clinton administration so assiduously tried to reach with its Health Security message.

Vague and evasive explanations of how the reformed health care
system would work left Americans open to alternative descriptions pur-
veyed by Health Security's fiercest opponents. A portrayal of the Clinton proposal as virtually government-free, as little more than a vast
set of voluntary associations, simply was not plausible. If that was all
President Clinton had in mind, why did he need to ask Congress to
enact a 1,342-page bill?

CHAPTER FIVE

MOBILIZATION AGAINST GOVERNMENT

Advocates of Health Security were disorganized and the Clinton administration did not adequately explain the changes it was proposing. But if this were all of the story, the President's attempt at comprehensive health reform might simply have faded away, dying with a whimper rather than a bang. Instead, the Health Security legislation—so conveniently laid out in detail for critics to pick over—became a perfect foil for mobilization against government.

Starting even before President Clinton announced his plan, groups with financial or occupational stakes in the present U.S. health care system amassed money, lobbyists, and field agents to peck away at the regulatory and financial innards of any serious health care reform. At first, such efforts by determined interest groups appeared scattered and mutually contradictory, yet they took their toll over time. Meanwhile, insurgent conservatives opposed to a strong domestic role for the federal government discovered that an all-out ideological attack on Health Security offered an excellent way for them to gain ground, first within the Republican Party and then in the general electorate. Counterattacks from stakeholders and ideologues became mutually reinforcing over the course of 1994 and shifted critical resources of money and energy toward a radicalized, much more conservative Republican Party.

Critiques of "government meddling" eventually resonated with mainstream public opinion, despite continuing popular concern about the national health care system. The cost-cutting implications of President Clinton's proposed Health Security legislation were so different from the generous new financial subsidies implied by President Franklin Roosevelt's Social Security legislation of 1935 that many individuals and groups came to see comprehensive health care reform as more of a possible threat than a solution. President Clinton undertook governmentally mediated social reform in a context of looming federal budget deficits and public distrust of government. He also attempted to reorganize a realm where many vested interests were firmly ensconced. Ironically, President Clinton thought he was being responsible and moderate to place the emphasis on regulations rather than new taxes, to focus on controlling and cutting health care costs as well as on extending social benefits. Yet he aroused widespread fears about possible federal government interventions in accustomed social and economic routines. Insurgent conservatives opposed to new—and existing—federal programs were waiting in the wings, ready to take advantage of these fears.

Threatened Stakeholders Mobilize

Stakeholder groups determined to modify or eviscerate President Clinton's proposal for comprehensive health care reform swung into action without delay or doubt. Groups with an occupational or financial stake in the $800 billion-per-year business of U.S. health care had long since aroused themselves to present concerns to Congress and to address the Clinton administration.[1] The minute the Clinton plan officially appeared—as soon as drafts of it starting leaking and circulating in the late summer of 1993—all these groups could quickly decide how disappointed or angry they were with each relevant detail of the vast blueprint. Their leaders and staffs geared up to notify members across America about threatening features of the proposed legislation.

The staffs of Washington-based interest groups ran press conferences and deployed hordes of lobbyists to ask the Clinton administration and Congress for changes in legislative provisions. Well-endowed and vitally threatened stakeholders formed coalitions with one another, and many used local contacts to promote grassroots agitation in individual congressional districts. The wealthiest and most determined groups also funded polling and advertising efforts designed to influence public opinion about key aspects of the Health Security proposal.

Techniques used by stakeholder groups to undercut the Clinton plan are well illustrated by the remarkable efforts of the Health Insur-

Courtesy Universal Press Syndicate

ance Association of America (HIAA), a beleagured yet resourceful association of midsized and small insurance companies, many of which would have been forced out of business if the Health Security legislation had passed in anything resembling its original form. At first glance, the HIAA might not have seemed a likely formidable player in the reform battle. But the kinds of leverage it could exercise turned out to be important.

An analyst dropping in from Mars in 1993 might have supposed that insurance interests were losing leverage in U.S. politics, because the industry was increasingly disunited.[2] Back in 1992, as national discussion of health care reform heated up in the wake of the Harris Wofford victory in the Pennsylvania special election, the HIAA was the peak association of the for-profit insurance industry. At that point, the HIAA turned toward policy advocacy and prophylactic efforts to shape public opinion in favor of merely incremental reforms along the lines of those then being pushed by the Bush administration.[3] But before long many small insurers opposed to any new insurance regulations split off from HIAA to form the Council for Affordable Health Insurance.[4]

More consequentially, America's "big five" insurance companies also withdrew from the HIAA: Cigna Corporation left in 1991, Aetna Life and Casualty and Metropolitan Life departed just as Bill Clinton was elected in November 1992, and Travelers Corporation and Prudential Insurance followed out the door in 1993.[5] The big insurers expected that their expanding stake in health maintenance organizations might flourish under new legislation. Complaining that HIAA was "paralyzed by small insurers who are opposed to national health care reforms," the big insurance companies formed the Alliance for Managed Competition to lobby on their own terms.[6] The HIAA was eventually left with members accounting for only about one-third of the nation's 180 million holders of private health insurance policies (one-third of the others were with the big five, and the other third with Blue Cross and Blue Shield). Worse, the HIAA's internal ranks remained restive, as second- and third-tier companies disagreed among themselves about whether they could live with various detailed provisions of looming health care reform bills.[7]

No matter. The HIAA's leadership had little to lose by throwing big money into a life-and-death struggle against core regulations within the Clinton health plan. The stripped-down association made up in feistiness, organization, and leadership savvy what it lacked in encompassing membership. In contrast to the White House and its allies—but like many other health stakeholder groups—the HIAA already had its resources and infrastructure in place well *before* the battle over the Clinton plan was fully engaged. In 1992 the association had already turned to political mobilization, using paid print and television advertisements to tout the HIAA's minimalist "Campaign to Insure All Americans" and hiring some fifteen organizers to build coalitions in key states and localities. HIAA organizers targeted such groups as insurance company employees, small businesses, veterans' groups, and older citizens, arguing that any reforms more comprehensive than those the HIAA endorsed "could cost jobs and would mean bureaucratic controls."[8]

Shortly after the November 1992 elections, the HIAA achieved a coup for its leadership. It persuaded ten-term Ohio Republican Congressman Willis D. Gradison, a respected member of the critical Subcommittee on Health of the House Ways and Means Committee, to resign just after his reelection and become the Washington-based head of the HIAA, and put him in charge of public relations and behind-the-scenes strategizing alike.[9] This happened just as the HIAA was gearing up to muscle the Clinton administration. Touting Gradison's reputation for amiability and compromise in Congress, the HIAA at first offered cooperation—if only the Clinton policy planners would avoid all regulations that could hurt the business of those HIAA member companies that made profits by "cherry picking" healthier subgroups of employees to insure at lower rates than those that could be offered by other insurance companies.[10] In effect, the HIAA said that if the Clinton administration would surrender hopes for serious health financing reform at the start, it would be nice in return.

When the Clinton planners refused to make the desired concessions, the HIAA quickly went on the attack. Grassroots lobbying and television ads to raise doubts about the emerging Clinton plan started in May 1993, including one controversial ad (dropped after a brief run) suggesting that "mandatory HMO systems" might be "the first step to socialized medicine."[11] After officials saw drafts of the still-unfinished Clinton plan in late August, the HIAA released the first installment of $14 to $15 million that would be spent on the infamous "Harry and Louise" television commercials. Starting in early September 1993 and stretching into summer 1994, the HIAA sponsored three waves of these commercials, periodically stopping them in hopes of extorting concessions from the Clinton administration or Congress, then restarting them or turning them to a new issue, to gain further leverage with public opinion. The HIAA spent some $14 to $15 million on its ads, the largest share of the more than $50 million devoted to print and air advertising during the 1993–94 debate, the majority of which "opposed rather than favored some facet of reform with more ads explicitly objecting to the Clinton plan than supporting it."[12]

Harry and Louise were an obviously well-off, forty-something middle-class white couple who, on TV, sat around reading the Clinton Health Security plan and discussing it between themselves (and, in one ad, with Harry's younger brother, "an underthirty yuppie").[13] What Harry and Louise found in the Clinton plan worried them (even though, like the HIAA, they claimed to support national health reform). "There's got to be a better way" Harry and Louise opined for the cameras, as they discovered the horrible possibilities of bureaucrats choosing their health plan ("They choose, we lose"), health plans that might run out of money, and higher premium costs for younger people (who might, after reform, have to pay the same "community rate" as older, sicker people). In one of the ads, the dialogue, driving home the antigovernment point, went as follows:

Louise: "This plan forces us to buy our insurance through those
         new mandatory government health alliances."
Harry: "Run by tens of thousands of new bureaucrats."
Louise: "Another billion-dollar bureaucracy."[14]

The Harry-and-Louise ads became veritable icons among political insiders, but *not* because they were originally seen by many American television viewers. They weren't, because the HIAA paid to place them only in a few markets: especially in the Washington–New York corridor, where key policy elites would watch, and in certain states, where there were swing congressional districts.[15] The ads became famous after Hillary Rodham Clinton attacked them as distortions. Then news media throughout the country reproduced the ads along with the arguments about them, for all Americans to see and hear. The controversy was not very enlightening, as Kathleen Hall Jamieson explains:

[President] Clinton and the HIAA . . . agreed that unresponsive, costly bureaucracy was the problem. There was only one catch. They disagreed on whose "bureaucracy" was to blame. Harry and Louise saw it as the "bureaucracy" of "these new mandatory government health alliances," Clinton as insurance companies "writing thousands and thousands of different policies, charging old people more than young people and saying who cannot get health insurance."[16]

Along with other negative advertisements, the Harry-and-Louise ads heightened public uneasiness, particularly since these ads raised questions about key aspects of the Health Security plan—alliances, premium caps, and community insurance rating—that the Clintonites did not adequately explain. But much of the HIAA's impact during the 1993–94 health reform debate, just like the impact of many other stakeholder groups opposed to aspects of the Clinton plan, depended on less-visible influences than national advertising. Using a technique that has now become standard for resourceful interest groups, the HIAA put more millions of dollars into grassroots agitation to affect the thinking of the public and congressional representatives in localities across America.[17] Such manufactured grassroots agitation (sometimes called "astro-turf" mobilization) targeted states or districts where opinion or votes could go either for or against comprehensive health care reform.

Activating Social Networks

Funded by the HIAA, an intergroup alliance, the Coalition for Health Insurance Choices (CHIC), was set up with an action plan that called for "enlisting local business leaders, particularly those with personal ties to Members [of Congress]; writing letters to the editor (with samples provided); and holding public meetings."[18] Existing social ties were activated to "increase the amount of information to our customers and employers and to various advisers or customers, [such as] agents, attorneys and accountants, working toward activating them on a broad scale. . . ."[19] Even as the Clinton administration said little about the nature of health alliances, CHIC spread the word that alliances could be personally threatening. As an HIAA official explained, we ask people " 'If you have a problem with your health plan, would you rather go to your employer's personnel office or to a state agency and deal with a state bureaucrat?' . . . When you talk to people in those terms they realize [the Clinton proposal] would be inventing a whole new mechanism that isn't necessary."[20]

This sort of grassroots tactic against national health care financing had been pioneered to stunning effect back in 1948 to 1950. That was when the American Medical Association had gone all out to defeat President Truman's plan for national health insurance. Reaching out to Americans via their ties to physicians, that classic AMA campaign had used doctors' offices to disseminate oppositional materials, including one million copies of a foldout pamphlet entitled "Compulsory Health Insurance—Political Medicine—Is Bad Medicine for America!"[21] While waiting to see their doctors, patients across the land in the late 1940s were left to contemplate the dangers of governmentally sponsored health insurance.

In the 1993–94 iteration of recurrent U.S. battles over whether to extend insurance coverage through government, the HIAA was far from the only stakeholder group that combined national efforts with locally oriented and socially embedded techniques to spread criticisms of proposed new health care reforms. Although less influential among all American physicians now, the AMA activated its lobbying and community ties once again, fighting against anything that might restrict the incomes of its members.[22] A dizzying array of other groups was also at work.

Some stakeholders in the health care system were associations of institutions with many ties into communities. To help fend off medical cost controls and cutbacks in Medicare revenues, each of the American Hospital Association's "4,900 member hospital administrators throughout the nation received a lobbying kit, with advice about how to mobilize the four million hospital employees and tens of thousands of volunteers. Hospital trustees [too] are an invaluable asset because they are among the most respected business and community leaders."[23] About 85 percent of U.S. hospitals are nonprofit, community facilities, most of which are members of the American Hospital Association.[24] In any local community, hospitals as well as doctors' offices were likely to be centers of social discussion about the meaning of impending health care reforms.

Similarly, "superlobbyist" Michael David Bromberg of the Federation of American Health Systems—an association of 1,400 for-profit hospitals and investor-owned health care companies—went well beyond intense shmoozing with countless Democratic and Republican members of Congress. Bromberg helped to found the Health Leadership Council (HLC) with membership "limited to the chief executives of 50 of the largest health care companies—drug manufacturers, hospital chains, medical suppliers, managed care and insurance companies." In turn the HLC worked to "minimize government regulation in any bill that does pass" by activating local people, such as hospital administrators, to influence newspaper editorialists and other influential citizens in the districts of "100 House members and 15 to 20 senators, most of them moderate Democrats in eight key [southern] states. . . ." As Bromberg explained to a reporter, when he was a congressional aide in his youth, he "learned that grass roots—paying attention to things in the district—was more important than all the myths of Washington lobbying."[25]

Other stakeholders with less-local institutional presence also found creative ways to spread the word. For example, the National Association of Health Underwriters would have been put out of business by health alliances. It had only 12,000 to 16,000 members and a mere $3 million to spend on a campaign to "Preserve Consumer Choice." But its president was a "political specialist" who devised a plan to enter into a coalition "with other agents' groups, insurers, and small business owners. The group . . . [would] pursue an agressive grassroots campaign . . . [to] enlist not only its far-flung members but also their customers; 120 million Americans have policies written by independent agents."[26]

The real impact of stakeholder efforts came from the *combination* of advertising, direct mailings, Washington lobbying, and grassroots activations that they were collectively able to mount. The examples could go on and on without changing much except the details of the groups and goals and social ties involved. Much effort was expended on getting messages out through social networks and into pivotal states and localities.

The nation's capital, meanwhile, was in perpetual frenzy, as the struggle over possible health care reform became "a bonanza for pollsters and pundits and analysts and number crunchers" along with lobbyists and as "a daily, unrelenting round of Health Care Events" was staged by "every interest group in the land . . . from dentists to the Christian Coalition."[27] Overall, according to a study done by the nonpartisan, good-government-oriented Center for Public Integrity, health care reform during 1993 and 1994 was "the most heavily lobbied legislative initiative in recent U.S. history." During 1993 and 1994, "hundreds of special interests cumulatively . . . [spent] in excess of $100 million to influence the outcome of this public policy issue."[28] And this is surely an underestimate, because the center's researchers had to rely on incomplete, publicly available records.

What difference was made by the cascading criticisms from health care interests? In the first weeks after the President launched the Health Security effort, public support for his approach weakened a bit as questions were raised about the contents of the President's plan. But political observers still thought some sort of comprehensive reform would be enacted, because the complaints of the many groups that had a stake in the existing health care system were taken as gambits in bargaining over the details of legislation to be hammered out in Congress. President Clinton himself kept saying that he was not wedded to all the details of his proposal, that he was prepared to make all sorts of possible changes. Many early critiques of particular provisions of the Health Security plan came from groups that the Clinton administration assumed it would be able to attract in due course with specific modifications in particular provisions of the Health Security plan. And virtually all early critiques of the Clinton plan were accompanied by disclaimers that their sponsors joined the President in wanting comprehensive reforms of some sort.

Most stakeholder groups *did* favor reforms provided that someone else paid the price in terms of limited profits or disrupted routines.[29] Physicians, including those in the American Medical Association, wanted universal coverage but not stringent cost controls or regulations giving advantages to managed care.[30] Big insurance companies, such as those in the Alliance for Managed Competition, wanted universal coverage but not premium caps or encompassing purchasing alliances, either or which would cut significantly into their profits.[31] Many smaller businesses strongly opposed any employer mandate to contribute to health coverage, while others would accept only a very modest requirement.

As for medium-sized and larger businesses, many favored regulations that might reduce costs for insurance and medical care, but tended to oppose a generously defined standard benefits package as well as the requirement that all but very large employers work through the regional health alliances. (This latter opposition was ironic, because the Congressional Budget Office wanted encompassing regional purchasing cooperatives precisely in order to hold down health-cost increases in the future.) During the 1980s, personnel and benefits officers had encouraged many companies to get involved in discussions about cost-reducing national health reforms. Yet during the 1993–94 debate many of these same officers feared particular reform provisions, such as the 5,000-employee cutoff for mandatory participation in regional alliances, which might have forced personnel and benefits people out of their corporate jobs.[32]

In short, substantial institutions and groups in American life favored comprehensive health care reform in principle, but strongly opposed any specifics that could step on their particular toes. No stakeholder was willing to make any substantial sacrifice of profits or of freedom from regulation. And the dynamics of gearing up for big battles in Congress exacerbated each group's inclination to dig into extreme positions, while avoiding discussions that might facilitate compromise.

Especially in the early months of the 1993–94 debate, stakeholder groups tended to focus on attacking the exact provisions of the Health Security plan that each group liked least, while nobody ever mentioned in ads or public statements the parts they supposedly liked.

Major stakeholders who somewhat favored reform, particularly the Alliance for Managed Competition and the Business Roundtable, also staked out their legislative position by endorsing the vague legislation championed by Representative Jim Cooper (with its small alliances, no premium caps, and no employer mandate), while refusing to endorse the Clinton Health Security plan "in its present form."[33]

Stakeholders' public efforts and legislative maneuvers worked together to sow anxiety about virtually *all* the core public regulatory features of the Clinton plan: regional alliances, premium caps, employer mandates, and community rating rules. By late spring, there was little determination in Congress to go forward with any of these features, certainly not in anything close to the forms originally proposed by President Clinton. The regulatory and financial content of health care reform was being eviscerated, even as many in the general public were increasingly confused and angry about the very features of the Clinton plan that were being abandoned in Congress as infeasible.[34]

An Ideological Crusade Is Born

For a time after the Clinton Health Security plan appeared, stakeholder groups may have focused their fire on one or another of its specific features, while implying a vague overall endorsement of some sort of national health care reform. Yet from very early on, there were hints of a much more hard-edged, total, and sincerely ideological opposition from the radical right wing of the Republican Party. In the very same October 3, 1993, *New York Times* article that announced "The Clinton Plan is Alive on Arrival" (the article that quoted prominent Republicans promising to work on compromises with the Clintons), there was also a sour and intransigent note from House Republican Whip Newt Gingrich, who "promised an attack over costs and big-government inefficiency."[35] The attack was soon forthcoming, even before the Clinton bill was published in late October.

On October 13, the *Wall Street Journal* carried a mocking letter from conservative Republican Dick Armey on "Your Future Health Plan." According to Representative Armey, far from promoting a "streamlined and simpler system" as it promised, "the Clinton health plan would create 59 new federal programs or bureaucracies, expand 20 others, impose 79 new federal mandates and make major changes

Courtesy Joe Sharpnack

in the tax code. . . . [T]he Clinton plan is a bureaucratic nightmare that will ultimately result in higher taxes, reduced efficiency, restricted choice, longer lines, and a much, much bigger federal government." Cleverly, Armey accompanied his letter with a flow chart and a Clinton-plan glossary allegedly illustrating the hierarchical and ramified administrative carapace that would tower over hapless patients should the Clinton plan be enacted. Of course, much of the complexity in the Armey charts came from already-existing governmental and private-insurance arrangements in the U.S. health care system. But no matter. Versions of the Armey chart soon appeared on television, inspired cartoonists and humor columnists, and became a staple of conservative attacks on the Clinton plan. An Armey-type chart was also used as a prop for the official Republican response to President Clinton's second State of the Union Address in January 1994.

Seemingly only marginal irritants at first, Gingrich and Armey turned out to be forerunners of a burgeoning right-wing crusade—a campaign to counter not only the Clinton Health Security plan but also the premise that America faced a "health care crisis" and needed any sort of comprehensive reform through government legislation. In late 1993, insurgent antigovernment Republicans realized that their ideological fortunes within their own party, as well as the Republican partisan interest in weakening the Democrats as a prelude to winning control of Congress and the presidency, could be splendidly served by first demonizing and then totally defeating the Clinton plan, along with any compromise variant devised by congressional Democratic leaders.

In November 1993, the Project for the Republican Future was launched "to frame a new Republicanism by challenging not just the particulars of big-government policies, but their very premises and purposes."[36] The project was chaired by William Kristol, a Ph.D. from Harvard University who was the son of neoconservatives Irving Kristol and Gertrude Himmelfarb and former chief aide to Republican Vice President Dan Quayle. In December Chairman Kristol started issuing a steady steam of strategy memos to "Republican Leaders" about "Defeating President Clinton's Health Care Proposal." Simple criticisms and congressional modifications of parts of the Health Security plan were not in Republican political interests, argued Kristol. The Clinton plan would "destroy the present breadth and quality of the American health care system," and "is also a serious *political* threat to the Republican Party."[37] If the Democrats succeeded in enacting health care reform, Kristol argued, they would "relegitimize middle-class dependence for 'security' on government spending and regulation" and "revive the reputation of . . . the Democrats . . . as the generous protector of middle-class interests."

Public support for the Clinton plan had begun to erode since the President's September speech, Kristol pointed out, and "an aggressive and uncompromising counterstrategy" by the Republicans could ultimately kill the plan, if it convinced middle-class Americans that there really was not a national health care crisis. Correctly noting that polls showed most Americans to be satisfied with their personal medical care, Kristol argued that Republicans should convince people to forget concerns about the system as a whole by arousing fears that the quality of their personal medical care would be fundamentally undermined should the Clinton plan succeed. Republicans, Kristol suggested, should attack the Clinton plan for promoting "tightly regulated managed care for most people, with an emphasis on efficiency over quality." They should "insistently convey the message that mandatory health alliances and government price controls will destroy the character, quality, and inventiveness of American medical care."[38]

Kristol's memorandum held out bright prospects for Republicans following "the unqualified political defeat of the Clinton health care proposal":

> Its rejection by Congress and the public would be a monumental setback for the president, and an uncontestable piece of evidence that Democratic welfare-state liberalism remains firmly in retreat. Subsequent replacement of the Clinton scheme by a set of ever-more ambitious, free-market initiatives would make this coming year's health policy debate a watershed in the resurgence of a newly bold and principled Republican politics.[39]

In short, Kristol advised Republicans that the 1993–94 debate should *not* be about how to reform the U.S. health financing system in the direction of universal coverage. Instead, Republicans should use the debate as an occasion to embarrass Democrats and ensure a political turnaround that would enable conservatives to replace the "welfare state" with "free-market initiatives." Kristol maintained this uncompromising stance even after Clinton's original proposal was off the table. *"Sight unseen, Republicans should oppose it,"* he wrote about a possible summer 1994 compromise in Congress. "Those stray Republicans who delude themselves by believing that there is still a 'mainstream' middle solution are merely pawns in a Democratic game. . . . Our enemy is no longer Clinton, it is Congress."[40] "Opposition Without Apology" should be the Republican byword, Kristol declared.

The Attack Spreads

Kristol's uncompromising vision proved influential, and we can trace some of the steps it took as typewritten memos turned into prophecy. This story tells us something important about American politics today. Antigovernment conservatives work from a web of organizations and networks. They are well connected, not just to one another but to communications media and federated groups based in local communities across (at least much of) the nation. Right-wing intellectuals can offer analyses and visions of change that do not just sit on the page or echo in the lecture hall. Conservative antigovernment themes spread—from think tanks to popular media and from elites to groups with a geographically dispersed grassroots presence.

Soon after Kristol's memos began to appear, the Heritage Foundation and other think tanks in the Republican orbit echoed his strategy of all-out opposition to Democratic-sponsored health care reform. Interestingly, the fall 1993 issue of the Heritage Foundation journal, *Policy Review*, rested content with outlining alternative market-oriented plans for achieving universal health care coverage.[41] But by its very next issue, *Policy Review* featured an interview with William Kristol, who outlined his view that

> Republicans have been too timid and defensive so far in their reaction to Clinton's plan. The goal over the next several months should not be simply to wound the proposal, to nitpick the numbers or criticize some of the most onerous provisions, but to defeat the Clinton plan root and branch. . . . We [at the Project for the Republican Future] want to use the health care debate as a model for routing contemporary liberalism and advancing an aggressive conservative activist agenda.[42]

Fitting right in with the Kristol strategy, there appeared in the same winter issue a smear article entitled "Clinton's Frankenstein: The Gory Details of the President's Health Plan." This came adorned with the picture and cartoon reproduced here and with the following bold-print declarations and picture captions scattered throughout the text:

> The power of the new federal bureaucracy the President has proposed to administer health care will rival any in the history of the republic.

> Under a picture of a mother and child with a pediatrician: "For many Americans, a basic concern is whether they will be able to keep their own doctors under the Clinton plan."

> Under side-by-side pictures of a man with a very smokey cigarette and two runners in jogging suits: "Under the Clinton plan's insurance rating system, everyone is equal. Heavy smokers will be rated exactly the same as dedicated joggers."

> Under a picture of President Clinton holding up a Health Security Card: " 'Health Security Cards' will be issued to every American as we are forced to purchase health insurance through our regional alliances."

Policy Review, Winter 1994, Number 67. "Clinton's Frankenstein: The Gory Details
of the President's Health Plan." Robert E. Moffit. Courtesy Archive Photos

Global budgeting for health care will inevitably lead to rationed
health care.[43]

The themes dramatized in "Clinton's Frankenstein" soon became
staples in stepped-up nationwide attacks on the Health Security plan.
Newspapers ran cartoons illustrating notions about health care
rationing and the supposed bureaucratic nightmares the Clinton plan
would bring.[44] The *Reader's Digest* (the "World's Most Widely Read
Magazine") regularly ran features offering scary portrayals of the Clinton plan and attacking governmental involvement in health care.[45]
For instance, the March 1994 issue of the *Digest* included "Your Risk
Under Clinton's Health Plan," an article featuring the following large-
print extracts:

It promises health care for everyone, but what kind of
health care and at what price?

Rhetoric to the contrary, the Clintons must know this plan
will result in rationing.

YOU HAVE TO EXPECT SOME CUTBACKS WITH THE CLINTON HEALTH PLAN...

Copyright © 1993 by Dayton Daily News and Tribune Media Services. Courtesy Grimmy, Inc.

The plan would actually increase costs and tax many jobs and businesses out of existence.

Quality will be a forgotten concept.

They are taking away our choice of doctor.[46]

This *Reader's Digest* article concluded by using alleged shortcomings of the Canadian single-payer health financing system to attack Clinton's approach. (This was highly ironic, because Clinton had explicitly rejected a Canadian-style approach, and his plan was much more market based.) Why should we ruin the best, free-enterprise-based health system in the world, the *Digest* article asked? A peroration from House Minority Leader Republican Newt Gingrich wrapped up the message: "At the very moment when we [in the United States] are on the threshold of even greater strides in medicine, the Clintons are telling us, Let's bureaucratize health."[47]

Portrayals of the Clinton plan as a bureaucratic takeover by welfare-state liberals became regular grist for Rush Limbaugh and other right-wing hosts of hundreds of talk radio programs. These programs constitute a set of mass outlets virtually independent of the established media. They reach tens of millions of listeners, and are an important channel for antigovernment communications. More than half the voters surveyed at polling places in the November 1994 election said they tuned to such shows, and the most frequent listeners voted Republican by a 3 to 1 ratio.[48]

Demonizing the First Lady and the Clinton Plan

On talk radio and in other popularly oriented outlets, attacks on the Health Security plan were often accompanied by vicious ridicule of Hillary Rodham Clinton.[49] The First Lady had been given a highly visible leadership assignment for health care reform. She was the President's wife, yet also an independent professional in her own right. Both Mrs. Clinton's relationship to her husband, and the prominent roles she took for health care reform were ripe for attack, especially as the Health Security proposal was publicly redefined as big-government "meddling" in private arrangements.

Highly educated, reform-minded women have a long history of advocacy on behalf of federal social programs in the United States. Arguably, there is no other Western democracy in which women reformers have played a greater role in shaping public social policies, from the nineteenth century to the present.[50] Hillary Rodham Clinton

Copyright © 1993 Copley News Service. Reprinted by permission

Berry's World

APOLOGIES TO DISNEY
© 1993 by NEA, Inc.

Copyright © 1993 by NEA, Inc. Courtesy Newspaper Enterprise Association, Inc.

walked in the footsteps of Jane Addams, leader of the Social Settlement movement of the early 1900s, and in those of Julia Lathrop, the founding head of the U.S. Children's Bureau, which administered some of the first major federal programs for mothers and children.[51] Hillary Rodham Clinton's prominence was reminiscent of Frances Perkins, Secretary of Labor under President Franklin Delano Roosevelt, and of First Lady Eleanor Roosevelt and the many other female reformers who influenced social reforms during the New Deal.[52] Anyone who studies the history of these earlier U.S. women reformers will soon discover that all of them became subject to vicious ridicule combining political and sexual themes. Like all of these predecessors, Hillary Rodham Clinton could easily be targeted for misogynist attacks by those who hated the idea of expanded public social provision in the United States.

In Mrs. Clinton's case, moreover, the possibilities for pillorying were greater than ever, because of the president-husband with whom she enjoyed influence and the tenseness of gender relationships in our time. Bill Clinton had not served in the military during the Vietnam War, and he had tried to promote fairness for homosexuals in the armed services. Consequently, his own traditionally understood "manhood" was questioned by many in America. The late twentieth century, moreover, is an era of changing gender relationships, accompanied by much tension about newly assertive women—and wives. Hillary Rodham Clinton could easily appear "too strong" in relation to a husband many thought was "too weak." She also symbolized the increasing presence and assertiveness of career women, whom many people—including men in elite, professional positions—secretly or not so secretly fear and hate.

At the start of the 1993–94 health reform debate, Mrs. Clinton seemed for a time to have avoided negative imagery. She was always careful to be as personally charming and polite as possible in her dealings with people in Congress and the world of health care stakeholders. She was obviously competent and knowledgeable about health care, yet at the same time seemed to have a warm personal touch, especially when she held "town meetings" to talk with ordinary citizens or referred to individual concerns raised in the hundreds of thousands of letters sent to her during 1993–94. Hillary Rodham Clinton at first seemed to be bringing the caring image of the good mother to the health reform process, as well as a nonthreatening version of professional competence.

The tables started to turn, however, once attacks on the Health Security proposal began in earnest toward the end of 1993. Suddenly, the sorts of attacks on Mrs. Clinton that conservatives had initially tried out back in 1992 during the early months of the presidential campaign and at the 1992 Republican presidential convention, reappeared and began to spread. This was the same period, moreover, when Mrs. Clinton's image as a caring person was undermined by media portrayals of her as a scheming stock-market manipulator in the Whitewater affair.[53]

Increasingly over the course of 1994, the First Lady's visible role as leader of the Task Force on Health Care Reform and as continuing public advocate for Health Security made her a perfect foil for those opposed to comprehensive reform. By using Hillary Rodham Clinton as a target, cartoonists and talk radio hosts could ridicule the Clinton plan for its alleged governmental overweeningness—and in the process subliminally remind people how much they resent strong women. Hillary Clinton was the ideal demon. Or perhaps it would be better to say that she was the made-to-order Evil Queen for opponents of Health Security!

Nor were high-brow publications necessarily resistant either to misogynist mockery of the First Lady or to extreme propaganda about the Clinton proposal. The editorial pages of the *Wall Street Journal* featured one caricature and extreme commentary after another. Then there was the *New Republic*, whose mockery of Hillary Rodham Clinton we noted in the Introduction. In its February 7, 1994, issue, this magazine published—indeed featured on its cover—a lurid article called "No Exit" by Manhattan Institute intellectual Elizabeth McCaughey, a woman who some months later would be elected the Lieutenant Governor of New York on the Republican ticket. "No Exit" purported to answer the question "Under the Clinton plan how exactly will your coverage and treatment change?"[54] This article was later much discussed and reprinted in places like the *Reader's Digest*.

McCaughey's article exactly followed the Kristol game plan, seeking to frighten middle-class Americans currently covered by health insurance into believing that the Clinton reforms would, if enacted, force them into low-quality managed-care plans with long waiting lines and an emphasis on cost cutting through denial of needed care. McCaughey included outright lies about the Health Security bill, for example, falsely stating that it would prevent patients and doctors from dealing with one another outside of officially approved insurance plans.[55] Her accusations about bureaucratic regulations forcing middle-class people into low-cost managed-care plans were in fact much more true of the Cooper bill than of Clinton's Health Security. But the editors of the *New Republic* favored the Cooper plan and were happy to use McCaughey's smear piece to sully public perceptions of Clinton's proposals.[56]

Locally Rooted Conservative Agitation

During 1994, the hard-line conservative attack on Clinton's Health Security plan brought together more and more allies and channeled resources and support toward antigovernment conservatives within the

Republican Party. Well-organized, locally rooted conservative constituencies—especially the Christian Coalition and small businesses that
did not provide health insurance to their employees—fully engaged
in the battle. They featured opposition to Health Security as they
simultaneously aroused their troops for the electoral battles coming
later in the year.

Evangelical Christians, making up as much as a fifth to a quarter of
the national electorate, were the popular constituency that stood most
steadfastly with Republican George Bush in the 1992 presidential election.[57] At the organizational core of this constituency is the Christian
Coalition, launched in 1989 out of the debris of Pat Robertson's failed
presidential bid in 1988. The founding executive director of the Christian Coalition was Ralph Reed, honey faced and smooth talking, a
Ph.D. in American history from Emory University and former head of
College Republicans there, and a former member of Jack Kemp's staff.
Reed led Evangelical conservatives in fresh directions that promised
to pay off well in U.S. politics.

Like many advocacy groups on the liberal side of the spectrum,
earlier right-wing Christian organizations had concentrated on
national direct mail and lobbying in Washington. But the Christian
Coalition took a new approach, building from the grass roots up.[58] It
mobilized people around local causes, including school board elections; and it taught activists how to canvass voters, define issues, capture nominating party caucuses, and win local and state elections. All
this happened relatively quietly at first, yet within an overall organizational network defined by a shared ideological vision, a certain Christian understanding of "pro-family values."[59]

The election to the presidency of Bill Clinton, a Baptist southerner
given to using Biblical references in his speeches, aroused the Christian Coalition along with other conservative Republicans, perhaps
because Clinton was a potentially tough, culturally close political
competitor.[60] New efforts paid off, so that "by early 1993 the Christian
Coalition was adding ten thousand new members and activists to its
rolls every week."[61] Organizational activists evinced a special hatred
for Bill and Hillary Clinton, and often featured scripturally expressed
condemnations of their persons as well as their policies at local and
national meetings.[62] In late 1993, the Christian Coalition boasted of
some 450,000 members each paying $15 a year in dues, plus some
300,000 more affiliated activists; and it had "what amounts to a

national precinct organization, thanks to its listing of 35,000 churches it can contact to disseminate its messages."[63] By the middle of 1994, the Coalition's national organization enjoyed a budget of $20 million, and its nationwide ranks had grown to some 1,200,000 supporters (more than half of them dues paying) organized in 872 chapters, with at least one chapter in every state, and full-time field staffs in 19 states.[64]

The Christian Coalition became involved in the drive against Health Security partly because of members' hatred for the Clintons yet mostly because the Coalition is an integral part of the conservative wing of the Republican Party. As the spokesman for Newt Gingrich put it, the "organized Christian vote is roughly to the Republican party today what organized labor was to the Democrats. It brings similar resources: people, money and ideological conviction."[65] From their own perspective, moreover, "the Coalition and its allies are conducting a long march through the Republican party."[66] By 1994, the Coalition had a dominating presence in eighteen state Republican organizations and wielded substantial influence in thirteen others.[67]

In July 1993, Robertson and Reed announced that the Coalition would move out from its sole emphasis on "core family issues" (defined as antiabortion, support for prayer in the schools, and opposition to special protections for homosexuals) to take stands on broader social and economic issues such as anticrime measures, reduced taxes, term limits, and welfare reform.[68] As Democratic President Clinton undertook to make good on the economic and security promises that had won him the 1992 election, the Christian Coalition decided to stake out its own positions on overlapping turf. Clearly, its leaders also sought central influence within conservative Republicanism and aimed to make their movement as appealing as possible to middle-of-the-road Americans.

As part of the broadening of the Christian Coalition's focus, Ralph Reed mobilized his troops during the summer of 1993 against the Clinton budget, and then signaled clear opposition to the Clinton health care reforms.[69] In September 1993, the *Wall Street Journal* reported that the Coalition intended "to weigh in on health-care reform, fighting funding of elective abortions in any national plan, opposing mandatory membership in health cooperatives that might limit families' choice of doctors and resisting requiring small businesses to pay for employees' health coverage."[70] Later, once the all-out conservative assault on Health Security was plotted, the Christian Coalition devoted substantial resources to it. On February 15, 1994, Ralph Reed "announced a $1.4 million campaign to build grass-roots opposition to the Clinton plan," with tactics to "include 30 million postcards to Congress distributed to 60,000 churches; radio commercials in 40 Congressional districts and print advertisements in 30 newspapers."[71] The Christian Coalition ran full-page newspaper ads in the *Washington Post* and *USA Today*, and its postcards were distributed through Catholic as well as Evangelical Protestant churches.[72] In short, the Christian Coalition used the anti-Health Security campaign as one more prong in its overall effort to reach out beyond its core evangelical base.[73]

Other right-wing opponents of Health Security were also at work in local communities, especially in the South and West.[74] The central conservative theme of opposition to government "bureaucracy" proved attractive to those very small business owners who did not already insure their employees. The National Restaurant Association had 28,000 members, most of them strongly opposed to the Clinton plan's call for employers of part-time workers to contribute a pro-rated amount to their health coverage.[75] Yet the most tenacious and effective small-business opposition came from the National Federation of Independent Businesses (NFIB), whose 600,000 members were typically enterprises employing six or seven people (to whose health coverage, if any, the employer usually did not contribute).[76] Not only were NFIB members and other small-business people worried about paying new charges under universal employer mandates; many were in principle opposed to the idea that employers should contribute to health care costs.[77]

In a poll taken back in 1991, many small-business owners frankly told Bob Blendon and his associates that they would contribute money and mobilize politically to defeat any attempt to impose such a requirement.[78] After Bill Clinton's election, so determined was the NFIB to fight off an employer mandate that it refused to meet with the Clinton Task Force on Health Care Reform and started at once to lobby Congress against reforms that included any sort of requirement for universal employer contributions to health insurance. While the Clinton plan and alternatives to it were debated during 1993–94, the NFIB worked closely with the HIAA, the Restaurant Association, and others to pressure congressional representatives on key committees. "From mailings and faxes to town meetings and phone campaigns, they ... brought enormous pressure on 'swing' members of Congress."[79] In local communities, the NFIB also agitated among fellow small-business people, unrelentingly pressing the case against new government requirements for employers. Already staunchly pro-Republican, the NFIB steadily moved into an ever closer alliance with congressional militant Newt Gingrich and the organizations he created to train insurgent activists and raise funds for conservative candidates competing in the 1994 elections.[80]

Undercutting Moderates Who Might Compromise

Because of the ways in which interest associations and congressional politics are structured in the United States, national leaders who might want to work out compromises on comprehensive legislation can be outflanked on the side and undercut from below. This is part of what happened during 1994 to the Clinton Health Security plan, as well as to any conceivable compromises that might still have furthered cost containment and universal coverage.

People who planned health care legislation in the Clinton administration endeavored mightily to sound out business groups, moderate Republicans, and conservative Democrats with whom they might compromise on national health reform. If all possible compromises toward the center could not be embodied in the original Health Security proposal (for example, because of the need to satisfy the CBO about cost controls), then projected compromises might come into play later, as legislation worked its way through Congress. The Clinton administration thought it had actual or potential compromises worked out with key national business associations and with swing members on key congressional committees.

But a number of possible compromises came undone. Sometimes this happened when major national associations, such as the Business Roundtable and the National Association of Manufacturers, allowed their internal associational decision making to be captured by particular business sectors that were most likely to oppose premium caps, substantial health alliances, or significant employer mandates. Business is predisposed to fear new governmental regulation. And decision making inside the Business Roundtable was, for example, directed by the chief executive officer of Prudential, so it is not really very surprising that the Roundtable eventually spurned Clinton administration overtures and endorsed the Cooper-Breaux bill rather than any version of Health Security.[81]

But the most telling instances of collapsing compromises occurred when fiercely antigovernment forces such as the NFIB and insurgent conservative Republicans undercut the moderate national leaders of locally rooted associations that were amenable to accomodations with the Clinton administration (or the Democratic congressional leadership). Leaders of the Chamber of Commerce and the American Medical Association were certainly affected by conservative undercutting. So were middle-of-the-road Democrats and Republicans in Congress.

One dramatic incident was an outright turnaround by the Chamber of Commerce. On February 3, 1994, Robert Patricelli, head of the Health Committee of the Chamber, was scheduled to testify before the House Ways and Means Committee. As is often done, he submitted a copy of his testimony in advance, a statement that reflected support for a compromise version of comprehensive health care reform. "We accept the proposition that all employers should provide and help pay for insurance on a phased-in basis," the Chamber's prepared statement read.[82]

Leaders of the Chamber had some definite disagreements with the Clinton Health Security proposal; for example, they wanted alliances to be voluntary for firms with more than one hundred employees, and they wanted a 50 percent employer contribution rather than 80 percent. Nevertheless, the Chamber's 1991 to 1993 leadership had charted a conciliatory course, endorsing the principles of universal coverage and a mandate for all employers to contribute employee health coverage. In turn, people in the Clinton Task Force on Health Care Reform had courted Chamber leaders. Various provisions the Chamber wanted had been included in the original Health Security proposal, and it was understood that further movement toward Chamber positions (for example on the 50 percent mandate) might occur as Congress modified the original Health Security proposal.

But before Robert Patricelli could appear in Congress, determined conservative Republicans learned of his potential testimony and arranged for Chamber officials to be bombarded by local business members angry about the national leadership's acceptance of modest employer mandates. So intense was the pressure that the President of the Chamber of Commerce ordered a rewrite in the House testimony to back off from endorsing employer mandates. By late February, moreover, the Chamber responded to antimandate sentiment spreading at the grass roots by officially repudiating its earlier support for both universal coverage and employer mandates. In April 1994, key Chamber leaders who had plotted a compromise course since 1991 were fired or resigned. "For the next five months, the Chamber used its considerable resources to kill any chance of universal health insurance."[83]

What happened? Why did the national Chamber of Commerce cave in? A federated association of local and state groups encompassing some 200,000 businesses, many of them small and medium sized, the Chamber was subjected over many months prior to February 1994 to a double whammy. It experienced what scholars call "cross lobbying" from the NFIB, along with "reverse lobbying" from right-wing politicians.[84] (Normally, we think of groups like the Chamber as lobbying politicians, but in the Health Security struggle conservative Republicans lobbied the Chamber and other conciliation-minded stakeholder groups; hence the term "reverse lobbying.")

Businesses that were members of the Chamber of Commerce

"Won't all these new rules impact adversely on the viability of small businesses with fewer than fifty employees?"

tended to be somewhat larger than the tiny enterprises of the NFIB, and by 1993 some "67 percent . . . provided health insurance for their employees and were being hurt by rising premiums and by competition from other small businesses that didn't provide insurance."[85] The national Chamber leadership had carefully worked out a moderate position that reflected one understanding of the interests of a majority of Chamber members. But of course the Chamber remained vulnerable to competition from the NFIB, which was working hard at the local level to take its members away. Some businesses did defect, and the entire "National American Wholesale Grocers' Association resigned from the Chamber."[86] Other members complained to the national office; for example, the "National Retailers Federation urged each of its members to pressure the Chamber."[87] Overall, the NFIB's intense message against employer mandates "found a particularly warm reception among Chamber members that didn't provide health insurance," and that 30 percent became "the most vocal."[88]

NFIB cross-pressure on the Chamber was, moreover, greatly reinforced by a full-court press from conservative Republicans. Treated as traitors to a party they normally support, conciliatory Chamber leaders were (as John Judis aptly puts it) "pilloried" in the *Wall Street Journal* and other conservative publications, ridiculed on talk radio shows, and subjected to unrelenting pressure from "the 75-member House Conservative Opportunity Society, chaired by Representative John Boehner of Ohio" (the congressman who ultimately took the lead in blowing the whistle on the prepared February testimony).[89] House Republicans told national Chamber leaders that it was their "duty to categorically oppose everything that Clinton was in favor of." Meanwhile, "Boehner, Representative Richard Armey of Texas, and Representative Chris Cox of Ohio contacted local and state Chambers to organize opposition . . . , even urging that local Chambers leave the national organization."[90] Faced with all this, it is hardly surprising that the U.S. Chamber of Commerce eventually abandoned possibilities for compromise on universal health coverage.

Cross- and reverse-lobbying were not restricted to the Chamber of Commerce, as we can see by looking briefly at two more instances where possible compromises were undermined by such efforts. During the spring of 1994, the House Energy and Commerce Committee tried to work out a compromise health reform bill, one that would meet many stakeholders' objections yet retain some employer contributions to help pay for expanded coverage. As political scientist Cathie Jo Martin explains, the "committee's chair, John Dingell, was highly motivated to enact reform . . . [and he] made many concessions: making alliances voluntary in order to allow insurers to stay in business, introducing community rating slowly, and exempting small businesses from mandates."

> But the National Federation of Independent Businesses (NFIB) sent action alerts to all of its members in the 10 districts with swing legislators, urging that the legislators be told to oppose Dingell. The group also sent faxes to about 10 percent of its members requesting phone calls and arranged meetings between legislators and select members. NFIB also did action alerts in a series of moderate Republicans' districts as a kind of preventative measure. . . . [And the] National Restaurant Association . . . arranged for the restauranteurs to fax their legislators en mass from a national meeting in Chicago.[91]

In the end, the Energy and Commerce Committee was unable to report out any bill. The final vote on a compromise was one short, in significant part because a major target for the NFIB and conservative Republican pressure was committee member Jim Slattery, Democrat of Kansas, who "was running for governor . . . and worried about alienating the small businessmen in his state."[92]

By July 1994, things were looking very bleak for any sort of compromise legislation, so reformers were heartened when a coalition of nationally prestigious associations—the American Medical Association, the AFL-CIO, and the American Association of Retired Persons—joined together to run ads that endorsed "universal coverage with a standard set of comprehensive health benefits for every American by building on our current employment-based system . . . with a required level of employer contributions."[93] But before this could give a fillip to congressional legislative efforts, the AMA was subjected to intense reverse- and cross-lobbying. Conservative "House Republicans, led by Representative Newt Gingrich, attacked AMA leaders in a letter to all 450 members of the association's House of Delegates."[94] "We are dismayed," the Republican letter said, "by the actions of the leadership of the A.M.A." It is "out of touch with rank and file physicians."[95]

The NFIB also worked in local communities to influence physicians—often, in effect, small business people, many of whom employ staff assistants without contributing to their health insurance. Beyond that, NFIB officials "met with representatives of more than half a dozen state medical associations. They encouraged NFIB state affiliates to warn their AMA counterparts that if employers were compelled to pay for health insurance, they would pressure the government to limit medical fees."[96] Undercut by such grassroots agitation and inter-organizational lobbying, the national AMA leadership deemphasized mandates and universal coverage during what remained of the 1993–94 debate.

Finally, it is worth noting that moderate Republicans in Congress who might have been prone to compromise on significant health care reform were outflanked on the right within their own party. Retreat by moderate Republicans in the face of conservative Republican calls for all-out opposition certainly helped make it impossible for conciliatory leaders of normally pro-Republican groups such as the Chamber of Commerce and the American Medical Association to continue to support searches for legislative agreements. At various points, morever, moderate Republicans, such as Bob Packwood of Oregon and David Durenberger of Minnesota, backed off from possible compromises that embodied legislative ideas they had previously endorsed.[97] Still, the Republican backpedaller who mattered most was the Senate Minority Leader, Bob Dole.[98]

Courtesy Tribune Media Services

In the fall of 1993, Dole publicly pronounced his readiness to work out approaches to achieving universal health coverage, and from time to time thereafter he nominally endorsed bills in Congress that aimed for comprehensive reform. But Dole had presidential ambitions within the Republican Party, and as soon as the right-wing counterattack against health care reform gathered steam, he started scuttling searches for effective compromises. Early in 1994, Dole briefly echoed William Kristol's argument that maybe there was no national health care crisis, after all. Then Dole appeared to drop that line and endorse possible "mainstream" efforts. Yet he never would commit to supporting any funding for extended health insurance coverage, so his public gestures toward compromise were effectively meaningless.

By late May of 1994, during a retreat over Memorial Day weekend, Dole and other Republican congressional leaders accepted the assessment of pollsters and consultants that their party would do better electorally by refusing to compromise with the congressional Democrats. Sensing that big victories lay ahead in November 1994, congressional Republican leaders in effect accepted the Gingrich-Armey-Kristol formula for all-out opposition. Any time the Clinton administration moved toward them, they backed away. A tiny number of moderate Republicans, including Senators Chafee and Danforth, continued to explore compromises until the bitter end. But they were not supported by most Republicans, including Minority Leader Dole.

A Historical Perspective on the Public's Defection

Despite all the resources—money, moral commitment, and grassroots communications networks—that the antigovernment right could mobilize, the question remains why such attacks proved as broadly influential as they did over the course of 1994, seeping bit by bit into the general public's perception of the Clinton Health Security plan. Middle-class Americans were (and remain) concerned about both the security of their personal access to affordable health care and the overall state of the nation's health financing system. As we have seen, centrist Democrat Bill Clinton endeavored to define a market-oriented, minimally disruptive approach to national health care reform; and his plan was initially well received. Nevertheless, by midsummer 1994 and on through the November election, many middle-class citizens—not members of far-right groups, but Independents, moderate Democrats and Republicans, and former Perot voters—had come to perceive the Clinton plan as a misconceived "big government" effort that might threaten the quality of U.S. health care for people like themselves.

The ultimate defection of the American public came in the late spring and early summer, when majorities began to tell pollsters that they would rather Congress did *not* enact health reforms "this year."[99] More and more Americans wanted Congress to "continue to debate the issue and act next year." By then, as we have learned, elite impulses toward compromise had faded, and forces opposed to reform were thoroughly aroused in many congressional districts. The only thing that might have prompted Congress to act anyway would have been steadfast majority public support to do something "now" about comprehensive health care reform. But that was gone by the time the Democratic congressional leaders finally got bills to the floor of the House and the Senate.

To produce the retreat of public opinion on the desirability of going forward during 1994 with major health care reform, it took more than agitation from the NFIB and Christian right groups, more than memos from Bill Kristol, and more than strident articles in *Policy Review* and the *New Republic*. But what did it take? A historical perspective on U.S. political struggles at first glance only deepens the mystery here. After all, 1994 is hardly the first time that political conservatives and business groups have used lurid antistatist rhetoric to attack Democratic-sponsored social security initiatives.

Ideological and rhetorical counterparts to William Kristol, the Heritage Foundation, Rush Limbaugh, and business opponents of taxes and bureaucracy can easily be found, not only in all previous episodes of attempted health insurance reforms but also back in 1934–35, when Social Security was formulated and enacted very much as Bill Clinton must have hoped would happen with his own Health Security proposal. In 1934–35, an intragovernmentally centered commission planned an omnibus bill, which Congress debated and modified only a little before enacting it several months after it was introduced. Although hundreds of groups and individuals made their views known during the 1935 congressional hearings on Social Security, most demands for changes or alternatives to the Roosevelt administration's proposals were ignored or defeated in Congress. If anything, antigovernment conservatives argued with greater emotion in 1935 than in

1994 that the American way of life would come to an end if Social Security were enacted. Congress passed it anyway.

Yet the overall governmental situation that Franklin Roosevelt and the Democrats faced in debating Social Security in the mid-1930s was instructively very different from the context in which President Clinton fashioned and fought for his Health Security program in the mid-1990s. It is not just that Democrats enjoyed much greater electoral and congressional majorities in 1935 (after all, many Democrats back then were southern conservatives who often opposed federal government initiatives). The more important differences between Social Security and Health Security have to do with the kinds of governmental activities they called for and how their respective program designs related to preexisting stakeholders and social relationships in the given policy area.

Some officials and experts involved in planning the Social Security legislation introduced in 1934 wanted to include a provision for health insurance, but President Roosevelt and his advisors wisely decided to set that aside. Because physicians and the American Medical Association were ideologically opposed to governmental social provision and were organizationally present in every congressional district, Roosevelt feared that they might sink the entire Social Security bill if health insurance were included.[100] Instead, Social Security focused on unemployment and old-age insurance and public assistance.

Parts of Social Security called for new payroll charges, yet these were tiny and came at a time when most U.S. employees paid few taxes and were mainly worried about getting or holding onto jobs. Of course, business leaders hated the new payroll taxes; but in the midst of the Great Depression business opposition carried little weight with public opinion or elected officials, and could be overridden.

Beyond promising employed citizens new insurance protections, Social Security also offered federal subsidies to public assistance and health programs that already existed or were being enacted by most of the states. Roosevelt administration policymakers wanted to accompany the new subsidies with a modicum of national administrative supervision, but Congress stripped most such prerogatives out of the bill before it became law.

In the end, the Social Security Act primarily promised to distribute money. Citizens were wooed with promised pension benefits they did not already have, and not threatened with the reorganization of services to which they already felt accustomed. Indeed, the sole national program created in 1935, retirement insurance for older employees, was launched on entirely open policy terrain, for neither the states nor most employers had created such benefits prior to 1935. In addition, state and local officials were desperately strapped for revenues to deal with the crying social needs of the Great Depression. These officials could be depended on to encourage Congress to enact an omnibus law that would channel new federal monies into their programs, without subjecting states and localities to many new federal regulations.

Think of the contrast between Social Security and President Clinton's Health Security proposal. Clinton's plan was formulated during the post-Reagan political and governmental era, when taxes are electorally anathema and public budgeting is extraordinarily tight. Thus the proposed Health Security legislation was deliberately designed to offer little new federal revenue to anyone; and it would have cut back on projected federal spending for Medicare and Medicaid.

What is more, the Clinton Health Security proposal was put forward in the midst of a U.S. health care system which was already crowded with many institutional stakeholders and in which most middle-class employees already enjoyed health insurance coverage of some sort (even if it was increasingly costly and insecure). Although the Clinton plan offered new coverage to millions of uninsured Americans and promised new choices and security to those already insured, it also entailed a lot of new regulations that would push and prod insurance companies, health care providers, employers, and state governments. These new regulations were designed in an intricate and fairly tight way precisely to ensure that rising private and public health care costs would come down. This was the rationale for including both premium insurance caps and mandatory regional purchasing alliances in the Clinton proposal.

Given that there were such intricate and interlocked governmental regulations and given that they were not accompanied by vast new subsidies from the federal treasury, the Clinton Health Security plan was bound to arouse much more widespread consternation than the Social Security legislation put forward in 1934–35. Even groups that the Clinton administration thought it was helping—such as big employers with large pools of early retirees, whose health care expenses would be partially shifted to the public purse—could easily become riveted on the ways that particular regulatory aspects of the new Health Security plan might prove cumbersome or disruptive to preexisting arrangements. Such employers and their corporate benefits officers might, for example, become preoccupied with the standardized benefits package or the requirement that they switch to purchasing insurance through regional health alliances (or, if they remained outside the regional alliances, pay a small fee for that privilege).

Similarly, doctors and hospitals could become obsessed with possible cutbacks in Medicare revenues, potential federal rules encouraging the spread of managed care, or possible new regulatory mechanisms for keeping down costs in health care. As each institutional stakeholder in the present U.S. health system became concerned, moreover, its leaders and intermediate-level employees spread worrisome messages to millions of middle-class Americans, employees and patients alike. As we have seen in this chapter, this happened as much through informal social networks as it did through deliberate lobbying or media advertising. The two kinds of communications, in any event, reinforced one another.

Historically, Americans have been perfectly happy to benefit from federal government spending, and even to pay higher taxes to finance spending that is generous and benefits more privileged groups and citizens, not just the poor.[101] Such benefits are especially appealing if they flow in administratively streamlined and relatively automatic ways. But Americans dislike federal government regulations not accompanied by generous monetary payoffs. Individual citizens dislike means tests or cumbersome application procedures. Business owners profoundly resent regulatory oversight of their workplace operations. State and local officials dislike "unfunded mandates," rules about particular federal-state programs laid down by congressional committees and federal oversight agencies. Such resentment has only grown since 1980, as federal subsidies have become less and less generous, while federal rules have persisted or proliferated.

Ironically, precisely because Bill Clinton, a reformist Democrat, was working so hard to save money, he inadvertently ended up designing a health care reform plan that appeared to promise lots of new regulations without widespread payoffs. Established participants in the current U.S. health care system became increasingly worried that the Clinton plan might squeeze or reorganize the way they were accustomed to delivering, financing, or receiving health care. Many organized interests and individual citizens came to fear that the Clinton plan—or worse, some hodepodge amended version that Congress might enact at the last minute—would deliver new regulations without many (or any) new benefits, except to the currently uninsured.

Of course, the hard-right opponents of the Clinton Health Security plan did everything they could to magnify all sorts of potential worries and focus them on an overall ideological critique of meddlesome governmental "bureaucracy." The job of mobilizing opposition was made easier by the fact that the Clinton administration put out a detailed 1,342-page bill without conducting a credible public campaign to explain its key elements, such as health alliances. Over the course of 1994, more and more middle-class Americans crystallized worries about "too much bureaucracy" and threats to quality health care from the Clinton plan. The bureaucracy message resonated not simply with fear of national governmental action in general—after all, the same citizens continued to love Medicare and Social Security—but with fear of new federal regulations designed to control costs and promote reorganizations in the existing, organizationally dense health system.

The Albatross of "Managed Care"

A final feature of the situation in 1993–94 also helps to explain what may have happened to the Clinton plan in the eyes of average citizens. Not only did the Clinton plan end up provoking worries about federal regulations without payoffs, it also took on the baggage of whatever fears Americans currently had about the spread of "managed health care." The Clinton plan aimed to save public and private money in large part by using federal and state regulations of the insurance market to encourage the spread of high-quality managed-care forms of health care delivery. Such delivery forms were already well established in certain parts of the United States, especially in the West and parts of the Midwest, but were hardly present in the South and many parts of the East.[102] At the time when Clinton's Health Security plan was being formulated and launched in 1992 and 1993, Americans remained unenthusiastic about the notion of controlling costs through

"You don't get a room, Mr. Rheinschreiber, because you don't pay for a room! That's the whole idea of same-day surgery!"

managed care and managed competition. As Robert Blendon explained using a late 1992 poll, managed-care forms (such as HMOs)

> still do not enjoy widespread public appeal, principally because Americans are satisfied with their current health care arrangements and lack familiarity with the concept. When those not currently enrolled in an HMO (85% of the public) were asked how interested they would be in joining such a plan, only 7% said "very interested" ... [while] 20% were "hardly interested" and 43% of respondents were "not at all interested" in joining. . . . [A]bout half of all Americans feel that joining a health plan that restricts their choice of physicians to the most cost-effective is not a desirable method of controlling high health costs.[103]

Managed care was especially new to, and likely to be seen as worrisome by, well-insured upper-middle-class people in the East, and particularly in New York City, the heart of the nation's media empires and the nub of the constituency of Senate Finance Committee Chairman Daniel Patrick Moynihan. The Clinton plan included all sorts of safeguards to ensure that managed-care medicine would be of high quality; and it also ensured every American employee a choice among health plans, including at least one that preserved traditional fee-for-service medicine. But such features of the Clinton plan got lost in the superheated, overwrought ideological battle that the right launched against it.

Journalists and other writers were wont to stoke Americans' worries about managed care, while implying that more low-quality versions of such care was what President Clinton had in mind for all of us. A steady stream of editorials and features in the *New Republic* certainly took this tack, including the famous "No Exit" diatribe discussed above. Other magazines also ran scary articles about managed care, implicating the Clinton plan in its possible spread.[104] And then there was the best-selling novel *Fatal Cure*, by well-known medical mystery author Dr. Robin Cook. Appearing in January 1994, smack in the middle of the health care reform debate, this novel made the *New York Times* bestseller list and became a main selection of the Literary Guild and the Doubleday Book Club, as well as an alternate selection of the Mystery Guild.[105]

Fatal Cure told the story of two idealistic, young married doctors, David and Angela Wilson, with a little girl suffering from cystic fibrosis. David and Angela graduated from medical school in Boston and took posts in an idyllic Vermont community called Bartlet, only to discover that hospital administrators and managed-care bureaucrats were squeezing revenues out of the hospital where they worked. Worse, as the young doctors gradually discovered, these officials were killing off patients with potentially expensive ailments when the patients entered the hospital with minor compaints! Their own daughter nearly became the next victim.

The proximate villains in *Fatal Cure* are all greedy health care capitalists and private-sector administrators working for profits. Nevertheless, every few pages the novel stops to editorialize about the ways in which new federal government regulations in health care are pushing the capitalists and administrators into harmful—indeed, in this story, murderous—cost-cutting practices. Nor did reviewers of *Fatal Cure* miss this aspect of its message. As the *Detroit News* declared, this is a "hair-raising, cautionary tale about the possible pitfalls of impending health-care reform in America."[106]

If all of the United States in 1993–94 had been like California in terms of the organization of health care delivery, such scare stories about managed care might not have been so potent. But during the period when Clinton's Health Security proposal was being debated, many Americans did not have positive images of high-quality managed care. So they found negative projections about possible new doctor-patient relationships into which they might be prodded quite worrisome. There was, in short, a ready audience for the messages about rationing and reduced quality of health care that the Health Insurance Association of America and the Project for the Republican Future were delivering. And part of the reason why there was such a receptive audience is that many Americans are worried about changes going on today in the private health care market. Ironically, therefore, President Clinton's proposed reforms could be blamed for bureaucratic things capitalists are doing, as well as for new bureaucratic things that the federal government might do.

Health Security, the Compromise That Boomeranged

Given an extraordinary opportunity to unite in opposition to the Clinton Health Security plan, America's assorted antigovernment conservatives pulled together into a thunderous juggernaut dedicated to winning big in the midterm elections and reversing decades-long momentum toward public regulations and social protections in U.S. capitalism. In a remarkable turnabout from the fall of 1993 to the fall of 1994, Health Security became not a likely landmark but a probable turning point in the history of twentieth-century U.S. social policy. It became an albatross rather than a rallying point for the beleagured Democratic party.

From a broad historical perspective, we can see why Clinton's Health Security plan embodied the seeds of its own political destruction. The very societal and governmental contexts that originally made it quite rational for a centrist Democratic president to choose a reform approach emphasizing firmly regulated "competition within a budget," simultaneously made that approach ideal for political countermobilization by antigovernmental conservatives. Well-organized and morally determined right-wingers were, by the early 1990s, already lying in wait to defeat the Democratic Party and dismantle the U.S. social-security programs whose best features Bill Clinton aspired to extend. Ambitiously launched but poorly explained by its own sponsors, Health Security gave antigovernment conservatives exactly the target they were looking for—a proposed federal initiative that could be portrayed as threatening to the American middle class.

CHAPTER SIX

LEGACIES AND LESSONS

The victory of Bill Clinton in 1992 kindled enormous hope for people who want to address America's deepening social ills and inequities in part through public initiatives. Just possibly this moderate yet populist Democratic governor from Arkansas could lead the nation in overcoming the civic decline furthered by the raucous market forces and unrealistic public policies of the 1980s. Clinton called for responsibility and initiative by all individuals and families, yet he did not propose simply to leave increasingly hard-pressed working Americans to their own devices. He projected a new synergy among culturally revitalized families and communities, vital market forces, and reformed public programs designed to open opportunities and ensure a modicum of security to all Americans.

The economic and budgetary policies of Republicans Ronald Reagan and George Bush had displayed their shortcomings for all to see. Whatever U.S. global triumphs they facilitated, at home the Reagan-Bush policies furthered a burgeoning public debt, the decay of public services, sluggish national economic growth, and increasing social inequality. American voters seemed to have repudiated Reaganism in 1992. Although the election generated no simple majority for any candidate, postelection public sentiment was clear enough: substantial majorities of Americans wanted the Clinton presidency to succeed. Americans called for the newly elected President to work with the Democratic Congress to overcome gridlock and "get the nation moving again." Popular expectations were especially high for job-promoting economic growth and for comprehensive reform of the national health system.

But in truth the ghosts of Ronald Reagan and his fellow conservative Republicans were in no way banished in 1992. A huge federal budget deficit and ever deeping distrust of the role of government in American life are the Reagan legacies that matter most. To be sure, debt and disillusionment with the federal government were growing before the 1980s.[1] But the Republican ascendancy of that decade exploded the deficit and deliberately encouraged cynicism about public efforts to address national problems. Grappling with those inherited conditions haunted all that President Clinton tried to do during his first years in office. The Clinton administration's hopes to "invest" in education, national service, and job training were dashed against the rocks of fiscal austerity, as were its plans for welfare reforms that included job training and child care for single mothers as they were pushed off public assistance. Nowhere, moreover, were the debilitating legacies of the Reagan era more apparent than in *both* the formulation and the resounding demise of the Clinton Health Security plan.

"Reagan's Revenge" is the title of a very insightful essay published in June 1994 by Columbia University historian Alan Brinkley. "For generations," Brinkley explained, "American conservative leaders— from Herbert Hoover to Barry Goldwater—had appealed for support by warning of the dangers Government programs posed to individual freedom. But attacking Government programs had failed to topple the liberal order. Almost everyone had a stake in some of them. The biggest and most expensive programs—Social Security, Medicare, veterans' benefits and others—had the strongest support."[2] During the 1970s, however, certain antigovernment conservatives figured out that attacking taxes—and the politicians and "bureaucrats" who spent them in supposedly "wasteful" ways—would work much better than frontal assaults on government programs. Conservatives seeking to defeat liberals and roll back government programs could promise huge tax cuts and starve existing public undertakings of resources. This approach was pioneered very successfully by businessman Howard Jarvis and embodied in the antitax movements that started in California and spread across a dozen states in the late 1970s. Then the crusade went national, as Ronald Reagan made tax cuts, along with attacks on "welfare" for the poor, the centerpiece of his successful drive for the presidency.

A huge federal tax cut was hastily put through in 1981 by a Congress frightened at the results of the 1980 elections. Ideas as well as electoral results were at work. "Supply-side" publicists offered an ideological rationale for sharply cutting taxes while maintaining most federal domestic expenditures and sharply increasing defense spending. Supply-siders asserted that tax cuts would so thoroughly unleash private investments that federal tax revenues would grow rather than shrink. The modest federal deficits that Reagan had inherited—a $59 billion annual deficit and $914 billion national debt in 1980—could still be reduced in the near future, the supply-siders promised. This, despite the fact that most Americans, and especially the rich, would be paying significantly lower amounts into the federal treasury. And this despite the fact that President Reagan did not want to face the political risk of recommending sharp decreases in domestic social spending, and especially not in the heftiest parts of it that went to middle-class citizens and business interests. Reagan promised to cut taxes, keep spending, and reduce deficits, too. It was, after all, "Morning in America," and anything was possible.

Rosy supply-side projections turned out to be nonsense. Within twelve years after 1980, the U.S. annual deficit would grow to over $300 billion, and the national debt would stand at over $3 trillion.[3] As reported in the memoirs of President Reagan's first Budget Director, David Stockman, many people in the Reagan administration realized early on that supply-side projections were (as George Bush once put it) "voodoo economics."[4] Yet as Alan Brinkley explains, although the 1981 "tax cut was not supposed to increase the deficit,"

> many of its supporters were not very troubled when it did. Major figures in the Reagan administration, unlike many of the people who had voted for them, had no faith in Government and no love for its programs. Some began quietly to see real advantages in the skyrocketing debt. The fiscal crisis . . . undercut support for starting new Government programs, and even for sustaining old ones, less by discrediting the programs than by pitting them against the need to reduce a huge and growing national debt.[5]

Ironically, the full antigovernment effects of the huge Reagan budget deficits came about partly because Democrats remained ensconced in the Congress and in many local and state governments. Democratic politicians and constituencies tied to them had powerful vested interests in hundreds of particular governmental programs. Throughout the 1980s, they used leverage in Congress to preserve programs, despite the fact that those programs were increasingly starved for funds needed to operate efficiently or to realize effectively their declared objectives. Programs were preserved, but hobbled. What is more, Democrats and moderate Republicans continued to use government to address economic and social problems. They simply used regulations and mandates on business or on state and local governments more readily than revenues. With no money to throw at problems, federal rules were thrown at them instead.

All this fueled the arguments pressed by insurgent conservative Republicans that government is an inefficient and cumbersome way to get things done. Public programs starved for funds did, indeed, become less efficient: offices were not computerized, and the qualifications and morale of administrators deteriorated. Detailed federal rules became increasingly irritating, especially when not accompanied by ever more generous subsidies. Throughout all this, Reagan Republicans and other still more fervent antigovernment conservatives such as Newt Gingrich, bashed away at government programs and at the allegedly greedy, inefficient "bureaucrats" who ran them. Raising taxes became more and more out of the question, because new revenues would just be "wasted" on badly run programs or unnecessary meddlesome agencies.

As Brinkley sums up, the "tax revolt was a product . . . of growing cynicism about politics and politicians. Its results, ironically, . . . greatly increased that cynicism." By the time Bill Clinton got ready to run for the presidency, Americans' distrust of the federal government was at an all-time high. When the newly elected President arrived in Washington, D.C., his administration, the "first . . . in nearly 30 years with an expansive power to do good . . . [found] itself imprisoned within a fiscal environment that makes it difficult for Government to do anything."[6]

In this book, we have seen how powerfully Bill Clinton's Health Security initiative was affected by Reagan's revenge. As a 1992 Democratic presidential contender, Governor Clinton had excellent reasons for promising comprehensive health care reform. His fellow citizens wanted it, and comprehensive reform was a way simultaneously to make Americans more secure and the national economy more efficient. Inclusive health reform also promised to overcome class and racial divisions within the Democratic Party; and its favorable results might well, over time, rekindle faith in government as an agent of the common good.

Still, even the original promises Clinton made about health care reform were influenced by antigovernment Reagan legacies. Clinton and his 1992 campaign advisors were obsessed with avoiding the word "taxes," so the candidate had to find a road to national health reform that appeared not to involve direct taxing and spending by government. Furthermore, after Clinton settled on managed competition within a budget as his "way through the middle," he refused openly to discuss the inevitable role of public rules of the game in his reform plan. So determined was Clinton to avoid the delegitimated subject of "government," that he and his advisors could barely acknowledge the governmental contents of their health care plan to themselves, let alone talk openly and convincingly about them to the American citizenry.

It wasn't just avoidance of "taxes" and "government" that mattered for Health Security, though. In a supreme irony, federal budgetary procedures put in place in the wake of the Reagan fiscal debacle pushed the Clinton administration toward including more rather than less governmental regulation in the full-fledged Health Security legislation. Reagan's revenge was a double bind, and it delivered a double whammy. In order to avoid a highly visible role for the federal government while still extending health coverage and dealing with the problem of the deficit, the Clinton planners substituted regulations for revenues, and governmental indirection for an out-front public presence in health care financing.

As we have learned, the Clinton Health Security proposal was no simple triumph of liberalism. Big cuts in two existing public health insurance programs, Medicaid and Medicare, were included in Health Security to help make the out-year budget projections look convincing. Still more telling, encompassing regional health alliances, contingent premium caps, and all sorts of charges to "recapture" private-sector health savings for the federal budget were included in the Health Security legislation largely in order to satisfy the deficit-neutrality rules of the Congressional Budget Office. CBO rules and other budget procedures had been devised as a response to the wild fiscal excesses of the Reagan era. Operating within these rules, and pursuing his own fiscal goals, President Clinton had to make a convincing case that health care reform would reduce the huge, looming national debts bequeathed to him (and all of us) from the 1980s.

A political boomerang resulted from President Clinton's efforts at governmental indirection and fiscal stringency. In large part because the Clinton administration's Health Security proposal was intricately designed as a series of interlocking regulations, right-wing government haters could argue that this set of reforms would hurt businesses, individuals, and health providers, interfering with their "liberties." Proclaimed threats of possibly rising taxes and governmental inefficiency could be spiced with pronouncements that big, intrusive government would destroy our freedom and the quality of the "best health care system in the world." Designed to get around and through the antigovernment and fiscal legacies of the Reagan era, the Clinton Health Security proposal—in its ultimate irony—gave new life to the outcries about "governmental tyranny" that Barry Goldwater had once presented so ineffectively.

Could They Have Done It Differently?

In the aftermath of defeat, many people have not hesitated to pronounce what President Clinton and other supporters of health care reform should have done differently. Humility is more in order, however, because it is not clear that any alternative course would have resulted in success—if by success we mean an extension of coverage to many currently uninsured citizens along with the institution of effective cost controls in U.S. health care. Alternative scenarios are useful to consider, though, because they help to further clarify the implications of the analysis I have offered in this book. So let me briefly consider pronouncements about "what they should have done" from various points in the political spectrum.

Some radicals and liberal Democrats have an "I told you so" attitude about the recent Health Security debacle. Above all, adherents of the single-payer approach to health care reform are sure that the President would have done better to champion their cause, especially by expanding existing provision for older citizens into "Medicare for all." The central ideas of single payer are easy to explain, they argue, because single payer reduces bureaucracy, cuts costs, and lets patients choose doctors and hospitals freely. Even if single payer had gone down to defeat, presidential advocacy of this approach would have set the stage for a congressional compromise that ensured some sort of universal coverage.

I have long been sympathetic to single payer as a readily under-standable way to finance health care for all. In retrospect, however, I do not find it even slightly plausible that President Clinton would or could have taken this route. Given his centrist-Democrat leanings and fear of mentioning taxes, I cannot conceive of Bill Clinton sincerely embracing any variant of single-payer health reforms. More important, the same restricted means of political communication that made it hard for the Clinton administration to tell the American public about its approach would have made it equally or more difficult to convey an accurate portrayal of a single-payer plan. Even a proposed nation-wide move toward "Medicare for All" could easily have been carica-tured by fiscal conservatives—such as those in the Concord Coalition—as a "budget buster," a new "entitlement" that was bound to get out of control.

Had a single-payer plan been put forward by President Clinton, threatened stakeholders and the populist right would also have carried on a devastating scare campaign about a "government takeover" of medical care. Many middle-class Americans would have found the message plausible, because the administrative disruptions of any sin-gle-payer scheme would have frightened millions of employees whose jobs or employer-provided health coverage would have to be abolished during the changeover from private to public insurance. Congress would have recoiled in horror.

Monday-morning quarterbacking has come from another political direction, too. Conservative Democrats and other self-styled "middle-of-the-roaders" have been sure that Clinton was unwise to push for universal coverage. They think the President should have gone for incremental market reforms along the lines of the Cooper plan, and thus supposedly cemented bipartisan support right at the start. But I have already suggested that it makes no sense for a Democratic presi-dent to advocate changes in health insurance that do not push toward universality but leave many low-income workers out in the cold. Like-wise, it was (and is) dangerous for a Democrat to advocate minor regu-latory changes in the existing private insurance market that may leave more and more middle-income Americans facing ever higher premi-ums for the same, or less, coverage. After some years, such minimalist regulatory approaches could leave people more, not less, disillusioned with governmental solutions. Finally, we should also keep in mind that the Cooper bill turned out to be full of internal contradictions, when the Congressional Budget Office sat down to "cost it out" and assess its impact on the economy and the federal deficit. The Cooper bill also entailed as much, if not more, regulation than the Clinton plan; and Cooper would have in effect raised taxes on many employed Americans already enjoying the best health benefits. In the end, the supposedly moderate Cooper approach to health care reform was little more than a fig leaf for stakeholders who wanted to pretend support for serious reform without really delivering it. The Cooper plan had more support in the New York Times than it ever had in Congress or the country.

In the light of the institutional and historical analysis I have offered in this book, other retrospective possibilities have a bit more plausibility than the ones single-payer supporters or market-oriented conservative Democrats have advocated.

President Clinton conceivably could have tried to further managed competition within a budget through a ten-to-twelve-person bipartisan commission. Such a commission might have functioned as the policy planner instead of the Task Force on Health Care Reform. More plausibly, the commission might have been handed the results of the Task Force's deliberations and asked to review and revise them. Either way, such a commission would have had to include key congressional players from both parties, experts willing to explain inclusive versions of managed competition, and carefully selected institutional actors, such as a big-business executive, an insurance company leader, a well-respected physician, a union leader, and someone from the AARP. The President might have been able to structure the mandate and staffing of a commission to make it likely that it would report out something acceptable to him as well as to Congress and major stakeholders. Had this sort of process worked, the President would have been able to claim a broader, even bipartisan, mandate from the start, perhaps educating public opinion and focusing congressional efforts more effectively.

But a commission approach might not have worked. The Clinton administration would have had a devil of a time deciding whom to invite—and whom to leave out and thus offend. Key Republicans might have refused to join or worked to keep the commission from reaching agreement. As I have already discussed, the United States is not institutionally amenable to corporatist-style policy formulation. President Clinton could have appointed a commission, only to see a relatively consensual proposal emerge and later fall apart, dissected to death by congressional committees and undermined by dissident groups such as the NFIB that could mobilize in local congressional districts. The same forces that undermined the Health Security proposal itself could just as easily have undermined a top-down, "bipartisan" agreement endorsed by a commission.

If, somehow, a commission process had resulted in a consensual proposal that survived, the resulting reform proposals surely would not have been as intricately and tightly constructed as those President Clinton put forward in the fall of 1993. A commission would probably have designed an approach emphasizing insurance regulations, health alliances for smaller businesses only, and some tax-financed subsidies for small-business and low-income workers, but *not* mandatory health alliances for larger employers or premium caps for private insurance. Commission-designed proposals would not have "added up" to federal budgetary savings; thus the President would have had to raise new revenues or else undertake substantial cuts in existing government spending.

Another possibility is that Bill Clinton could have gone forward with the first approach he temporarily advocated during his 1992 presidential campaign, a version of play or pay that incorporated contingent cost controls of various sorts. Play or pay already had support and understanding among key congressional players and Democratic constituencies, so it might have been easier to rally reform advocates around it. Arguably, too, the President could more readily have explained the central mechanism of this approach to citizens—and to the employers and physicians who might, in turn, have signaled acceptance or tolerance to employees and patients. Every employer, the President could have declared, has to pitch in somehow, either by sharing the costs of insurance with employees or by paying a modest fee to help cover the uninsured. The entire public campaign for health reform could have been focused on this simple call for universal employer "responsibility." Meanwhile, "pay" fees for small businesses could have been set early on at a definite, low level, and this might have provoked less ideological countermobilization than a regulatory employer mandate (which was easily made to look like "bureaucratic intrusion").

Within a modified play-or-pay scheme, President Clinton could also have encouraged health purchasing cooperatives, setting them up as voluntary cost-controlling mechanisms for business and public-sector participants in the revised health care financing system. He could, in short, have made a modest start at creating "health alliances," hoping that they would eventually come to be seen as familiar and desirable administrative mechanisms to promote lower costs and higher quality in a gradually transformed health system.

Like the sort of loose managed competition that might have emerged from a Clinton-appointed commission, this loose sort of play-or-pay approach (seasoned with voluntary health alliances) would have required the promise of greater federal revenues at the start. President Clinton would have had to sweeten the transition for insurance companies and businesses, acknowledging that universal health coverage costs money. All along, this was something that the American public believed, so the President might have gained credibility by talking straightforwardly about public financing. To do this, President Clinton would have had to give up the notion that comprehensive health care reform could be sold, up front, as a federal deficit cutting measure.

For Bill Clinton and the Democratic Party, it would ironically have been politically wiser to have been less fiscally responsible—or else to have chopped away parts of the existing federal budget to free up money for health care reform. Either a looser version of managed competition or a version of play or pay that might have been acceptable to Congress needed to be greased with federal revenues if it was to be politically feasible. I conclude that President Clinton should have been less worried about pleasing deficit and budget hawks. He should have done what his conservative critics falsely charged him with doing—acted more like a Democrat in the New Deal tradition, by combining new federal regulations with generous subsidies to those affected.

But was this possible? In this book we have seen why the alternative scenarios I have just outlined were not likely. Along with the anti-"entitlement" climate fostered by the Concord Coalition and its echo chamber in the elite media, the budgetary side of Reagan's revenge is the reason. Back in the spring and summer of 1993, the Clinton administration thought it was impossible to put much new federal money into health care; and it was certainly obsessed with federal deficit cutting. That is why President Clinton finally proposed such an intricate and tightly regulated version of managed competition within a budget. He devised a perfect target for conservative counter-mobilization against government, because he was trying to deal with the aftereffects of previous conservative attacks on government.

What Happens Next?

Americans who voted in the 1994 midterm elections continued to care deeply about governmentally sponsored health care reform. According to an election-night survey of voters, sponsored by the Kaiser Family Foundation, health care reform remained even more of a voter priority than it was in 1992.[7] Even in the immediate wake of the Health Security debacle, hefty majorities of voters continued to favor definite steps toward covering the currently uninsured, especially children and low-income people. Most also opposed any cuts in government spending on Medicare and Medicaid, as well as opposing cuts in Social Security. At least in late 1994, President Clinton and the Democrats lost the public's former faith that they were the ones to take the lead in reforming U.S. health care. Yet the voters still wanted legislators and politicians to preserve government's financial contributions to health care and extend coverage to more Americans. Subsequent opinion studies have confirmed that such public expectations persisted through 1995. For example, even to balance the budget, most Americans do not want huge cuts in Medicare for the elderly.

Americans may have the foregoing concerns and hopes, but there is scant reason to believe that these citizen expectations are going to determine what happens in the foreseeable future. After their November 1994 triumph, Republicans claimed a very different "mandate" — focused on cutting the size of government radically and hobbling governmental decision makers for the future. Half or more of Americans had never even heard of the Republican "Contract with America," yet many Republicans and media commentators treated it as a blueprint for governing, as a set of considered citizen expectations that should be enacted very rapidly by the Congress. The Contract had nothing to say about health care reform; it overwhelmingly emphasized welfare

cuts, destruction of federal regulations, and huge tax cuts disproportionately targeted on business and the top income quintiles.[8] The
promises of the Contract would require massive shrinkage in the federal budget, over one trillion dollars in cuts by early in the next mil-
lenium.

In order to achieve the order of tax and public spending cuts they
promised in 1994, congressional Republicans set out to slash funding
for and fundamentally restructure Medicaid and Medicare. Indeed,
conservatives have for some time been highly critical of Medicare,
holding that it wastefully encourages older people to go to the doctor
too often and not "take responsibility" for their own health and financial planning. Despite Medicare's popularity with the U.S. public,
therefore, many conservatives have in mind abolishing this universal
federal program in favor of tax-subsidized vouchers or individual medical savings accounts, combined with efforts to encourage older citizens to enroll in for-profit managed-care plans. There is a certain irony
in all this, given that during the 1993–94 health care debate, a prominent argument used by conservatives was that President Clinton allegedly wanted to force everyone into managed care.

The real effect of Republican plans would be to starve Medicare for
funds and "cream off" the wealthier and healthier older citizens into
for-profit health plans. Those who remained in Medicare would face
sharply deteriorating service, and this would set the stage for further
arguments that "government programs do not work." Meanwhile,
Republican Medicaid proposals would destroy the national medical
safety net for the poor, and throw increasing numbers of low-wage
working people into the ranks of the uninsured.

Health care remains potentially a good issue for Democrats. The
uninsured continue to rise; their numbers now stand at some 41 million, two to three more million than during the debates over the Clinton reform proposals.[9] What is more, as private corporate and
insurance interests impose their own versions of managed care on
more and more employed Americans, people face fewer choices and
rising out-of-pocket costs. These trends are likely to continue, indeed
accelerate, as the antigovernment Republican ascendancy locks into
place. Consequently, issues about the security and quality of health
coverage will remain a potential point of popular appeal for Democrats, as will a broader array of issues about the availability of jobs with

wages and benefits sufficient to sustain families.

But the Democrats are not likely to achieve credibility on health care or other issues until they come to terms with the overall political challenge they face. Politically engaged Americans who want progress toward adequate social protections for all citizens and families must face the fact that the United States has entered into a period of political upheaval and governmental transformation. In the wake of the failed Health Security effort of 1993–94 and the antigovernmental backlash it helped to fuel, there is no prospect of starting again with merely new tactics.

An extraordinarily resourceful politician, Bill Clinton may survive even the debacle the Democrats experienced in the 1994 elections. He may be reelected president in 1996. But, if so, it will be because he has thrown himself more completely than ever into the mode of politics that avoids explicit discussion of government as a positive force, that celebrates tax cuts and severe reductions in public spending to "balance the budget." Whether or not Bill Clinton is reelected, the antigovernment mood in America is remarkably ascendant.

Possibilities for revitalized social protections in America, including more inclusive health insurance, will remain open into the twenty-first century, because antigovernment conservatives have no prospect of solving the nation's domestic problems. Unregulated market competition alone will not produce opportunity and security for most American families. Still deeper tax cuts for the wealthy, financed by slashing away at valuable as well as outmoded federal programs, will not suddenly produce the intact families raising healthy, well-educated children that conservatives claim to want. An opening remains in U.S. politics for political forces that can project a convincing vision of a revitalized and more egalitarian civic society for America. An opening exists for leaders who can address the very real insecurities of families in the bottom three-fifths of the income distribution, people who are working longer hours, sacrificing time with children, in return for less money and, at best, fragmentary social protections to help in humanly common episodes of illness, childbirth, and old age.

But deteriorating social and economic conditions do not, in themselves, determine political outcomes. Many liberals in America are sitting around waiting for conservative Republicans to falter, assuming that liberals will then come back to power, automatically. This is dead wrong. Absent a coherent progressive alternative to the ideas and political organization of conservatives, America in the twenty-first century could easily become a more and more unequal society, in which the rich and the upper-middle class go it alone without either paying for, or using, governmentally provided or financed social protections.

As much in this book has revealed, the Democratic Party is by now a relatively hollow political shell. In terms of both ideas and organized grassroots support, conservatives in and around the Republican Party vastly surpass progressives in and around the Democratic Party. If a progressive turnabout is to come in U.S. politics, therefore, much will first have to happen both intellectually and politically. Democrats and public intellectuals who care about civic life and the needs of most working Americans are going to have to go through a period of ferment. People must get away from mind-sets associated with long-term governmental incumbency. New ideas must be hammered out away from Washington, D.C., New York City, and the major university centers. Conversations in plain language, not insider jargon, will have to take place across the gaps between upper-middle-class progressives and Americans from all walks of life.[10] Discussions must go on in community centers, churches, schools, day care centers, and workplaces. Together, citizens and leaders may then put forward a convincing vision of the nation's problems and the ways that government as well as business and civic associations can contribute to solving those problems.

In isolation, even an issue like health care—central as it is for many Americans—will not bring about a political revival for Democrats or a resurgence of faith in government. As the failure of President Clinton's courageous effort in 1993–94 shows, the future of inclusive social policies, including health reform, depends on Americans' coming to believe that government can offer minimally intrusive solutions to the heartfelt needs of individuals and families. If progressives are to achieve any sort of inclusive policy changes in America's future, it will be because new rationales for the role of government, and new majority political alliances, have been achieved first. I believe that such new rationales and alliances can be forged, because most Americans still want government to function efficiently, compassionately, and fairly on behalf of everyone. Yet the new rationales for government, as well as the new majority political alliances, will necessarily have to be achieved on bases very different than the ones that prevailed in the aftermath of the New Deal.

A renewed social vision capable of inspiring majority political support must be honest and hard-hitting, and it must synthesize factual analysis with frank statements about social justice and moral values. Progressives must not fear speaking openly about the uses of public authority and—yes—the need for public revenues to be raised through well-designed taxes. There is no reason why a heartfelt case cannot be made. Governmentally enforced "rules of the game" really *are* necessary to ensure that capitalist markets and private investors contribute to a good society.[11] Taxes really *are* worthwhile, when they pay for the existing or newly designed governmental efforts in which all Americans have a stake. And the United States is not at all an "overtaxed" country.[12] Medicare and Social Security need to be revitalized; new protections for working families should be designed to replace outmoded welfare programs; and government needs to help Americans adapt to a rapidly changing economy through improved education and training. There are many progressive Americans who know that these things are true, and they need to start speaking up and working with one another, much as did conservatives in and around the Republican party back in 1964, after the apparently total defeat of their movement in the Goldwater-Johnson presidential election.

In putting forward his Health Security proposal, President Bill Clinton argued that this new public undertaking could contribute to the achievement of vital social and economic goals. Perhaps the formula the President and his administration devised was not exactly the right one. But it was America's loss that the civic conversation the proposal for Health Security might have started never did take place. Those who believe that governmentally mediated reform has a vital role to play in health care and beyond did not make their case forcefully enough. The national conversation was dominated by those who saw political advantage in using Health Security as one more occasion for attacking government.

There is room for much argument about what appropriate governmental efforts are or should be, as a changing America enters a new century. Many things need to be done not by government alone but through *partnerships* of national, state, and local governments with families, communities, and businesses. It will not do, however, to pretend that Americans do not need government. Americans needed and enormously benefited from federal government activities in the past, and all Americans together need revitalized and refocused government endeavors in the coming century as well.

NOTES

Introduction

1. Quotes from the President's speech come from the prepared text, as reprinted in Erik Eckholm, ed., *Solving America's Health-Care Crisis* (New York: Times Books, Random House, 1993), pp. 301–14.
2. According to Paul Starr, "What Happened to Health Care Reform?," *American Prospect*, no. 20 (Winter 1995): 20, the morning after the President's speech, "Stanley Greenberg, the President's pollster, crowed that the overnight surveys showed we were winning two-thirds approval." See also Daniel Yankelovich, "The Debate That Wasn't: The Public and the Clinton Plan," *Health Affairs* 14, no. 1 (Spring 1995), p. 11.
3. William Schneider, "Health Reform: What Went Right?" *National Journal*, October 2, 1993: 2404. This piece by Schneider bears close comparison to the summer 1994 retrospective analysis of health reform failure cited below in note 15. Like many pundits, Schneider cited almost exactly parallel explanations for "success" and "failure," shifting according to the winds of public opinion and other journalistic commentary at the moments he wrote.
4. Adam Clymer, "The Clinton Plan is Alive on Arrival," *New York Times*, Sunday, October 3, 1993, p. E3. All quotes in this paragraph are from this article.
5. Hilary Stout and David Rogers, "Outline of Compromise Is Dimly Discernible as Clinton Offers Plan," *Wall Street Journal*, September 23, 1993, pp. A1, A8.
6. *Contract with America: The Bold Plan by Rep. Newt Gingrich, Rep. Dick Armey, and the House Republicans to Change the Nation*, eds. Ed Gillespie and Bob Shellhas (New York: Times Books, Random House, 1994).
7. "National Election Night Survey" (Menlo Park, Calif.: Henry J. Kaiser Family Foundation, November 15, 1994, news release).
8. For the outlook from which current initiatives flow, see Newt Gingrich, *Window of Opportunity: A Blueprint for the Future* (New York: Doherty, 1984), especially chaps. 4–6. This book is similar to, yet also franker than, Newt Gingrich, *To Renew America* (New York: HarperCollins, 1995).
9. Jill Zuckman, "Gingrich Declares War on Social Programs," *Boston Globe*, Saturday, November 12, 1994, pp. 1, 6.

10. Robin Toner, "Gingrich Promises Medicare Tough Look, Bottom to Top," *New York Times*, Tuesday, January 31, 1995, pp. 1, A14.

11. Initially, Speaker Gingrich promised to leave Social Security alone for at least six years, but by March 24, 1994, he was declaring (on the CNN television program "Larry King Live") that he and his fellow Republicans would begin to revise Social Security after only two years.

12. Robin Toner, "Health Impasse Sours Voters, New Poll Finds," *New York Times*, Tuesday, September 13, 1994, pp. A1, A18. For additional detail on all the points in this paragraph, see Everett Carl Ladd, ed., *America at the Polls, 1994* (Storrs: Roper Center for Public Opinion Research, 1994), especially pp. 32–35, 38.

13. Stanley B. Greenberg, *Middle Class Dreams: The Politics and Power of the New American Majority* (New York: Times Books, Random House, 1995), p. 263.

14. Polling and focus group data supporting this appear in Stanley B. Greenberg, Al From, Will Marshall, and Tom Mirga, *Third Force: Why Independents Turned Against Democrats—and How to Win Them Back* (Washington, D.C.: Democratic Leadership Council, November 1994).

15. William Schneider, "Why Health-Care Reform May Be Beyond Saving," *Los Angeles Times*, August 14, 1994, pp. M1, M6. Schneider also claims in this piece that the public opposed Health Security as a "typical Democratic social-welfare program . . . that helps the poor." But there is no evidence that most Americans ever opposed universal coverage, or the extension of health insurance to the currently uninsured, most of whom are in low-wage working families. The Kaiser Family Foundation poll referenced in the next note documents, moreover, that strong popular support for extending coverage to the uninsured remained in place through the November 1994 election. U.S. elites tend to oppose universal coverage (as a "costly entitlement"), but the vast majority of ordinary Americans strongly favor it. Most Americans do not see health care as an optional consumer good. They see it as an ethical social good.

16. "National Election Night Survey," Henry J. Kaiser Family Foundation. On the issue of Americans' worries about being "worse off" if Democratic health care reforms had passed, see also Schneider, "Beyond Saving," p. M6. The Kaiser Foundation investigates health and social welfare issues, and has supported governmental health insurance reforms, including the Clinton plan.

17. "Total Quality Madness," *New Republic*, October 3, 1994, p. 7.

18. Ibid. In this piece, Magaziner is ridiculed as "comic" and Hillary Clinton is called "a tragic figure." The failed Clinton health plan is characterized as "Rodhamism," not "Clintonism." For background on Magaziner written before the failure of the reform effort, see Robert Pear, "An Idealist's New Task: To Revamp Health Care," *New York Times*, Friday, February 26, 1993, p. A14.

19. Schneider, "Beyond Saving."

20. Bob Woodward, *The Agenda: Inside the Clinton White House* (New York: Simon & Schuster, 1994), and Elizabeth Drew, *On the Edge: The Clinton Presidency* (New York: Simon & Schuster, 1994).

21. Bob Blendon, "The Gridlock Is Us," *New York Times*, Sunday, May 22, 1994, Op-Ed, p. E15.

22. Joshua M. Wiener, "What Killed Health Care Reform," *Brookings Review*, Winter 1995: 46.

23. Robert J. Blendon, Mollyann Brodie, Tracey Stelzer Hyams, John M. Benson,

"The American Public and the Critical Choices for Health System Reform," *Journal of the American Medical Association* 271, no. 19 (May 18, 1994), p. 1539. On the fact that Americans tend to support universal or extended health insurance coverage out of social concern as well as self-interest, see Mark Schlesinger and Tae-ku Lee, "Is Health Care Different? Popular Support of Federal Health and Social Policies," *Journal of Health Politics, Policy and Law* 18, no. 3 (Fall 1993), especially pp. 578–86; Lawrence R. Jacobs and Robert Y. Shapiro, "Public Opinion's Tilt Against Private Enterprise," *Health Affairs*, Spring, 1, 1994): 285–98; and Robert Y. Shapiro, Lawrence R. Jacobs, and Lynn K. Harvey, "Influences on Public Opinion Toward Health Care Policy: Self-Interest and Collective Concern" (Department of Political Science, School of International and Public Affairs, Columbia University, and Department of Political Science, University of Minnesota, 1994, typescript).

24. Robert J. Blendon, Mollyann Brodie, and John M. Benson, "What Happened to Americans' Support of the Clinton Plan," *Health Affairs* 14, no. 2, (Summer 1995), pp. 15–17.

25. For opinion on taxes, see ibid; Lawrence R. Jacobs and Robert Y. Shapiro, "Don't Blame the Public for Failed Health Care Reform," *Journal of Health Politics, Policy and Law* 20, no. 2, (Summer 1995): Table 5, 419; and Gene Koretz, "Americans Would Chip in for Universal Health Coverage," *Business Week*, January 10, 1994, p. 23.

26. This argument is cogently made in Jacobs and Shapiro, "Don't Blame the Public."

27. See the description of the Social Security planning process in Edwin F. Witte, *The Development of the Social Security Act* (Madison: University of Wisconsin Press, 1963).

28. The Social Security planners made many anticipatory concessions to farmers, certain business sectors, and southern congressional representatives, and the Health Security planners (as we shall see) attempted to propitiate big business, elderly lobbies, and key congressional blocs of supporters of single payer reforms or incremental market reforms.

29. For cogent arguments to this effect, see Henry J. Aaron, *Serious and Unstable Condition: Financing America's Health Care* (Washington, D.C.: Brookings Institution, 1991), and Joseph White, *Competing Solutions: American Health Care Proposals and International Experience* (Washington, D.C.: Brookings Institution, 1995).

30. For a "Consumer Choice Plan" that the Heritage Foundation advocated during the 1993–94 health care reform debate, see Stuart M. Butler, "Have It Your Way," *Policy Review* no. 66 (Fall 1993): 54–59. This plan would legally require all Americans to buy insurance, and it would be financed with massive tax subsidies.

31. Mary Ruggie, "The Paradox of Liberal Intervention: Health Policy and the American Welfare State," *American Journal of Sociology* 87, no. 4 (January 1992): 919–44.

32. Lawrence R. Jacobs, "Politics of America's Supply State: Health Reform and Technology," *Health Affairs* 14, no. 2 (Summer 1995): 143–57.

33. Paul Starr, *The Logic of Health Care Reform: Why and How the President's Plan Will Work*, rev. and enl. ed. (New York: Penguin Books, 1994; 1st. ed. 1991), p. 7, citing studies done by the Employee Benefits Research Institute on 1992 census data.

34. Elaborations of such arguments appear in Peter G. Peterson, *Facing Up: How to*

Rescue the Economy from Crushing Debt and Restore the American Dream (New York: Simon & Schuster, 1993), and Ross Perot, *Not for Sale at Any Price: How We Can Save America for Our Children* (New York: Hyperion, 1993). I discuss the Concord Coalition's analysis and influence in "Remaking U.S. Social Policies for the 21st Century," the Conclusion to my *Social Policy in the United States: Future Possibilities in Historical Perspective* (Princeton, N.J.: Princeton University Press, 1995).

35. The best description of the Clinton plan, offered by one of the key people involved in devising it, appears in Paul Starr, *The Logic of Health Care Reform.*

36. For reflection on the paradox, see Lawrence R. Jacobs, "Health Reform Impasse: The Politics of American Ambivalence toward Government," *Journal of Health Politics, Policy and Law,* no. 18 no. 3 (Fall 1993): 629–55.

37. Daniel Yankelovich, "The Debate That Wasn't: The Public and the Clinton Plan," *Health Affairs* 14, no. 1 (Spring 1995), pp. 12–13. Further documentation of this point appears in chapters 1 and 2 of this book.

38. See Figure 1 in chapter 4.

Chapter One

1. On the early episodes, see Ronald L. Numbers, *Almost Persuaded: American Physicians and Compulsory Health Insurance, 1912–1920* (Baltimore: Johns Hopkins Press, 1978); Daniel S. Hirshfield, *The Lost Reform* (Cambridge, Mass.: Harvard University Press, 1970); and Monte M. Poen, *Harry S. Truman versus the Medical Lobby* (Columbia: University of Missouri Press, 1979). For an indication of what the political patterns of these past failures portended for the 1990s effort, see Theda Skocpol, "Is the Time Finally Ripe? Health Insurance Reforms in the 1990s," reprinted as chap. 9 in Theda Skocpol, *Social Policy in the United States: Future Possibilities in Historical Perspective* (Princeton, N.J.: Princeton University Press, 1995). In this 1993 article, I predicted that the 1990s effort would fail in the face of an ideological counterattack for which health reformers would, as repeatedly in the past, not be prepared.

2. Theodore R. Marmor, *The Politics of Medicare* (Chicago: Aldine, 1970).

3. Paul Starr, *The Social Transformation of American Medicine* (New York: Basic Books, 1982), bk., 2, chap. 4.

4. Paul Starr, *The Logic of Health-Care Reform,* 1st ed. (Knoxville, Tenn.: Grand Rounds Press, Whittle Direct Books, 1991), p. 16.

5. Ibid., p. 18.

6. Ibid., p. 24.

7. Ibid., p. 22.

8. Ibid., p. 17.

9. Ibid., p. 19.

10. Robert Wood Johnson Foundation, *Challenges in Health Care: A Chartbook Perspective,* 1991 (Princeton, N.J.: Robert Wood Johnson Foundation, 1991), pp. 102–5.

11. See the discussion in Robert J. Blendon and Karen Donelan, "The 1988 Election: How Important Was Health?" *Health Affairs* 8, no. 3 (1989): 6–15.

12. Steven M. Gillon, "The Travail of the Democrats: Search for a New Majority," in *Democrats and the American Idea: A Bicentennial Appraisal,* ed. Peter B. Kovler (Washington, D.C.: Center for National Policy, 1992), pp. 298–99.

13. Robert J. Blendon and Karen Donelan, "Public Opinion and Efforts to Reform the U.S. Health Care System: Confronting Issues of Cost-Containment and Access to Care," *Stanford Law and Policy Review,* Fall 1991, p. 146.

14. Mary Matalin and James Carville (with Peter Knobler), *All's Fair: Love, War, and Running for President* (New York: Random House, 1994).

15. Employment-related coverage declined every year after 1988, and the loss of coverage would have been worse had not Medicaid expanded during those years. See Laura Summer and Isaac Shapiro, "Trends in Health Insurance Coverage, 1987 to 1993" (Washington, D.C.: Center on Budget and Policy Priorities, 1994), pp. 4–6.

16. Ibid., p. 147.

17. Paul Starr, *The Logic of Health Care Reform,* rev. and enl. ed. (New York: Penguin Books, 1994), p. 5.

18. Sidney Blumenthal, "Populism in Tweeds," *New Republic,* November 25, 1991, p. 10.

19. Ibid.

20. Ibid.

21. From Wofford's June 1, 1991 acceptance speech, as quoted in Mark Shields, "A Pitch to the Middle Class," *Washington Post National Weekly Edition,* November 11–17, 1991, p. 29.

22. Matalin and Carville, *All's Fair,* p. 71.

23. Dale Russakoff, "How Wofford Rode Health Care to Washington," *Washington Post National Weekly Edition,* November 25–December 1, 1991, p. 14.

24. On Thornburgh's mistakes, even more than mentioned here, see Blumenthal, "Populism in Tweeds," pp. 12–15.

25. Matalin and Carville, *All's Fair,* p. 71.

26. The story of the ad appears especially in Russakoff, "How Wofford Rode Health Care," p. 14.

27. The points and quotes in this paragraph come from ibid., pp. 14–15.

28. Ibid., p. 14.

29. Robert J. Blendon, Ulrike S. Szalay, Drew E. Altman, and Gerald Chervinsky, "The 1991 Pennsylvania Senate Race and National Health Insurance," *Journal of American Health Policy* 2, no. 1 (January–February 1992), p. 21.

30. Russakoff, "How Wofford Rode Health Care," p. 14; and Julie Kosterlitz, "Health Care: The Issue for 1992?" *National Journal,* November 16, 1991, p. 2805.

31. Russakoff, "How Wofford Rode Health Care," p. 15, quoting political scientist G. Terry Madonna. Of course, it is also possible that a state with many union members and older people would be a place where the idea of national health care reform was familiar, because the AFL-CIO and the American Association of Retired Persons had been supporting comprehensive reforms for some time. Social scientists often suppose that people support governmental reforms when they "need" them in some economic sense. But it may be more accurate to hypothezize that they support them when they are already accustomed to government programs (such as Medicare) or are members of groups that openly discuss the desirability of governmental social reforms. If this latter interpretation is true, then Pennsylva-

nia in 1991 was *more likely* than most U.S. states to have voters amenable to the aim of national health care reform.

32. Ibid.

33. Ibid., pp. 14–15.

34. Shields, "Pitch to the Middle Class," p. 29.

35. John W. Kingdon, *Agendas, Alternatives, and Public Policies* (Boston: Little, Brown, 1984).

36. Kosterlitz, "Health Care: The Issue for 1992?" *National Journal*, November 16, 1991, p. 2805; emphasis added.

37. Blendon, et al., "Pennsylvania and Health Insurance," p. 24.

38. A list of "Proposals for Universal Health Coverage Introduced in the 102nd Congress Through August 2, 1991, and Selected Recent Bills" appears in Robert J. Blendon, Jennifer Edwards, and Andrew L. Hyams, "Making the Critical Choices," *Journal of the American Medical Association* 267, no. 18 (May 13, 1992), Table 6, pp. 2514–16. See also Mark A. Peterson, "Report from Congress: Momentum toward Health Care Reform in the U.S. Senate," *Journal of Health Politics, Policy and Law* 17, no. 3 (Fall 1992), pp. 553–73.

39. Table 5 in Blendon, Edwards, and Hyams, "Making the Critical Choices," pp. 2512–13, outlines a selection of such proposals.

40. American Medical Association, *Health Access America: The AMA Proposal to Improve Access to Affordable, Quality Health Care* (Chicago: AMA, 1990), as explained in James S. Todd, S. V. Seekins, J. A. Krichbaum, and L. K. Harvey, "Health Access America—Strengthening the U.S. Health Care System," *Journal of the American Medical Association* 265, no. 19 (May 15, 1991), pp. 2503–6.

41. Provisions of such market-oriented plans are listed in Tables 5, 6, and 7 of Blendon, Edwards, and Hyams, "Making the Critical Choices."

42. Robert Pear, "Bush Health Plan Would Be Financed by Medicare Curb," *New York Times*, Monday, February 3, 1992, p. A1. For earlier difficulties in Bush administration efforts to come up with a plan, see Robert Pear, "Agreement on Health Care Eludes Panel," *New York Times*, Tuesday, December 3, 1991, p. B10.

43. George Bush, *The President's Comprehensive Health Reform Program* (Washington, D.C.: The White House, 1992).

44. Bill Gradison, "Statement by the Hon. Bill Gradison Before the House Ways and Means Committee," March 3, 1992 (typescript obtained from Gradison's office), p. 1.

45. Sharon Mcllrath, "Everyone Finds Something to Dislike in Reform Plan," *American Medical News*, February 24, 1992, p. 9.

46. Criticisms are summarized in ibid. and Richard A. Knox, "Health Care Leaps to Top of Political Agenda," *Boston Globe*, Sunday, December 29, 1991, pp. 1, 16. Testimony on the Bush proposals before House and Senate committees in March 1992 is summarized in *Social Insurance Update* (Newsletter of the National Academy of Social Insurance), no. 22 (March 1992), pp. 4–5.

47. See note 50 for a clear statement by Theodore Marmor, and see Rashi Fein, "Health Care Reform," *Scientific American* 267, no. 5 (November 1992): 46–53. Various single-payer plans introduced in Congress are summarized in Blendon, Edwards, and Hyams, "Making the Critical Choices," Tables 5 and 6.

48. K. Grumbach, T. Bodenheimer, D. U. Himmelstein, and S. Woolhandler, "Liberal Benefits, Conservative Spending: The Physicians for a National Health Pro-

gram Proposal," *Journal of the American Medical Association* 265, no. 19 (May 15, 1991), pp. 2549–54.

49. H.R. 1300, "Universal Health Care Act of 1991." For the features of this and other single-payer bills introduced in Congress, see Blendon, Edwards, and Hyams, "Making the Critical Choices," Tables 5 and 6.

50. Theodore R. Marmor and Jerry L. Mashaw, "Canada's Health Insurance and Ours: The Real Lessons, the Big Choices," *American Prospect*, no. 3 (Fall 1990), pp. 18–29.

51. Robert Kerrey, *Health USA Act of 1991* (Washington, D.C.: U.S. Senate, 1991), which is explained in Robert Kerrey, "Why America Will Adopt Comprehensive Health Care Reform," *American Prospect*, no. 6 (Summer 1991), pp. 81–90.

52. An engaging story about Bill Clinton's brief consideration and quick rejection of single payer in November 1991 appears in Tom Hamburger, Ted Marmor, and Jon Meacham, "What the Death of Health Reform Teaches Us About the Press," *Washington Monthly*, November 1994, p. 35. Clinton rejected single payer at that point, and never reconsidered it.

53. For a cogent explication of the approach and its practical rationale, see Ronald Pollack and Phyllis Torda, "The Pragmatic Road Toward National Health Insurance," *American Prospect*, no. 6 (Summer 1991), pp. 92–100.

54. On the Pepper Commission, see Kosterlitz, "Year of Soundbite," p. 182; "A Call for Action: The Pepper Commission, U.S. Bipartisan Commission on Comprehensive Health Care: Final Report, September 1990" (Washington, D.C.: U.S. Government Printing Office, 1990); and the explanation in Senator John D. Rockefeller IV, "A Call for Action: The Pepper Commission's Blueprint for Health Care Reform," *Journal of the American Medical Association* 265, no. 19 (May 15, 1991): 2507–10. On "Health America," see the explanation offered by Senator Edward M. Kennedy the day after he and Senators George Mitchell, Don Riegle, Jay Rockefeller, and others introduced the bill in the Senate: "An Affordable Health Care Plan for All," *Boston Globe*, Thursday, June 6, 1991, p. 21.

55. "Already, Big Business' Health Plan Isn't Feeling So Hot," *Business Week*, November 18, 1991, p. 48. All quotes in this paragraph are from this article.

56. Peterson, "Report from Congress," pp. 570–71.

57. Ibid., pp. 562–63.

58. Julie Kosterlitz, "Democrats Split on Health Bill," *National Journal*, May 16, 1992, pp. 1186–87; and Julie Kosterlitz, "Less Radical Surgery," *National Journal*, September 19, 1992, p. 2150.

59. Blendon, Edwards, and Hyamns, "Making the Critical Choices," p. 2509.

60. Jacobs and Shapiro, "Public Opinion's Tilt", and the discussion of poll results in Julie Kosterlitz, "Dangerous Diagnosis," *National Journal*, January 16, 1993, p. 128. Kosterlitz pointed out that, while the public had general faith in Clinton to control costs and ensure universal access to health care, it did not, as of late 1992, know what his reform plan would be or necessarily support its likely tenets.

61. The plans being discussed in the late winter of 1991–92 and early spring of 1992 by Democratic presidential contenders Bill Clinton, Bob Kerrey, and Paul Tsongas are outlined in Blendon, Edwards, and Hyams, "Making the Critical Choices," Table 4, p. 2511.

62. This comes from the back page of the DLC's magazine, *New Democrat* 7, no. 3 (May 1995).

63. The Clinton synthesis is discussed in Stanley B. Greenberg, *Middle Class Dreams: The Politics and Power of the New American Majority* (New York: Times Books, Random House, 1995), chap. 7.

64. Diane D. Blair, *Arkansas Politics and Government: Do the People Rule?* (Lincoln: University of Nebraska Press, 1988), and Roy Reed, "Progressive Politics in Dogpatch," in *The Clintons of Arkansas*, ed. Ernest Dumas (Fayetteville: University of Arkansas Press, 1993), pp. 148–60.

65. "Announcement Speech," Old State House, Little Rock, Arkansas, October 3, 1991, as reprinted in Governor Bill Clinton and Senator Al Gore, *Putting People First: How We Can All Change America* (New York: Times Books, 1992), p. 193, passim.

66. See "A New Covenant," Governor Bill Clinton, Democratic National Convention, New York City, July 16, 1992, as reprinted in Clinton and Gore, *Putting People First*, pp. 217–32; and Gwen Ifill, "Clinton's Standard Campaign Speech: A Call for Responsibility," *New York Times*, Sunday, April 26, 1992, p. 24.

67. As quoted in Peter Goldman, Thomas M. DeFrank, Mark Miller, Andrew Murr, and Tom Mathews, *Quest for the Presidency 1992* (College Station: Texas A&M University Press, 1994), p. 77.

68. Some background on Carville, Begala, Grunwald, and Greenberg appears in "It's the Money, Stupid," *Business Week*, November 15, 1993, pp. 163–74. (I do not endorse the innuendo in this article that these people have been mainly looking for money in their association with Clinton.)

69. Stanley B. Greenberg, "Reconstructing the Democratic Vision," *American Prospect*, no. 1 (Spring 1990): 82–89. Quotes in this paragraph come from pp. 86, 87, passim. For a full statement of Greenberg's analysis of contemporary U.S. politics and the dilemmas faced by the Democratic Party, see his *Middle Class Dreams*.

70. Personal communication from Stan Greenberg.

71. Bill Clinton for President Committee, "Bill Clinton's American Health Care Plan: National Insurance Reform to Cut Costs and Cover Everybody" (n.d., typescript), p. 7. I received my copy of this from Clinton's Little Rock campaign headquarters in April 1992.

72. "Bill Clinton's American Health Care Plan," p. 2.

73. Robert Pear, "Two in Bush Cabinet Attack Democrats on Health Care," *New York Times*, January 29, 1992, p. A12.

74. The story of the working out of this "message" is told in Goldman et al., *Quest for the Presidency 1992*, part II, especially chaps. 12 and 13. My account of Clinton's embrace of inclusive managed competition during the campaign draws insights from chap. 4 of Jacob Stewart Hacker, "Setting the Health Reform Agenda: The Ascendance of Managed Competition" (senior honors thesis, Harvard College, Committee on Degrees in Social Studies, November 1993), which is now being revised into a book to be published by Princeton University Press.

75. Published in fall 1992 as Clinton and Gore, *Putting People First*.

76. This discussion draws from Jacob Hacker's senior thesis and forthcoming book.

77. Clinton and Gore, *Putting People First*, pp. 107–10. See also another statement finished in July: Bill Clinton, "The Clinton Health Care Plan," *New England Journal of Medicine* 327, no. 11 (September 10, 1992): 804–7, followed by experts' assessments on pages 807–11.

78. Greenberg, *Middle Class Dreams*, pp. 195–96.

79. These and other originally confidential campaign memos are selected and reprinted in Goldman et al., *Quest for the Presidency 1992*, "Appendix: The Campaign Papers." The specific quotes here are from Greenberg, "The Centrality of Reassurance," p. 707, and "We Have No Right Losing Ground," p. 714.

80. Stanley Greenberg and Celinda Lake, "Take the Battle to Bush," in Goldman et al., *Quest for the Presidency 1992*, p. 711.

81. The *Times'* editorial campaign on health reform is discussed in Hacker, "Setting the Agenda," pp. 62–67; and Julie Kosterlitz, "The Times's Prescription," *National Journal*, January 9, 1993: 82–83.

82. Alain Enthoven and Richard Kronick, "A Consumer Choice Plan for the 1990s," *New England Journal of Medicine* 320, no. 1 (January 5, 1989): 29–37; 320, no. 2 (January 12, 1989): 94–101. See also Dana Priest, "A Primer on Managed Competition," *Washington Post National Weekly Edition*, March 15–21, 1993, p. 33.

83. Julie Kosterlitz, "A Sick System," *National Journal*, February 15, 1992, pp. 377, 379.

84. Ibid. and Kosterlitz, "Less Radical Surgery." The Tsongas plan, called "Health For All Americans Plan," was detailed in statements from the Tsongas Committee, Boston, Mass., 1992.

85. Key criticisms are summarized in Priest, "Primer."

86. For the full story of the emergence of what Hacker calls the "liberal synthesis" version of managed competition, see Hacker, "Setting the Agenda," chap. 3, as well as the fascinating Preface to Paul Starr, *The Logic of Health Care Reform*, rev. ed. Starr's book also does the best job I know of explaining the mechanism and logic of inclusive managed competition. Another excellent discussion of different varieties of managed competition is to be found in Joseph White, *Competing Solutions: American Health Care Proposals and International Experience* (Washington, D.C.: Brookings Institution, 1995), chaps. 7–9.

87. See "California Health Care in the 21st Century: A Vision for Reform," (John Garamendi, Insurance Commissioner of California, February 1992, typescript).

88. All quotations come from "Remarks by Governor Bill Clinton (D-AR) at Merck Pharmaceuticals, Rahway, New Jersey Concerning Health Care," Thursday, September 24, 1992, Federal News Service, Federal Information Systems Corporation, 1992.

89. Robert J. Blendon, Tracey Stelzer Hyams, and John M. Benson, "Bridging the Gap Between Expert and Public Views on Health Care Reform," *Journal of the American Medical Association* 269, no. 19 (May 19, 1993), pp. 2573–78.

90. See Goldman et al., *Quest for the Presidency 1992*, p. 715; and Greenberg, *Middle Class Dreams*, p. 267.

Chapter Two

1. *Health Security Act* (Washington, D.C.: Government Printing Office, 1993).

2. This budget story is featured in Bob Woodward, *The Agenda: Inside the Clinton White House* (New York: Simon & Schuster, 1993).

3. Julie Kosterlitz, "OK, Bill, It's Time to Pick Your Remedy," *National Journal*, January 23, 1993, pp. 200–1.

4. Ira C. Magaziner, "Preliminary Work Plan for Interagency Health Care Task Force," The White House, January 25, 1993, p. 5.

5. Ibid.

6. Ibid., p. 13.

7. Ibid.

8. This position was taken, after the fact, by former chairman of the House Ways and Means Committee Representative Dan Rostenkowski, "Rostenkowski Analyzes Health Reform Failure," speech prepared for delivery at the Harvard School of Public Health, December 5, 1994.

9. People who believe that big-business support was the key to successful moderate national health care reforms tend to take this point of view. See, for example, John B. Judis, "Abandoned Surgery: Business and the Failure of Health Care Reform," *American Prospect* no. 21 (Spring 1995), p. 72.

10. This point is made in Robert D. Reischauer, "Lessons from the Health Reform Debate," Maxwell School, Syracuse University, October 7, 1994, pp. 18–19. As then head of the Congressional Budget Office, Reischauer found that many of the alternatives to the Clinton plan hastily worked out in Congress during 1994 were not technically coherent because "health staffs of Congress . . . lack the breadth and depth of expertise found in the Executive branch."

11. For example, according to Ira Magaziner (interview of March 1, 1995), in the spring of 1993 Clinton administration policy planners approached moderate Republican Senator John Chafee of Rhode Island about the possibility of collaborating on a health care reform bill. But Chafe preferred to propose a separate bill, and then ultimately compromise in Congress. According to Magaziner, conservative Democrats such as Representative Jim Cooper of Tennessee and Senator John Breaux of Louisiana took the same stance. While I have not checked this out with the senators and representatives involved, it makes sense, given the way credit claiming works in U.S. politics. Why would key players in Congress want to join the administration effort from the start, when they could visibly claim credit for "improving" the final version of health care reform by hanging back first and compromising later? After-the-fact commentators wish the compromise had been made from the start, but they may be imagining incentives for up-front bargaining that do not exist, institutionally speaking, in U.S. politics.

12. Robert H. Salisbury, "Why No Corporatism in America?, in *Trends Toward Corporatist Intermediation*, eds. Philippe C. Schmitter and Gerhard Lehmbruch (Beverly Hills, Calif.: Sage Publications, 1972), pp. 213–30.

13. Center for Public Integrity, *Well-Healed: Inside Lobbying for Health Care Reform* (Washington, D.C.: Center for Public Integrity, 1994), p. 53. In 1965, when Medicare was debated, the AMA enlisted about 65 percent of U.S. physicians. In the early 1990s, the AMA remained the largest single medical association. But in due course, ten other groups with a combined membership surpassing the AMA would endorse the Clinton Health Security plan, while the smaller American College of Surgeons endorsed a single-payer approach. See Robert Pear, "10 Doctors' Groups Endorse Clinton's Health Plan," *New York Times*, Friday, December 17, 1993, p. A26; and Julie Kosterlitz, "Stress Fractures," *National Journal*, February 19, 1994, p. 414.

14. After a law is passed, moreover, there are many ways in which it can be interpreted during implementation. Groups contending over enactments tend to know that — another thing that makes up-front binding bargains difficult to devise.

15. Diane D. Blair, *Arkansas Politics and Government* (Lincoln: University of Nebraska Press, 1988), pp. 260–61.

16. Discussion with the First Lady and a staff person on July 21, 1995. See also President Clinton's characterization of the First Lady's role in his September 22, 1993 speech launching Health Security.

17. "Town meetings" held by the First Lady could receive very warm and detailed coverage in the local press. See, for example, the coverage of the First Lady's visit to Maine in the *Bar Harbor Times*, February 10, 1994. In addition to a news article on pp. A1 and A11, Mrs. Clinton's February 7 substantial speech at the University of Maine at Orono was reprinted in its entirety, consuming several pages of this weekly newspaper.

18. Quoted from Office of the Press Secretary, the White House, "Address by the President to the Joint Session of Congress," February 17, 1993.

19. Kaiser-Harris poll of March 11, 1993.

20. *U.S. News and World Report* poll of April 21, 1993 (Storrs, Con.: Roper Center for Public Opinion Research, 1993).

21. Interviews on March 1 and May 3, 1995, with Ira Magaziner, who has letters detailing the kinds of compromises that stakeholder groups were willing to make when it looked as if President Clinton had enormous public support for health care reform.

22. In chapter 3, I discuss the worries that task-force leaders had from early in 1993 about the timing of getting reforms through Congress. Still, public expectations for the administration to devise an initiative *were* high in 1993. My point here is that these high public expectations bolstered the will to proceed with a presidentially controlled planning process.

23. Paul Starr, *The Logic of Health Care Reform*, rev. and enl. ed. (New York: Whittle Books in association with Penguin Books, 1994), pp. xxix, xxx. Of course, the model of a top-down corporate restructuring was not a very good one for designing a proposal that had to make its way through the U.S. legislative system! When chief executives in a corporation hire an outside consultant to design changes, those executives have the potential authority to impose the new design from above. But no U.S. president—still less one elected by 43 percent of the vote—has anything like that kind of authority. To be fair, I am convinced from talking to him and reading his 1993 memos that Magaziner knew the Task Force on Health Care Reform was doing a different kind of planning. He tried to envisage all sorts of compromise changes that could be made in the proposal as it worked its way through Congress. But there were nevertheless inescapable contradictions between an omnibus, policy planning effort centered inside the executive branch and the utterly unmanageable political processes through which the Clinton proposal would have to pass on the way to becoming legislation.

24. Ibid., p. xxx.

25. Ibid., pp. xxx–xxxi.

26. According to the *National Journal*, June 26, 1993, p. 1657, the "White House has said that the working groups were made up of 412 federal employees, 82 'special' or 'temporary' employees and 17 'consultants.'"

27. Magaziner, "Work Plan," p. 13.

28. Julie Kosterlitz, "The Big Sell," *National Journal*, May 14, 1994, p. 1120. I am not

endorsing the truth of these claims by lobbyists, just pointing out that, whether sincerely made or not, such retrospective claims were very likely in the wake of informal task-force consultations with stakeholders. The structure of the situation invited such claims.

29. Interviews with Ira Magaziner on March 1 and May 3, 1995.

30. To this day, as I can attest from conversations, Ira Magaziner can explain in detail the logic—both technical and political—of every single step the Clinton policy planners took. He understandably feels as he did in August 1993, when he wrote in an internal memo: "Our strongest asset may be the merits of our case. . . . [A]n unprecedented national discussion will reveal that we have the best policy. The more people understand it, the more supportive they will be." This appeared in Ira C. Magaziner, Walter Zelman, and Lynn Margherio, Memorandum to the President and Hillary Rodham Clinton on "Positioning of September Health Reform Introduction," August 30, 1993, p. 3. In the wake of the defeat of Health Security, commentators have labeled this attitude of Magaziner's "arrogant." I think it makes more sense to see that people asked to do a huge policy plan would naturally think their work made sense and want to explain it to others. Magaziner's chief error may have been his supposition that there would be "an unprecedented national discussion" of the Clinton proposal, as opposed to a war of stereotypes and symbols. Politics is never simply, or mainly, a "discussion!"

31. Interview with Ira Magaziner, March 1, 1995.

32. This was published as The White House Domestic Policy Council, *The President's Health Security Plan*, with an introduction by Erik Eckholm (New York: Times Books, Random House, 1993). Modifications were introduced before the final version of the Health Security bill appeared in late October, but this September 7 draft received wide circulation, and can be considered the product of the task-force planning process launched in January 1993.

33. Julie Kosterlitz, "Middle-of-the-Road Vehicle," *National Journal*, September 18, 1993: 2274.

34. Ibid.

35. Choices that had to be made within the overall rubric of "managed competition" are clearly spelled out in John Judis, "Whose Managed Competition?" *New Republic*, March 29, 1993: 20–24; and Julie Kosterlitz, "Encrypted Signals," *National Journal*, May 1, 1993: 1030–34. I draw on these overviews in the following discussion.

36. Joe White has pointed out to me that during the debate over Health Security, Enthoven moved toward the Cooper position. See Enthoven's critique of the Clinton plan in Alain C. Enthoven and Sara J. Singer, "A Single-Payer System in Jackson Hole Clothing," *Health Affairs* 13, no. 1 [Spring (I) 1994]: 81–95. By 1995, moreover, once Clinton's approach to universal coverage had definitively failed, Enthoven and the Jackson Hole group easily jettisoned their earlier call for an employer mandate to allow such coverage. See Paul M. Ellwood and Alain C. Enthoven, " 'Responsible Choices': The Jackson Hole Group Plan for Health Reform," *Health Affairs* 14, no. 2 (Summer 1995): 24–39. To me, this latest revision suggests that the Jackson Hole group has been, all along, not truly committed to covering all Americans, but instead has been primarily concerned with promoting insurance-company-run managed care through laws that will, as Ellwood and

Enthoven put it (p. 39), "accelerate the reforms already taking place in the market."

37. Starr, *Logic of Reform*, pp. 87–90, cogently explains why Cooper-type reform provisions, especially small and purely voluntary alliances, probably would have backfired in practice, fueling ever rising costs without spreading coverage to many small businesses or uninsured people. For further analysis of the internal contradictions of the Cooper approach, see Joseph White, *Competing Solutions* (Washington, D.C.: Brookings Institution, 1995), chap. 8; and Congressional Budget Office, "An Analysis of the Managed Competition Act" (Washington, D.C.: Government Printing Office, May 4, 1994).

38. Woodward, *The Agenda*, p. 316. Memos written by Ira Magaziner and his staff over the course of the summer seem to have been trying to stave off death by delay for health care reform.

39. An important example of such a "recapture" provision was a proposed 1 percent "payroll assessment" on those very large employers who chose to form their own "corporate alliances" and thus stay out of the regional alliances. The purpose of this according to Walter A. Zelman, "The Rationale behind the Clinton Health Reform Plan," *Health Affairs* 13, no. 1 [Spring (I) 1994], p. 26, was so that these corporate alliances would "contribute their share to academic medical centers and to support more needy and higher-cost individuals insured in regional alliances."

40. Judis, "Business and Failure of Reform," p. 67; and interview with Ira Magaziner, May 3, 1995.

41. Interview with Ira Magaziner, May 3, 1995.

42. Interview with Ira Magaziner, May 3, 1995.

43. Starr, *Logic of Reform*, p. 74.

44. Good explanations of the reasons for encompassing alliances appear in Starr, *Logic of Reform*, pp. 85–90, and Zelman, "Rationale," pp. 17–19. As Zelman explains, cutoffs for the alliances at one hundred employees, such as proposed by Cooper, would encourage two tiers in the insurance market, decrease insurance portability for employees, greatly increase administrative complexity for medium and small companies, and necessitate—in the end—more rather than less government regulation. This latter point, I think, never was made clearly in the national discussions of 1993–94. Supporters of much smaller purchasing cooperatives always proclaimed that they were taking a "less bureaucratic" route, and they were never challenged on the accuracy of their claims.

45. See above all the excellent discussion of budgetary constraints and procedures in Joseph White, "Budgeting and Health Policy Making," in *How Congress Shapes Health Policy*, eds. Thomas E. Mann and Norman Ornstein (Washington, D.C.: Brookings Institution, 1995), chap. 3. Also of great interest are White, *Competing Solutions*, pp. 200–2; Allen Schick, *The Federal Budget: Politics, Policy, Process* (Washington, D.C.: Brookings Institution, 1995); Viveca Novak, "By the Numbers," *National Journal*, February 12, 1994: 348–52; and Linda T. Bilheimer and Robert D. Reischauer, "Confessions of the Estimators: Numbers and Health Reform," *Health Affairs* 14, no. 1 (Spring 1995): 37–55.

46. In my *Protecting Soldiers and Mothers: The Political Origins of Social Policy in the United States* (Cambridge, Mass.: Belknap Press of Harvard University Press, 1992), chap. 7, I discuss reformers' (often unavailing) efforts to anticipate and get around

court objections to maximum-hours and minimum-wage legislation during the early 1900s. New Dealers who devised plans for both Social Security and the Wagner National Labor Relations Act also tried to anticipate what the U.S. Supreme Court would ultimately accept.

47. It is important to realize that, in practice, the CBO's decisions have more weight against, than for, social policy proposals. If a proposal doesn't "cost out," it may die, especially if it is in a politically tenuous position anyway. (If such a failed proposal is popular in Congress, it may simply be changed to do better with the CBO rules.) On the other hand, an idea that is very cost-effective according to CBO scoring may not get anywhere anyway if it steps on politically powerful toes. Thus the CBO gave a very positive "scoring" to single-payer health legislation sponsored by Representative Jim McDermott (Democrat of Washington) and Senator Paul Wellstone (Democrat of Minnesota). But the mere fact that their approach would save the people of the United States a lot of money, more than enough to ensure health coverage for all, was not enough to make this approach politically viable in Congress (or inside the Clinton administration).

48. Congressional Budget Office, "An Analysis of the Administration's Health Proposal: A CBO Study" (Washington, D.C.: Government Printing Office, February 1994).

49. See especially Congressional Budget Office, "Managed Competition and Its Potential to Reduce Health Spending: A CBO Study" (Washington, D.C.: Government Printing Office, May 1993).

50. See CBO, "Analysis of the Managed Competition Act."

51. Starr, *Logic of Reform*, chap. 5, pp. 85–90.

52. See CBO, "Managed Competition and Its Potential," for a discussion of regulatory features that such plans needed to have if they were to promote extended coverage and reduced costs. Among the desirable features (pp. 14–15) were encompassing Health Insurance Purchasing Cooperatives that would "establish a single insurance pool for each region" of the country.

53. Interview with Ira Magaziner, May 3, 1995. According to Magaziner, the President would often ask if there were such moderate legislative precedents for particular features of the emerging Health Security bill, because if possible, he was looking for ways to be and seem bipartisan.

54. Kosterlitz, "Middle-of-the-Road Vehicle." This one-page overview of the Health Security plan is the best brief characterization available. For an excellent full discussion, see White, *Competing Solutions*, chap. 9.

Chapter Three

1. In addition to Table 1, see Robert J. Blendon, "What Happened to Americans' Support of the Clinton Plan?" *Health Affairs* 14, no. 2 (Summer 1995), pp. 9–11; and Karlyn H. Bowman, *The 1993–1994 Debate on Health Care Reform: Did the Polls Mislead the Policy Makers?* (Washington, D.C.: American Enterprise Institute, 1994), pp. 32–33, Table 21.

2. Media concentration on the arcane Whitewater scandal made things worse in late 1993 and early 1994, because trust in President Clinton and Hillary Clinton was undercut and everyone was distracted from rational discussion of health care

reform (on this point, see Kathleen Hall Jamieson, "Health Care Drowns in Whitewater," *Philadelphia Inquirer*, Saturday, April 9, 1994). But I do not believe that Whitewater was the principal cause of the erosion of public faith in the Health Security plan.

3. Douglas Jehl, "Clinton Opens Major Push to Sell His Health Program," *New York Times*, Wednesday, April 6, 1994, p. A18; and Julie Kosterlitz, "The Big Sell," *National Journal*, May 14, 1994, p. 118–23.

4. I am referring to the visits recorded in the October 3 *New York Times* article cited at the beginning of this book.

5. William Schneider, "Health Care Reform: What Went Right?" *National Journal*, October 2, 1993, p. 2404.

6. Interview with Ira Magaziner, March 1, 1995. See also the plan for "Media/Message and Introduction of Health Reform," memorandum from Bob Boorstin to Ira Magaziner of July 1, 1993.

7. Elizabeth Drew, *On the Edge: The Clinton Presidency* (New York: Simon & Schuster, 1994), pp. 310–11; and Office of the Press Secretary, the White House, "Remarks by the President and the First Lady on Delivering the 'Health Security Act of 1993' to Congress," Statuary Hall, U.S. Capitol, Washington, D.C., October 27, 1993.

8. Office of the Press Secretary, the White House, "State of the Union Address by the President" (Washington, D.C., January 25, 1994, typescript), p. 8.

9. Ibid.

10. Gwen Ifill, "Clinton Campaigns Hard for Health Plan as 'Outsider,'" *New York Times*, Sunday, April 10, 1994, p. 33.

11. Charles O. Jones, *The Presidency in a Separated System* (Washington, D.C.: Brookings Institution, 1994), chap. 5.

12. Drew, *On the Edge*, chap. 24.

13. Ibid., chap. 25.

14. Ibid., chap. 22. An alternative might have been to seek revisions of the treaty and put off pushing for congressional approval until 1994.

15. Bob Woodward, *The Agenda* (New York: Simon & Schuster, 1994), pp. 318–19.

16. Heartfelt arguments, which were very prescient about how delays might kill the opportunity for national health care reform, appear in "Health Reform and the Economic Package," memorandum from Ira Magaziner to the President and First Lady, March 7, 1993.

17. Speaking through James Fallows in "Triumph of Misinformation," *Atlantic Monthly* 275, no. 1 (January 1995): 26–37, Hillary Rodham Clinton and Ira Magaziner acknowledged that regular conversations should have taken place with members of the press during the task force's deliberations. The White House's decision not to allow "inside briefings" of the sort that elite Washington-based reporters tend to expect invited charges of arrogance and secrecy and made it that much harder for reporters to gain an understanding of the inner logic of the intricate Clinton Health Security proposal.

18. For example, Paul Starr spent time in the summer of 1993 preparing a rationale statement about the contents of the Health Security plan. This could have been used to explain the plan to educated elites in the media, academia, and private-sector institutions. But Starr's statement was never used for its arguably crucial educational purpose. American opinion leaders would of course not have all

agreed that the Clinton Health Security plan was desirable. But the quality of the public debates that started abruptly in September would certainly have been better if more educated Americans in leadership positions had at least *understood* the Clinton plan!

19. Ira C. Magaziner, "Health Reform Timing," memorandum to Mack McLarty, David Gergen, and George Stephanopoulos, July 22, 1993, p. 1.

20. Drew, *On the Edge*, p. 309.

21. Starr, "What Happened to Health Care Reform?" *American Prospect*, no. 20 (Winter 1995), p. 25.

22. Ruy A. Teixeira, *The Disappearing American Voter* (Washington, D.C.: Brookings Institution, 1993), and Larry J. Sabato, *The Rise of Political Consultants: New Ways of Winning Elections* (New York: Basic Books, 1981). Excellent overviews of recent trends appear in Richard M. Valelly, "Vanishing Voters," *American Prospect*, no. 1 (Spring 1990), pp. 140–50; and Marshall Ganz, "Voters in the Cross Hairs: How Technology and the Market are Destroying Politics," *American Prospect*, no. 16 (Winter 1994), pp. 100–109. Both are reprinted in *The American Prospect Reader in American Politics*, ed. Walter Dean Burnham (Chatham, N.J.: Chatham House, 1995).

23. See, for example, the telling portrayal in Robert Dreyfuss, "How Money Votes: An Oklahoma Story," *American Prospect*, no. 19 (Fall 1994), pp. 42–57.

24. Richard Freeman, ed., *Working Under Different Rules* (New York: Russell Sage Foundation, 1994), p. 16.

25. J. David Greenstone, *Labor in American Politics* (New York: Knopf, 1969); and James C. Foster, *The Union Politic: The CIO Political Action Committee* (Columbia: University of Missouri Press, 1975).

26. For an organizationally grounded discussion of the New Deal Democratic coalition, see David R. Mayhew, *Placing Parties in American Politics* (Princeton, N.J.: Princeton University Press, 1986), chap. 11.

27. Margaret Weir and Theda Skocpol, "State Structures and the Possibilities for 'Keynesian' Responses to the Great Depression in Sweden, Britain, and the United States," in *Bringing the State Back In*, eds. Peter Evans, Dietrich Rueschemeyer, and Theda Skocpol (Cambridge and New York: Cambridge University Press, 1985), pp. 107–63; and Theda Skocpol, *Social Policy in the United States: Future Possibilities in Historical Perspective* (Princeton, N.J.: Princeton University Press, 1995), chaps. 5–7.

28. Theodore R. Marmor, *The Politics of Medicare* (Chicago: Aldine, 1970).

29. For an overview, see Thomas Byrne Edsall and Mary D. Edsall, *Chain Reaction: The Impact of Race, Rights, and Taxes on American Politics* (New York: Norton, 1991).

30. John B. Judis, "The Pressure Elite: Inside the Narrow World of Advocacy Group Politics," *American Prospect*, no. 9 (Spring 1992), as reprinted in *The American Prospect Reader in American Politics*, Burnham, p. 257.

31. Karen Paget, "Citizen Organizing: Many Movements, No Majority," *American Prospect*, no. 2 (Summer 1990), as reprinted in *The American Prospect Reader in American Politics*, Burnham, p. 241.

32. Ibid. The AARP has since grown still larger.

33. Center for Public Integrity, *Well-Healed: Inside Lobbying for Health Care Reform* (Washington, D.C.: Center for Public Integrity, 1994), p. 67.

34. Ibid.

35. Robert D. Putnam, "Bowling Alone: Democracy in America at the End of the Twentieth Century," (Harvard University, Cambridge, Mass., March 1995, typescript).

36. Paget, "Citizen Organizing," pp. 250–51.

37. Paget, "Many Movements, No Majority," pp. 249–50.

38. Freeman, *Different Rules*, pp. 16–17.

39. "Media/Message and the Introduction of Health Reform," memorandum from Bob Boorstin to Ira Magaziner, July 21, 1993; "Positioning of September Health Reform Introduction," memorandum for the President and Hillary Rodham Clinton from Ira C. Magaziner, Walter Zelman, and Lynn Margherio, August 30, 1993; and a huge "Strategy" book prepared for the President starting in September 1993 (with sections added throughout the fall).

40. The DNC effort and intraparty criticisms of it are discussed in Center for Public Integrity, *Well-Healed*, pp. 64–65.

41. Julie Kosterlitz, "Once a Health Plan is Unveiled, What Then?" *National Journal*, May 29, 1993, p. 1299; and Julie Kosterlitz, "The Democratic Steamroller That Wasn't," a special box inserted in "The Big Sell," *National Journal*, May 14, 1994, p. 1122.

42. Kosterlitz, "Steamroller That Wasn't," and a January 1995 telephone interview with Heather Booth at the Democratic National Committee.

43. Kosterlitz, "Steamroller That Wasn't," p. 1122.

44. Ibid.

45. Ibid; and Heather Booth interview. A decision was apparently made to devote further DNC efforts to television advertising, rather than grassroots mobilization — a decision which may have prompted Celeste's departure. See Center for Public Integrity, *Well-Healed*, p. 65.

46. Center for Public Integrity, *Well-Healed*, p. 65.

47. See the ad cosponsored by the AARP, the AMA, and the AFL-CIO, which appeared in the *Washington Post* and other papers on July 21, 1994. The ad endorsed "universal coverage with a standard set of comprehensive health benefits for every American," to be attained "by building on our current employment-based system . . . with a required level of employer contributions." It also supported the right of patients to "choose from a wide range of physicians and health plans" and reliance on "governmental and market forces" to control increases in health costs.

48. Douglas Jehl, "Clintons Asking Elderly to Support Health Plan," *New York Times*, Thursday, February 17, 1994, p. A20; and Robert Pear, "Clinton Fails to Get Endorsement of Elderly Group on Health Plan," *New York Times*, Friday, February 25, 1994, pp. A1, A15.

49. As quoted in Pear, "Clinton Fails," p. A1.

50. Ibid., p. A15.

51. Center for Public Integrity, *Well-Healed*, p. 67.

52. Interviews with Ira Magaziner of March 1 and May 3, 1995.

53. Pear, "Clinton Fails"; personal communication from Stan Greenberg; and Blendon, Brodie, and Benson, "What Happened?" Exhibit 1, p. 10, which shows that support for the Clinton plan among those sixty-five and over dropped from 62 percent approval in September 1993 to only 37 percent approval in April 1994.

54. Pear, "Clinton Fails to Get Endorsement," p. A1.

55. Personal communication from Stan Greenberg, July 27, 1995. Greenberg Research did focus groups to document the confusing effects of the AARP ads. According to Greenberg, the results were shown to the AARP staff, which replicated them in its own research. No matter, the AARP still did not change its ads to an outright endorsement of the President's proposals.

56. Center for Public Integrity, *Well-Healed*, p. 54.

57. Robert Pear, "10 Doctors' Groups Endorse Clinton's Health Plan," *New York Times*, Friday, December 17, 1993, p. A26.

58. "Interest Group Positioning," memorandum from Mike Lux to President Clinton, December 15, 1993, p. 1.

59. Ibid., p. 3.

60. Ibid.

61. Ibid., p. 4.

62. Center for Public Integrity, *Well-Healed*, p. 73.

63. In order, my examples of the following three ads appeared in *New Republic* on March 7, 1994, p. 15; March 21, 1994, inside the front cover; and April 18, 1994, p. 8.

64. The full-page ad was on p. A13.

65. Hilary Stout, "Many Don't Realize It's the Clinton Plan They Like," *Wall Street Journal*, Thursday, March 10, 1994, pp. B1, B6.

66. Reformers in the Clinton administration always expected that this is what would happen in Congress. Indeed, I think it is fair to say that, as of late 1993, just about everyone in America expected that Congress would work out some sort of modified version of Health Security or a substitute for it.

67. Robin Toner, "Images and Action Weighed at Democrats' Retreat," *New York Times*, Saturday, January 29, 1994, p. A9.

68. "Hyperpluralism" and its effects are dissected in Jonathan Rauch, *Demosclerosis* (New York: Time Books, Random House, 1994).

69. Frank R. Baumgartner and Jeffery C. Talbert, "From Setting a National Agenda on Health Care to Making Decisions in Congress," *Journal of Health Politics, Policy and Law* 20, no. 2 (Summer 1995), pp. 439–41.

70. Allen Schick, "How a Bill Didn't Become a Law," in *Intensive Care: How Congress Shapes Health Policy*, eds. Thomas E. Mann and Norman J. Ornstein (Washington, D.C.: Brookings Institution, 1995).

71. Julie Kosterlitz, "OK, Here's the Clinton Plan: Now What?," *National Journal*, September 25, 1993, p. 2312.

72. Julie Kosterlitz, "The Left Has Its Own Prescription," *National Journal*, April 3, 1993, p. 845. See also Alissa J. Rubin, "Two Ideological Poles Frame Debate Over Reform," *Congressional Quarterly* 52, no. 1 (January 8, 1994), pp. 23–25, which includes a list of the ninety-one House cosponsors of single-payer legislation (ninety Democrats plus Independent Bernie Sanders of Vermont).

73. The many activities of single-payer supporters are well surveyed in a nationally circulated newsletter, *Action for Universal Health Care*, put out monthly by the Northeast Ohio Coalition for National Health Care, United Labor Agency, Cleveland, Ohio. See also Congressman Jim McDermott's *American Health Security News*, put out weekly in Washington, D.C.

74. Schick, "How a Bill Didn't Become a Law," pp. 213, 260.

75. Hilary Stout and David Rogers, "Tennessee Democrat's Rival Health-Care Plan Inspires Industry Support, Administration Wrath," *Wall Street Journal*, Friday, December 3, 1993, p. A14; and Trudy Lieberman, "The Selling of 'Clinton Lite'," *Columbia Journalism Review*, March–April 1994, pp. 20–22.

76. Center for Public Integrity, *Well-Healed*, pp. 35–36.

77. For the CBO report on Cooper's bill, see Congressional Budget Office, "An Analysis of the Managed Competition Act," (Washington, D.C.: Government Printing Office, May 1994). On Frist, see David E. Rosenbaum, "G.O.P. Unleashes Its New Weapon: Winning Candidates," *New York Times*, Sunday, November 13, 1994, sec. 4, p. 1. Dr. Frist has since gone on to play a leading role in the Republican effort to dismantle Medicare in favor of public contributions to the purchase by older citizens of private health coverage—which would, of course, be a huge windfall for the for-profit health industry.

Chapter Four

1. Karlyn H. Bowman, *The 1993–1994 Debate on Health Care Reform: Did the Polls Mislead the Policy Makers?* (Washington, D.C.: American Enterprise Institute, 1994), pp. 26–27 (including Table 16).

2. Report to the White House from Stan Greenberg on an "Issue Poll" done May 24–25, 1993, with 1,000 respondents. Six percent of the voters surveyed said "Don't Know." For more on Americans' distrust of government during the relevant period, see Bowman, *Debate*, pp. 19–24; and Robert J. Blendon, Mollyann Brodie, and John M. Benson, "What Happened to Americans' Support of the Clinton Plan?" *Health Affairs* 14, no. 2 (Summer 1995), pp. 12–13.

3. This point has been both stressed and repeatedly documented by Robert Blendon and his associates. See the text and references in Mollyann Brodie and Robert J. Blendon, "The Public's Contribution to Congressional Gridlock on Health Care Reform," *Journal of Health Politics, Policy and Law* 20, no. 2 (Summer 1995), pp. 403–10.

4. Blendon, Brodie, and Benson, "What Happened?" Exhibit 3, p. 13.

5. Memorandum from Stan Greenberg to David Wilhelm, Democratic National Committee, September 23, 1993.

6. This point has been made by Robert Blendon in various articles and talks. In his latest version of the point (in Blendon, Brodie, and Benson, "What Happened?" pp. 15–16) Blendon suggests that the administration should have called only for a mandate covering full-time workers (on the ground that Hawaii took many years to move, in phases, from that form of the mandate to one involving part-timers as well). But I do not think it was necessary for the administration to dump its proposal for partial employer contributions for part-time workers. The Hawaiian example shows that such a mandate works, too. The point is that real-world examples of workable governmental regulations should have been highlighted.

7. See the prepared text of the September 22, 1993 Health Security speech as reprinted in *Solving America's Health Care Crisis*, ed. Erik Eckholm (New York: Times Books, Random House, 1993), p. 312.

8. Blendon, Brodie, and Benson, "What Happened?" p. 16.

9. Ibid.

10. This photograph appears in Eric Weissenstein, "Last Year's Legacy for Healthcare Reform," *Modern Healthcare*, December 19–26, 1994, pp. 42–44.

11. Mark A. Peterson, "The Health Care Debate: All Heat and No Light," *Journal of Health Politics, Policy and Law* 20, no. 2 (Summer 1995), p. 428.

12. Interview with Ira Magaziner, May 17, 1995.

13. This argument is made in Center for Public Integrity, *Well-Healed: Inside Lobbying for Health Care Reform* (Washington, D.C.: Center for Public Integrity, 1994), p. 64.

14. Greenberg, Issue Poll of May 24–25, 1993.

15. Memorandum to Ira Magaziner from Stan Greenberg on "The Health Care Joint Session Speech," September 14, 1993, p. 2.

16. Stan Greenberg has argued this in personal conversations. In addition, see Blendon, Brodie, and Benson, "What Happened?" pp. 18–19.

17. Elizabeth Drew, *On the Edge: The Clinton Presidency* (New York: Simon & Schuster, 1994), p. 191; and interview with Ira Magaziner, May 17, 1995.

18. I discuss this further in chapter 5.

19. "Talking About Health Care," (National Archives, Walter Zelman's files, n.d., typescript marked "Draft"). I received my copy of this from Jacob Hacker. According to Ira Magaziner (May 3, 1995 interview), this may have been a message memo circulated internally in the fall of 1993.

20. Greenberg, Report on May 24–25, 1993 Issue Poll.

21. Interview with Ira Magaziner, May 17, 1995.

22. Stan Greenberg memorandum to Ira Magaziner, "Re: The Health Care Joint Session Speech," September 14, 1993, pp. 1–3. Greenberg indicated that this memo's "observations reflect the research and discussion among the political advisors and, hopefully, will assist the speech-writing effort."

23. "Talking About Health Care," p. 3.

24. Robin Toner, "Shift in Health Strategy: Give Details to Congress," *New York Times*, February 13, 1994, p. 26.

25. "Talking About Health care," p. 1.

26. Ibid. This was the first "general point" listed.

27. Ibid., p. 2.

28. Also distributed during the same period was a video called "Health Security: Challenge to America," featuring President Clinton "and a host of real people telling horror stories about their health care," as Richard Wolf put it in "Democrats do their health-care homework," *USA Today*, Tuesday, November 23, 1993.

29. Mandy Grunwald, "Health Care Message Statement," internal White House memorandum, February 22, 1994. This appeared as part of the summary on the last page of the memo. Statements of this sort appeared periodically to guide speeches and presentations given by people in the Clinton administration.

30. Congressional Budget Office, "An Analysis of the Administration's Health Proposal: A CBO Study," (Washington, D.C.: Government Printing Office, February 1994), p. 70.

31. Ibid.

32. For background, see Theda Skocpol, *Social Policy in the United States: Future Possibilities in Historical Perspective* (Princeton, N.J.: Princeton University Press, 1995), especially chap. 4 (with G. John Ikenberry), "The Road to Social Security."

33. Lawrence R. Jacobs, *The Health of Nations and the Making of American and British Health Policy* (Ithaca, N.Y.: Cornell University Press, 1993), chap. 9.

34. On this point, there is no more cogent authority than the Congressional Budget Office's "Analysis of the Administration's Health Proposal."

35. Robert Blendon, Mollyann Brodie, Tracey Stelzev Hyams, and John Benson, "The American Public and the Critical Choices for Health System Reform," *Journal of the American Medical Association* 271, no. 19 (1994), p. 1543. See also the discussion in Blendon, Brodie, and Benson, "What Happened?" pp. 18–19. Opinion analysts, including Blendon and Stan Greenberg, tend to presume that because the public never registered approval of alliances during 1993–94, these entities could not have been explained. "Was it possible for the president to have educated the public about the merits and need for health alliances?" ask Blendon, Brodie, and Benson. "We think not. . . ." But, of course, the President and his allies never *tried* to explain alliances. So how do we know? What we do know is that proposing but not explaining regional health alliances contributed to political disaster for Health Security.

36. Gwen Ifill, "Clinton Campaigns Hard for Health Plan as 'Outsider'," *New York Times,* Sunday, April 10, 1994, p. 33.

37. Toner, "Ever Fainter Beat," p. A14.

38. Marshall Ganz, "Voters in the Crosshairs," *American Prospect,* no. 16 (Winter 1994), as reprinted in *The American Prospect Reader in American Politics,* ed. Walter Dean Burnham (Chatham, N.J.: Chatham House, 1995).

39. Of course, sometimes special rules apply that encourage decisions within a given time frame, as they do in annual budget debates in Congress.

40. Tom Hamburger, Ted Marmor, and Jon Meacham, "What the Death of Reform Teaches Us about the Press," *Washington Monthly,* November 1994; Kathleen Hall Jamieson and Joseph Cappella, "Newspaper and Television Coverage of the Health Care Reform Debate, January 16–July 25, 1994" (Annenberg Public Policy Center, funded by the Robert Wood Johnson Foundation, Philadelphia, August 12, 1994); and Joseph N. Cappella and Kathleen Hall Jamieson, "Public Cynicism and News Coverage in Campaigns and Policy Debates" (paper presented at the Annual Meeting of the American Political Science Association, New York, September 4, 1994).

41. See "Media Coverage of Health Care Reform: A Final Report," Kaiser Health Care Media Monitoring Project, Supplement of the *Columbia Journalism Review,* March–April 1995, pp. 1–2.

42. As documented in an article I discussed at the end of chapter 3: Hilary Stout, "Many Don't Realize Its the Clinton Plan They Like," *Wall Street Journal,* Thursday, March 10, 1994, pp. B1, B6.

43. Stan Greenberg, "Issue Priorities," memorandum to the White House, July 30, 1993. Keeping control of the debate, Greenberg cautioned, would require a "full-time strategic and communications operation."

44. As quoted in Toner, "Shift in Health Strategy," p. 26. This is an absolutely fascinating example of historically misguided wishful thinking. Presumably, John F. Kennedy was a positive role model for Begala, as for his boss, President Clinton. But the times were obviously different, and so were the types of policies involved in this comparison.

Chapter Five

1. Center for Public Integrity, *Well-Healed: Inside Lobbying for Health Care Reform* (Washington D.C.: Center for Public Integrity, 1994), p. 35.

2. As revealed by their own internal memos (see especially the memorandum cited in chapter 3, note 58), members of the Clinton administration took heart at the increasing fragmentation among oppositional stakeholders, especially in the insurance industry. But as this chapter shows, such fragmentation could work against presidentially sponsored reforms by freeing threatened groups to go all-out in opposition and do end runs around more cooperative groups (or factions within groups).

3. Julie Kosterlitz, "Insurers Are Gearing Up," *National Journal*, March 25, 1992, pp. 706–7.

4. Julie Kosterlitz, "Policy Divisions," *National Journal*, April 25, 1992, pp. 1007, 1010.

5. Julie Kosterlitz, "Trade Group's Pulse's Fading," *National Journal*, November 7, 1992, p. 2529.

6. Ibid; and Julie Kosterlitz, "Itching for a Fight?" *National Journal*, January 15, 1994, p. 106.

7. Kosterlitz, "Itching?" p. 107.

8. Kosterlitz, "Gearing Up," pp. 706–7.

9. Julie Kosterlitz, segment in "Capitol Hill Watch," *National Journal*, January 16, 1993: 142; and the interview reported in Julie Kosterlitz and Viveca Novak, "Why Bill Gradison's Heading Downtown," *National Journal*, January 30, 1993, pp. 290–91. See also Robin Toner, "Changing Roles in the Health Care Debate: The Man Behind 'Harry and Louise'," *New York Times*, Wednesday, April 6, 1994, p. A18.

10. Kosterlitz, "Itching?" p. 107.

11. Ibid.

12. Annenberg Public Policy Center, "The Role of Advertising in the Health Care Debate: Part Two: Accuracy" (Philadelphia: Annenberg Public Policy Center, University of Pennsylvania, July 25, 1994), p. 1. According to the report (p. 2), the "ads opposing the Clinton plan focus[ed] on five fears: increased taxation, rationing (e.g., waiting lines), big bureaucracy-government control, diminished choice of plan/doctor, and massive job loss." This report also notes (p. 2) that "with few exceptions, the most histrionic and demonstrably false assertions occur not in print or broadcast ads but in direct mail addressed to older Americans."

13. Julie Kosterlitz, "Harry, Louise, and Doublespeak," *National Journal*, June 25, 1994, p. 1542.

14. As quoted in John Carroll, "Health Care Ads Hazardous to Clinton," *Boston Globe*, Monday, February 7, 1994, p. 47.

15. Kathleen Hall Jamieson, "When Harry Met Louise," *Washington Post*, August 15, 1994, p. A19. For the full research background on which this draws, see Annenberg Public Policy Center, "The Role of Advertising in the Health Care Debate: Part Three: The Effect of 'Harry and Louise' on the Press, the Public and the Political Process" (Philadelphia: Annenberg Public Policy Center, University of Pennsylvania, August 1, 1994).

16. Annenberg Public Policy Center, "The Role of Advertising in the Health Care Reform Debate, Part One: A Preliminary Report of Research Funded by the Rob-

ert Wood Johnson Foundation" (Philadelphia: Annenberg Public Policy Center, University of Pennsylvania, July 18, 1994), p. 3.

17. Kosterlitz, "Itching?" p. 110.

18. Ibid., p. 109.

19. HIAA President David Hurd, as quoted in ibid., p. 110.

20. HIAA Executive Vice President Charles N. Kahn, as quoted in ibid.

21. Monte S. Poen, *Harry S. Truman Versus the Medical Lobby* (Columbia: University of Missouri Press, 1979), p. 145.

22. Center for Public Integrity, *Well-Healed*, pp. 53–54.

23. Ibid., p. 56.

24. Ibid., p. 55.

25. All quotes are from Sandra G. Boodman, "Health Care's Power Player," *Washington Post National Weekly Edition*, February 14–20, 1994, p. 6.

26. Julie Kosterlitz, "A New Commander for an Uphill Battle," *National Journal*, August 21, 1993, p. 2093.

27. Robin Toner, "Gold Rush Fever Grips Capital as Health Care Struggle Begins," *New York Times*, Sunday, March 13, 1994, p. A1, including a quote from White House aide Robert Boorstin.

28. Center for Public Integrity, *Well-Healed*, p. 1.

29. See the excellent discussions on this point in Julie Kosterlitz, "Excess Baggage," *National Journal*, January 9, 1993, p. 99; and Julie Kosterlitz, "Stress Fractures," *National Journal*, February 19, 1994, pp. 412–17.

30. Center for Public Integrity, *Well-Healed*, pp. 53–54. For the AMA's first official reaction to the Health Security plan, see the open letter to all AMA members and the public released on September 24, 1993, with a cover letter signed by the AMA's top officers.

31. For information on big insurance company positions and activities, see Center for Public Integrity, *Well-Healed*, pp. 35–47, passim.

32. Cathie Jo Martin, "Together Again: Business, Government, and the Quest for Cost Control," *Journal of Health Politics, Policy and Law* 18, no. 2 (1933): 359–93; and "Mandating Social Change: The Business Struggle Over National Health Reform," (February 1995, typescript). Of course, many of these corporate benefits officers would probably have been employed by the new regional health alliances envisaged by the Clinton plan. But individuals could not know that in advance; and they might not have found such a change appealing, even if they had envisaged it.

33. Center for Public Integrity, *Well-Healed*, pp. 35–36; and John Judis, "Abandoned Surgery: Business and the Failure of Health Reform," *American Prospect*, no. 21 (Spring 1995), pp. 70–71.

34. See the telling discussion of Montana Senator Max Baucus's visit home in June 1994: Dana Priest, "Anger, Angst and Confusion About Clinton's Health Plan," *Washington Post National Weekly Edition*, June 13–19, 1994, p. 12.

35. Clymer, "Clinton Plan Alive," p. E3.

36. William Kristol, "Memorandum to Republican Leaders: Defeating President Clinton's Health Care Proposal" (Washington, D.C.: Project for the Republican Future, December 2, 1993, typescript), p. 1.

37. Ibid., p. 2.

38. Ibid., p. 3.

39. Ibid., p. 4.

40. William Kristol, "Memorandum to Republican Leaders" (Washington, D.C.: Project for the Republican Future, July 26, 1994). This is reprinted in "Health: Congress is now more dangerous than Mr. Clinton," *Washington Times*, Wednesday, July 27, 1994.

41. Thus the "Heritage Foundation's Consumer Choice Plan" was outlined in Stuart M. Butler, "Have It Your Way: What the Heritage Foundation Health Care Plan Means for You," *Policy Review*, no. 66 (Fall 1993): 54–59, and the following article was Anna Bray, "You Better Shop Around: How Federal Workers Choose Their Health Care," *Policy Review*, no. 66 (Fall 1993): 60–63. Interestingly, the latter article described the Federal Employees Health Benefits Program, which in many ways functions like a Clintonian alliance would have functioned, offering employees alternative health plans from which they can choose each year.

42. "Kristol Ball: William Kristol Looks at the Future of the GOP," *Policy Review*, no. 67 (Winter 1993), p. 15.

43. Robert E. Moffit, "Clinton's Frankenstein: The Gory Details of the President's Health Plan," *Policy Review*, no. 67 (Winter 1994): 4–12. This was the leadoff article in the issue, written by the Deputy Director of Domestic Policy at the Heritage Foundation.

44. Many examples appear in Charles Brooks, ed., *Best Editorial Cartoons of the Year, 1994 ed.* (Gretna, La.: Pelican, 1994), pp. 35–50.

45. See the one-page "pictographs" that appeared in the *Reader's Digest*, March 1994 and July 1994. The former (p. 111) displayed a graph of waiting lists for surgery in Canada under the heading "Is This the Kind of Health Care We Want?" The latter (p. 139) presented a graph of rising costs under Medicare since 1967 under the heading "Beware of Health Care Cost Projections."

   The *Reader's Digest* has no sense of consistency or irony. Amidst its steady stream of anti-Clinton and anti-Canada health care features, the *Digest* also regularly ran human-interest "Book Section" features about desperately ill children. One of them, "Lionhart: Matthew's Story," appeared in the October 1993 *Digest* (along with an article pushing antigovernment "Medical Savings Plans"). In "Lionhart," the desperately ill son of a Canadian fisherman receives all kinds of extraordinary health care in the single-payer Canadian health system, and then is sent at Canada's expense to Britain for an experimental heart-lung transplant! In the United States, this child would almost certainly have been in an uninsured family, and thus would have been highly unlikely to receive such extraordinary "uneconomical" emergency care. The child died in the end. The woes of another child, this one in an uninsured U.S. family, are chronicled in the July 1994 "Book Section" feature, "When All They Had Was Love." The family in this story would have benefited enormously from the enactment of the Clinton Health Security plan.

46. Ralph Kinney Bennett, "Your Risk Under the Clinton Health Plan," *Reader's Digest*, March 1994, pp. 127–32.

47. Ibid., p. 132.

48. These facts come from Timothy Egan, "Triumph Leaves No Targets for Conservative Talk Shows," *New York Times*, Sunday, January 1, 1995, pp. 1, 22.

49. For a sense of how Rush Limbaugh discussed the Clinton plan, see his *See, I Told*

You So (New York: Pocket Star Books, 1993), especially pp. 167–74, where ridicule of Hillary Rodham Clinton is a running theme.

50. I make this argument in Theda Skocpol, *Protecting Soldiers and Mothers: The Political Origins of Social Policy in the United States* (Cambridge, Mass.: Belknap Press of Harvard University Press, 1992), especially part III.

51. Ibid., chap. 9.

52. For background on the strong women of the New Deal era, see Susan Ware, *Beyond Suffrage: Women in the New Deal* (Cambridge, Mass.: Harvard University Press, 1981), and Doris Kearns Goodwin, *No Ordinary Time: Franklin and Eleanor Roosevelt: The Home Front in World War II* (New York: Simon & Schuster, 1994).

53. For some right-wingers, at least, there was a well-understood connection between pushing the so-called scandal of Whitewater and undermining the Clintons at a crucial juncture for the fortunes of Health Security. As Rush Limbaugh put it on CNN's "Nightline" program on April 19, 1994, "I think Whitewater is about health care. . . . Character, the issue of character, was put on hold during the 1992 campaign. Nobody cared about it, because so many people were upset with the economic situation. They wanted a change, and now it's coming home to roost. Most people think that health care is a good idea, but they haven't read the plan. They're taking the President's word for it. Now I think if the President's word is what we are going to rely on for his policies, this isn't a debate in the area of ideas, . . . and if people are going to base their support for the plan on whether or not they can take his word, I think it's fair to examine whether or not he keeps his word. This is about people who would like to stop health care in a legitimate democratic sense, trying to compete for the minds and hearts of the American people. . . . The cattle futures business, all of those things that people are curious about are simply a window into whether or not . . . they're [i.e., the Clintons are] telling falsehoods today."

54. The line appeared on the title page of *New Republic*, February 7, 1994, introducing Elizabeth McCaughey, "No Exit," pp. 21–25.

55. Long after it was too late to make up the damage done, *New Republic* published a featured "TRB" commentary, "No Exegesis," by Mickey Kaus acknowledging the many falsehoods that appeared in the original McCaughey article. Kaus concludes: "She got some things right. But she got a lot wrong. In the process, she completely distorted the debate on the biggest policy issue of 1994." Of course, it was not just McCaughey who "distorted the debate." It was also the editors of *New Republic*, by their decision to publish—and feature—her obviously partisan and inaccurate article.

56. For cogent overviews of the bureaucratic intrusiveness and likely socioeconomic effects of the Cooper plan, see Joseph White, *Competing Solutions: American Health Care Proposals and International Experience* (Washington, D.C.: Brookings Institution, 1995), chap. 8; and Congressional Budget Office, "An Analysis of the Managed Competition Act," (Washington, D.C.: Government Printing Office, May 1994).

57. John C. Green, James L. Guth, Lyman A. Kellstedt, and Corwin E. Smidt, "Murphey Brown Revisited: The Social Issues in the 1992 Election," in *Disciples and Democracy: Religious Counservatives and the Future of American Politics*, ed.

Michael Cromartie (Grand Rapids, Mich.: Eerdmans, 1994), pp. 43–64.

58. See the accounts in Ralph Reed, *Politically Incorrect: The Emerging Faith Factor in American Politics* (Dallas, Tex.: Word, 1994), pp. 196–99; and Sidney Blumenthal, "Christian Soldiers," *New Yorker*, July 18, 1994, pp. 31–37. Another difference between the Christian Coalition and earlier counterparts, such as the Moral Majority, was the greater presence in the Coalition of pentacostal Christians more than rural fundamentalists. According to James M, Perry, "The Christian Coalition Crusades to Broaden Rightist Political Base," *Wall Street Journal*, Tuesday, July 19, 1994, pp. A1, A6, this makes it easier for the coalition to reach out to Catholics and racial minorities.

59. For a carefully phrased statement of the vision, see Ralph E. Reed, Jr., "What Do Religious Conservatives Really Want?" in *Disciples and Democracy*, pp. 1–15. I say "a certain Christian understanding," because many of us who happen to be Christians do not agree with the right-wing vision at all. We think that Christian values suggest very different conclusions about politics and public policymaking.

60. In my scholarly career, I have previously studied revolutions. It is well known that in such conflicts the fiercest struggles break out between the culturally or ideologically closest competitors, as for example, between the Shi'ite clerics who took power in the Iranian Revolution and the *Islamic* socialists or members of the Bahai faith (which claims to encompass Islamic religious truths along with others). For the galvanizing effect of the early Clinton presidency on conservatives, see Stanley B. Greenberg, "The Conservative Republican Surge and the Democratic Reaction" (Washington, D.C.: Greenberg Research, 1995).

61. Reed, *Politically Incorrect*, p. 200.

62. Perry, "Coalition Crusades to Broaden Base," p. A6; and Kenneth Jost, "Religion and Politics," *CQ Researcher* 4, no. 38 (October 14, 1994), p. 904. As Jost writes, the "Christian Coalition called Clinton's inauguration a 'repudiation of our forefathers' covenant with God.' "

63. Gerald F. Seib, "Christian Coalition Hopes to Expand by Taking Stands on Taxes, Crime, Health Care, and Nafta," *Wall Street Journal*, Tuesday, September 7, 1993, p. A18.

64. Blumenthal, "Christian Soldiers," p. 36.

65. As quoted in People for the American Way, *A Turn to the Right: A Guide to Religious Right Influence in the 103rd / 104th Congress* (Washington, D.C.: People for the American Way, 1994), p. 5.

66. Blumenthal, "Christian Soldiers," p. 37.

67. John F. Persinos, "Has the Christian Right Taken Over the Republican Party?" *Campaigns & Elections*, September 1994, pp. 21–24.

68. Perry, "Coalition Crusades to Broaden Base", and Seib, "Christian Coalition Hopes to Expand." See also Ralph Reed, Jr., "Casting a Wider Net," *Policy Review*, Summer 1993, pp. 31–35.

69. On Christian Coalition mobilization against the Clinton budget, see *Wall Street Journal*, August 6, 1993, p. A1.

70. Seib, "Coalition Hopes to Expand," p. A18.

71. Robin Toner, "Hillary Clinton Opens Campaign to Answer Critics of Health Plan," *New York Times*, Wednesday, February 16, 1994, p. A11.

72. Reed, *Politically Incorrect*, p. 200; Jost, "Religion and Politics," p. 906; and "Health Care Wars," *Christian Century*, March 9, 1994, p. 248.

73. All this was but preparatory to a full mobilization to elect friendly conservatives to Congress in the November 1994 election, and then a conservative Republican to the presidency in 1996. For the remarkable successes achieved by the religious right in November 1994, see People for the American Way, *Turn to the Right.*

74. According to the Center for Public Integrity, *Well-Healed*, p. 62, the National Federation of Independent Businesses was "especially effective in the southern and western states" during the health care reform debate.

75. Ibid., p. 60.

76. John B. Judis, "Abandoned Surgery: Business and the Failure of Health Care Reform," *American Prospect*, no. 21 (Spring 1995), p. 68.

77. C. P. Hall, Jr., and J. M. Kuder, *Small Business and Health Care* (Washington, D.C.: National Federation of Independent Businesses Foundation, 1990).

78. Jennifer N. Edwards, Robert J. Blendon, Robert Leitman, Ellen Morrison, Ian Morrison, and Humphrey Taylor, "Small Business and the National Health Care Reform Debate," *Health Affairs*, Spring 1992, p. 171.

79. Center for Public Integrity, *Well-Healed*, p. 62.

80. The NFIB's ideological and financial contributions during the 1993–94 election cycle are discussed in Christopher Georges, ". . . While Some Say Political Payoffs Helped Save the SBA from Extinction," *Wall Street Journal*, Friday, May 19, 1995, p. A16.

81. Judis, "Abandoned Surgery," pp. 69–71. See also Hilary Stout and Rick Wartzman, "Why Clintons' Effort to Woo Big Business to Health Plan Failed," *Wall Street Journal*, Friday, February 11, 1994, pp. A1, A14.

82. As quoted in Judis, "Abandoned Surgery," p. 68. The following account draws heavily on Judis.

83. Ibid., p. 69.

84. The concepts are defined and used in Allen Schick, "How a Bill Didn't Become a Law," in *Intensive Care: How Congress Shapes Health Policy*, eds. Thomas E. Mann and Norman Ornstein (Washington, D.C.: Brookings Institution, 1995), pp. 241–42.

85. Judis, "Abandoned Surgery," p. 67.

86. Ibid., p. 68.

87. Ibid.

88. Ibid.

89. Ibid.

90. Ibid.

91. Cathie Jo Martin, "Mandating Social Change: The Business Struggle Over National Health Reform," (February 1995, typescript version), p. 15.

92. Ibid.

93. This ad appeared in the *Washington Post* and other newspapers on July 21, 1994.

94. Schick, "Bill Didn't Become a Law," p. 242.

95. As quoted in Robert Pear, "Health Care Tug-of-War Puts A.M.A. Under Strain," *New York Times*, August 5, 1994, p. A18.

96. Schick, "Bill Didn't Become a Law," p. 242.

97. Julie Kosterlitz, "The Sound of Two Senators Waffling," *National Journal*, August 13, 1994, p. 58. This deals with Packwood and also with Nebraska Democratic Senator Robert Kerrey, whose turnaround on health care issues from 1991 to 1994 was the most amazing of anyone involved in the national debate. Kerrey went from

supporting a single-payer plan during 1991–92 to refusing to accept any kind of employer mandate or any version of universal health reform during 1994. Another Democratic backpedaler was Senator Bill Bradley of New Jersey, who changed his mind about supporting the employer mandate. See John Aloysius Farrell and Peter Gosselin, "Clinton Defends His Embattled Health Proposals," *Boston Globe*, Wednesday, June 22, 1994, p. 3.

98. Various of Dole's peregrinations are summarized in Martin, "Mandating Social Change," and Alissa J. Rubin, "Two Ideological Poles Frame Debate Over Reform," *Congressional Quarterly*, 52, no. 1 (January 8, 1994), p. 23.

99. NBC–*Wall Street Journal* poll of July 23–26, 1994, discussed in *American Enterprise* 5, no. 6 (September–October 1994), p. 109.

100. Daniel S. Hirshfield, *The Lost Reform: The Campaign for Compulsory Health Insurance in the United States from 1932 to 1943* (Cambridge, Mass.: Harvard University Press, 1970), chap. 2.

101. This argument is developed in Theda Skocpol, Targeting within Universalism: Politically Viable Policies to Combat Poverty in the United States," in *The Urban Underclass*, eds. Christopher Jencks and Paul E. Peterson (Washington, D.C.: Brookings Institution, 1981), pp. 411–36; also reprinted as chap. 8 in Theda Skocpol, *Social Policy in the United States: Future Possibilities in Historical Perspective* (Princeton, N.J.: Princeton University Press, 1995).

102. Maggie Mahar, "What Clinton's Health Plan Would Mean to You," *New York*, April 26, 1993, p. 31.

103. Blendon, Hyams, and Benson, "Bridging the Gap," p. 2576.

104. See the *Reader's Digest* article referenced in note 46. See also Ralph Kinney Bennett, "Questions to Ask Your Congressman About Health Care Reform," *Reader's Digest*, August 1994, pp. 33–38; and Vince Passaro, "On the Examining Table," *Harper's*, May 1994, pp. 63–70. It is also true that there were some published defenses of managed care and the approach to it in the Clinton Health Security plan. See Michael M. Weinstein, "The Freedom to Choose Doctors: What Freedom?" *New York Times Magazine*, Sunday, May 27, 1994, pp. 64–65; and Jane Bryant Quinn, "Health Reform: The Missing Story," *Newsweek*, March 21, 1994, p. 58.

105. Robin Cook, *Fatal Cure* (New York: Putnam, 1994).

106. This appears on the cover of the February 1995 paperback edition of *Fatal Cure* (New York: Berkeley, 1995).

Chapter Six

1. The best analysis of the dynamics of U.S. politics from the 1960s to the 1980s appears in Thomas Byrne Edsall and Mary D. Edsall, *Chain Reaction: The Impact of Race, Rights, and Taxes on American Politics* (New York: Norton, 1991).

2. Alan Brinkley, "Reagan's Revenge: As Invented by Howard Jarvis," *New York Times Magazine*, June 19, 1994, pp. 36–37.

3. Ibid., p. 37.

4. David Stockman, *The Triumph of Politics: The Inside Story of the Reagan Revolution* (New York: Avon, 1987).

5. Brinkley, "Reagan's Revenge," p. 37.

6. Ibid., p. 36.

7. "National Election Night Survey" (Menlo Park, Calif.: Henry J. Kaiser Family Foundation, November 15, 1994, news release.

8. *Contract with America*, ed. Ed Gillespie and Bob Schellhas (New York: Times Books, Random House, 1994).

9. Hilary Stout, "Contrasting Reactions to GOP Proposals to Cut Medicare, Medicaid Reflect Voting Blocs' Power," *Wall Street Journal*, Tuesday, May 30, 1995, p. A16.

10. See Jeff Faux, "A New Conversation: How to Rebuild the Democratic Party," *American Prospect*, no. 21 (Spring 1995), pp. 35–43.

11. Powerful documentation of this point appears in Richard Freeman, ed., *Working under Different Rules* (New York: Russell Sage Foundation, 1994). This book shows that increasingly unfettered market forces in the United States are leading to relatively lower incomes and great social insecurities for less-privileged working people, as well as the very poor. This collection presents empirically precise comparisons of the United States with Canada, Western Europe, and Japan during the 1970s and 1980s.

12. Gene Koretz, "High Taxes Are Not What's Ailing the U.S. Economy," *Business Week*, February 10, 1992, p. 20. This includes a chart, "America: Low Man on the Totem Pole," showing that total U.S. tax revenues were lower in 1989 as a proportion of Gross Domestic Product than taxes in seven other nations, including Japan. The profile may have changed a bit since 1989, but not much.

INDEX